Who was Hurricane Higgins?

Unravelling the mystery of a snooker genius

Tony Francis

HODDER & STOUGHTON

First published in Great Britain in 2011 by Hodder & Stoughton
An Hachette UK company

1

A CIP catalogue record for this title is available from the British Library

Hardback ISBN 978 1 444 70877 6
Trade Paperback ISBN 978 1 444 73385 3
Ebook ISBN 978 1 444 70879 0

Typeset in Fresco by Hewer Text UK Ltd, Edinburgh
Printed and bound by CPI Group (UK) Ltd, Croydon, CR0 4YY

Hodder & Stoughton policy is to use papers that are natural, renewable and recyclable products and made from wood grown in sustainable forests. The logging and manufacturing processes are expected to conform to the environmental regulations of the country of origin.

Hodder & Stoughton Ltd
338 Euston Road
London NW1 3BH

www.hodder.co.uk

To Ben, Barney, Alex, Oliver and Hermione

CONTENTS

ACKNOWLEDGEMENTS

At the risk of sounding like an Oscar winner, I'd like to thank a few friends who helped to make this book possible. Alex's ex-wife, Lynn, his daughter, Lauren, and his son, Jordan, have become my friends after tirelessly going though the script with me and indeed contributing generously to the story. It's not been an easy time for them, especially Lauren.

Similar thanks go to Alex's sisters, Isobel, Ann and Jean who made me feel at home in Belfast.

Although they had contrasting 'takes' on Alex, all the contributors were a joy to work with. I'll mention Barry McGuigan who, despite being (or maybe because he is) teetotal, initiated me into the Irish drinking culture, and the actor, Richard Dormer who performed his one-man play, "Hurricane" to standing ovations and told me the fascinating story of how he 'became' Alex Higgins.

I'd also single out Tom McCarthy, the one-armed taxi driver who unloaded the wild adventures he and Alex got up to in the Republic and introduced me to more extraordinary characters in Alex's life.

Not least, I'm grateful to the indestructible Roddy Bloomfield for his boundless enthusiasm, to his number two, Sarah Hammond for her cool appraisals, and to Henry Vines for the way he handled the publicity. If I may say, it was a very smooth operation all round.

Photographic Acknowledgements

The author and publisher would like to thank the following for permission to reproduce photographs:

Belfast Telegraph, Helen Coburn, Andrew Cowie/Colorsport, Jim Duxbury/Rex Features, Stewart Fraser/Colorsport, Dave Hodges/ Sporting Pictures/Action Images, Kevin Holt/Daily Mail, Paul Johnston, Paul McCambridge/Press Eye, Peter Marlow/Magnum Photos, Kippa Matthews, Mirrorpix, Peter Muhly/AFP/ Getty Images, David Muscroft/Rex Features, Phil O'Conner/Sporting Pictures/Action Images, Pacemaker Press, Jonathan Porter/Press Eye, Press Association Images, Alan Quigley, Trevor Smith Photography, SSPL/Getty Images, The Sun/News International, Bob Thomas/Getty Images, Mark Waugh, Eric Whitehead/ Snooker Images.

All other photographs are from private collections.

FOREWORD

by Lauren Higgins

They call my dad a genius. There's no precise definition of genius. It's possessed by someone with an exceptional natural capacity and creative power beyond the realms of most thinking men. I'm immensely proud of my father's success and his achievement in giving a slightly boring game mass appeal. I thank his fans all over the world, young and old, who have supported him. It was you he thrived off. He loved an audience. He brought excitement, charisma and a swagger to the game. I've lost count of the number of people who've told me what a lovely moment it was when Dad won the World Championship and beckoned my mum and me on stage. He had a natural sense of theatre.

Growing up as the Hurricane's daughter wasn't always easy, especially when he began to decline. I also found myself trying to defend his sometimes unacceptable behaviour. He certainly wasn't an angel. It always saddened me that he couldn't control his outbursts or listen to the advice of others. Nobody could tell him what to do. I tried but he rarely lent an ear until he grew older. Then it was only half an ear. We were both stubborn people. I reached an age where I started to give as good as I got. At first he didn't like it. He wasn't used to people standing their ground. Then he began to treat me like an adult.

I truly thought that Dad would go on forever and always wished that one day he'd behave like a normal person. But that wasn't his style. He lived in the overtaking lane. Although he had his highs, it upsets me to think there were so many lows. It's heartbreaking that he was on his own when he died.

To me he was my dad and I will always love him. Sometimes I imagine that he's still there. It helps me to come to terms with the loss. There was more to him than negative headlines in newspapers would have you believe - much more.

I'd like people to remember him for his talent, his personality and that X-factor which made him such a star. You either have it or you don't. My father oozed star quality.

He wouldn't have liked everything Tony has written in this book. Dad thought he was right and the rest of the world was out of step. I hope you enjoy the read. It's a very moving story.

1

HE WAS MY SUBJECT

If it was left to me, I'd erect a statue to Alex Higgins. I might have to. No-one else seems interested. I'd do it in the grounds of Belfast City Hall and *on* the grounds that he kept us interested for forty years. Not even Katie Price will match that. And Alex had talent.

Alas, my proposal didn't even merit a second reading at the monthly meeting of the City Council's General Purposes Committee. Inertia rules. Didn't they know how lucky they were to have a sporting legend in their midst? They named an airport after George Best, for heaven's sake. Couldn't they condescend to a boulevard? A railway platform? All right, then, a lampost? He must have propped up a few. I'm flogging a dead horse, aren't I? Now *there's* a thought. Judging by his account at William Hill's, he spent a plenty of time backing them.

If I can't give you a statue, Alex, please accept this book as my tribute. You suggested many years ago that I should write it if I outlived you, so here it is – the posthumously authorised story of your life, told by and through the people who knew you best. Some of them are snooker players; most of them aren't. All of them had a role, from the pal who agreed to supervise you when you were bound over to keep the peace, to the actor who *became* you and the daughter who loved you but found the words difficult to say. Each of them had a different perception. Which, if any of them, could say they had Alex Higgins to a tee? I guess you'd be the best judge of that, although pinpointing the real Alex Higgins was probably beyond you too. There were at least two versions. Readers can make up their own minds.

I'll ask them to half-close their eyes and picture this: a shadowy figure alights on a windblown platform, hat on head, rucksack on back, weapon in hand. With a swish of his mantle, he swoops down a dark alley and vanquishes the fastest cuemen in town. Stuffing tenners into his coat pocket, he dissolves into the foggy night ready for the next duel. It's the Wild West, it's 1930s Chicago, it's Don Quixote. Those who've read Cervantes' masterpiece will see the similarities.

Bored by the peasant life that ensnares him, Don Quixote re-invents himself as a medieval knight resolved to spice up his life with daredevil deeds. If it means charging at windmills, so be it. If it means rescuing damsels from imaginary peril, it's better than working for a living.

Well, guess what? Madrid erected a statue to Don Quixote - and he didn't even exist. What are the burghers of Belfast waiting for? Needless to say, they turned out by the phalanx six months after Alex died when his stage play was showing and the champagne flowed at Belfast Grand Opera House. It was the return, by popular request, of *Hurricane*, Richard Dormer's remarkable one-man epic. The actor's wife, Rachel O'Riordan, who directed the award-winning play, told the assembled throng what a joy it was to honour a famous son of Belfast. They nodded, applauded, raised a glass and settled down to enjoy the show. The following day they forgot him again.

Maybe it's the only tribute the city will pay. Let's be grateful for it. There's unlikely to be a play called *Steve Interesting Davis* or *Ray Dracula Reardon*, decent chaps though they are. Snooker isn't sexy enough for that. The storylines don't set the pulse racing. Not any more, they don't.

Few sportsmen have been the subject of plays or movies because few sportsmen could enthral an audience beyond the aficionados of their particular science. A good story needs drama, ecstasy, agony, love, tears and a moral. Cue Alex Higgins. George Best fitted the bill too. By one of those strange coincidences, Alex's funeral and the musical devoted to Best were showing at the same time. While mourners squeezed into Belfast Cathedral, a twenty-foot poster on a nearby wall advertised *Dancing Shoes*, the story of Belfast's other supremely gifted alcoholic waster, George Best.

Alex was the 'People's Champion', yet he died unnoticed in a warden-assisted flat. He was adored by women but spent most of his life in solitary. He pioneered the snooker revolution but was ostracised by colleagues who grew fat on the proceeds. He earned millions but couldn't afford a roof over his head. So who was this guy? Who *was* Alex Higgins?

To some, he was a horrible drunk. There's plenty of evidence to support that view. For instance, a Belfast bus driver I travelled with told me he'd 'met' the great man twice in his life. Alex first materialised as horizontal baggage heading towards the gutter. The driver in question, Joe Morgan, happened to be walking past Belfast's famous Crown liquor saloon as the customer in question was being ejected. Good Samaritan that he is, Joe went to the assistance of the unwanted collection of limbs, cloak and hat groaning in the gutter.

'Blimey, it's Alex Higgins,' he gasped, turning the body face-up. 'I don't believe this. You and George Best are the greatest sporting legends we've ever had.'

'Yeah,' came the heavily slurred response. 'Me number one, Best number two.'

Joe was so elated by the quick-fire response that he bounced off down Great Victoria Street, forgetting that Alex was in chronic need of assistance. To be honest, he'd seen enough.

Why, you might ask, would anyone build a monument to a gutter drunk? I'd tell you to get real. Alex wasn't always drunk

– only when he was awake! In any case, this *is* Ireland. If you give up the booze they call you a quitter. You've let the side down. The Great Irish Writers tour of Dublin is a thinly disguised pub crawl. Where else do you suppose the likes of Brendan Behan, James Joyce and J.P. Donleavy found their inspiration? If *we'd* invented Guinness, we might have come up with *Borstal Boy* or *Ulysses* ourselves. We might have played snooker like Alex Higgins.

By the way, the second time Joe Morgan saw Alex was on the back seat of his bus one morning. He was asleep with his cue in his hand. Alex was already into his radiotherapy by then. He looked dreadful.

Yet, to Alexandra, his six-year-old great niece who sang 'Somewhere Over the Rainbow' at Alex's memorial dinner, this urban inebriate was Uncle Sandy, her godfather. To Lauren Higgins he was 'my dad and I'll always love him'. To Siobhan, the girl he wanted to marry, he was 'the gentlest man I ever met'. The snooker official he decked for daring to request a urine sample may take a contrary view.

However, when Alexander Gordon Higgins sashayed into the arena, all twitch and testosterone, nobody could take their eyes off him. He was snooker's matador, dispatching his foe with lightning thrusts before tossing his severed pride to the baying multitude. Until Alex turned it into a TV soap, watching snooker was something the elderly or unemployed did to while away the days. Listening to grass grow fulfilled a similar role. I was lucky enough to present snooker on ITV while Alex was still on song. I sympathise with Hazel Irvine and the BBC as they try to inject jeopardy into a sport which bumps along the lower rungs of entertainment. It's roughly on a par with those low-grade antique and cookery shows which clog up the schedules. The World Professional Billiards and Snooker Association (WPBSA) needs another Hurricane to prevent snooker sliding into the nation's subconscious. Barry Hearn might disagree. I suppose that if he can make a success of Leyton Orient and fishing against the clock, anything's possible.

It's a sad fact of snooker history that Alex pushed open the door to an era of unprecedented popularity and prosperity but tripped over the step. He was years ahead of the game before television showed interest. He *was* the interest. By the time television fully embraced snooker in 1978, Alex was already thirty and in danger of missing out. Barry Hearn, the Romford accountant who once paid him £500 a time to challenge Steve Davis, established a snooker agency and opened lucrative new avenues for his client.

Davis, although a modest individual with limited star quality, found himself endorsing coffee and men's toiletries. Others joined Barry's stable. They included Jimmy White who, like Alex, was a rascal. And yet Higgins, the most dazzling star of the lot, the headline grabber who put more bums on more seats than anyone in the game, could only watch with increasing frustration as fellow players filled their boots. The rewards should have been his. He once told me: 'Watching Steve Davis marketing his own aftershave made me wonder why Hurricane Higgins missed the boat. When I'm dressed up and shaven, I'm not a bad looking bloke. It wasn't my job to come up with the marketing ideas. I'm only a snooker player. Davis can earn as much money in his sleep as he can at the table. I still have to flog myself around the country to make a decent crust.'

The other side of the coin is that by exposing – and eventually overexposing – the game, television chipped away at Alex's core business. He was essentially a cabaret act. He earned his fortune from challenge matches and exhibitions. His natural habitat was the working man's club and the British Legion. In the early seventies when *Pot Black* was the only alternative, Britain's industrial workforce flocked to see this rocket-fuelled phenomenon at their local saloon. Once snooker received wall-to-wall coverage, those guys could enjoy all the thrills from their armchair. Alex could no longer rely on one-man shows for the bulk of his income. He had to win tournaments to earn serious money.

With good reason, the new breed of opportunist agents were frightened of him. Alex had always worked to his own timetable, lived by his wits and made his own rules. How could he knuckle down to someone else's? The answer is, with extreme difficulty. He boasted that he never missed a tournament, despite a black eye, a busted foot or delayed rail connections at Darlington and Crewe.

Alex should have been a marketing man's dream. Alas, no-one had the vision, the courage or the patience to give it a go. I remember one of his agents, the unfortunate Howard Kruger, telling me that if you could market a white sheep, a black one should be easy. Nice theory, but how could you organise a photo-shoot with someone who doesn't do daylight? How would a chain-smoking, vodka-swilling hellraiser cut it with trendy advertising executives, and vice-versa? How could you take him to dinner when there was a warrant out for his arrest? Kruger learned the hard way. Both were declared bankrupt.

For the best part of two years, Alex was my subject as we explored the man inside the man for his autobiography, *Alex Through the Looking Glass*. Friends commiserated with me. Why attempt the impossible? If the prospect of this squirming mass of hypertension sitting down to analyse his life seemed remote at the start, it grew more remote as he battled with depression, loss of form and the break-up of his marriage. I certainly timed it well!

That's when I first noticed what a problem Alex had with eating. It hounded him for most of his life and contributed to his death. A few moments before he was due to appear live on ITV, he told me with obvious glee that he'd managed to force down a banana. I asked him if that was his dinner. He replied: 'No. That's what I've eaten today.'

My wife and I took Alex and an occasional girlfriend for a Chinese meal at one of the best restaurants in Nottingham. He was in his comfort zone. He liked Chinese restaurants, though for the life of me I can't understand why. He bypassed the food. Having humiliated the head waiter by threatening him with the 'Chinese Godfather' because he didn't have dim sums on the menu, Alex talked and smoked his way through the meal without once picking up a chopstick.

When the three of us had finished eating and the dishes in the centre of the table had turned cold, Alex poured their semi-congealed dregs, one by one into his own bowl. Diners at a neighbouring table, already intrigued by his presence, watched with a growing sense of alarm. So did we. To everyone's disgust, he raised the bowl to his lips and drank its contents. That was his way of eating.

On the way home, Alex and his girlfriend sat in the back of the car. Just before we reached his hotel, I looked in my rear view mirror and saw her head disappear downwards. Alex was already in the well of the car. There was some scuffling. Fortunately it was dark so we couldn't see what was going on. I told him we were getting close to the hotel and asked if he wanted me stop or should I drive around the block a few more times. There was an embarrassed buttoning and straightening going on in the silence before his girlfriend opened the car door and more or less fell out. Amazingly, he kept our interview appointment the next morning. Not only that, he was on good form.

Some of his thoughts that day were prophetic; others were off-beam. In view of what happened to Alex Higgins in the twenty-five years since I ghosted his autobiography, it's interesting to re-visit them.

Whatever they say about me, they'll never forget me. I'm a one-off; a mystery man who'd drive the world's best psychiatrist to his own consulting couch. Snooker sustains me as well as tears me apart. Sometimes I wake up in a cold sweat wondering what would happen if I was forced out of the game; if injury deprived me of what I love best. That's the biggest fear, not because I'd be destitute but because I wouldn't know what to do with myself.

Playing big match snooker can be as big a turn-on as sex. There's nothing more exhilarating than walking into a room bursting with people shouting my name. I know there's another ten million watching on television – a vast audience who weren't interested in snooker till I came along. I feel something wash over me that I can't explain. My mind is turbocharged. I'm part of another world.

Sport is showbiz now. It's all about entertaining the crowds. Where I can sometimes pot a ball that looks mathematically impossible, John McEnroe can hit a ball down the line with such precision it stays in by a fraction. Then the idiot of a line judge calls it out. No wonder McEnroe explodes. I'm made of the same stuff.

I turn crowds on like nobody else can. I need public acclaim to feed my ego. It's a hungry ego. My feeling for the game is raw. I hit the balls while I'm still moving. I go for impossible shots nobody else would attempt. It's the hunter hunting and the crowd shouting for more. It's like being high. In the early days I'd play all day and all night. I'd run out of partners in those lonely twilight hours when I was wide awake and the rest of the world was pushing out zeds. I'd come alive after the midnight chimes, like Dracula. That's when you see the real Hurricane. When daylight creeps in, it's time for me to go.

To the outside world I'm a hellraiser; a temperamental genius on the lookout for trouble. That's wrong. My mother and sisters think they're reading about a complete stranger when they pick up the papers. Underneath it all, I'm a shy, placid person, no different from when I was a kid. I've made a point of not trusting anyone unless I'm absolutely sure. If you put your trust in yourself, you don't need anyone else.

There are lots of things I don't like about myself but I have to live with them. The Irish are fairly short-fused so many of my blow-ups were inevitable. They usually happen when I'm supposed to have my mind on the job but some busybody gets in the way. That's when I snap and tell them to fuck off. People should have more consideration.

They say you reach your peak at this game when you're thirty. If that's the case, I'd better get my second wind quickly. The game's so different now. Everything's a five-furlong sprint so you've got to get into the groove quickly or you're dead. My life's been action-packed. I've done this for longer than anyone. It's taken its toll. Now I've got to decided which course to take. Am I the responsible adult who should be taking things easier and enjoying the fruits of my success – or am I the hustler's hustler till I drop? I wish I knew.

The year 1989 will be my watershed. I've promised myself that I'll stop the one-night stands when I reach forty. I'll play tournaments only, and be selective about them. I promise you, I'll still be in the top ten, possibly top four by then. It's good that so many young players are waiting to inherit the earth but I can hold them off for a while yet – long enough to bow out gracefully.

My business interests take care of themselves. I've invested money in factory units in Salford. I have a half share in three racehorses; a quarter share in a snooker club in Oldham and thousands of acres of forest in Scotland which I haven't seen. With more foresight and better advice, I'd have been into my umpteenth million by now, with a chain of snooker halls across the country.

Alex's moods fluctuated as fast as his feet danced from bar to bookmakers and back again. He would switch from easy camaraderie to ominous tension with no apparent trigger. You had to balance two separate people. I felt sure he must have a medical condition. Jim Meadowcroft, his ally from early days in Blackburn, came to that conclusion long before I did.

Jim is convinced Alex was at best bipolar, at worst schizophrenic. He wasn't alone in that thought. His sisters knew such extremes of behaviour were beyond normal parameters. Jean believes schizophrenia would have been the verdict if he'd been properly examined. Of course, we're guessing. The only time he was tested for mental illness was during his brief stay at Cheadle Royal following his first suicide attempt. Lynn, his wife at the time, is convinced the word 'schizophrenia' appeared on his medical report, but didn't get a chance to check it.

True to form, Alex insulted the doctor and discharged himself on the second morning. He'd sooner suffer stoically than allow doctors within touching distance. Until the last few months he thought he was indestructible. He thought he could treat coronary obstructive pulmonary disease with a Fisherman's Friend. He thought he could discharge himself from hospital while suffering from pneumonia and everything would be okay in the morning. Then he ran out of mornings.

Watching Richard Dormer's impersonation of Alex in a play which he said had been partly inspired by *Alex Through the Looking Glass*, it made me realise what a courageous battle Alex had waged against life and all its demons - not least himself. Not only did he possess a unique talent, but he had the courage to gamble everything on it. He would stand or fall by his ability to challenge other players and beat them. What's more, snooker wasn't the means to an end. There was no end. There was no master plan, no finishing tape. There would be no-one to welcome him across the line and say: 'Now you can take it easy and enjoy the fruits of your toil.' Without his toil he was nothing. Taking things easy was a foreign concept.

Alex reminded me of the unfortunate duellist in *Monty Python and the Holy Grail*. Though reduced limb by limb until all that remained was a head on the ground, the hapless warrior insisted the injuries were mere flesh wounds and urged his opposite number to fight on. Alex persevered as first cancer then starvation then pneumonia and finally chronic pulmonary disease reduced him to a motionless head on a pillow.

We suspected all along that he'd lose everything he ever had - his skill, his strength, his family, his fortune, his women and ultimately his life. Perhaps 'lose' is the wrong word. Alex *gave* it all away. Not in a spirit of generosity. That wasn't his style. He gave it away because he didn't know what else to do with it. For those last few years, when betting on the horses with different friends in different bars was all he had to look forward to, the citizens of Belfast had forgotten, if they ever knew, that he was twice champion of the world.

To them he wasn't The Hurricane. He wasn't a snooker player. He was just Higgy, a local character who lived in liquor saloons, sold signed photographs of himself to fund his gambling and was frequently asked to leave the premises. Zero to hero to zero.

Although he didn't discuss his illness or reveal anything about his attitude to death, Alex became more philosophical as his strength ebbed away. These words were among the last ones he uttered to his long-suffering sister: 'I didn't live my life, Ann. I only took part in it.'

2

HE WAS NO MORE

She sensed it in her nostrils when she opened the door. The pungent confirmation that time had run out. Death, having stalked her brother for twelve years, had finally claimed its victim. It was Saturday, July 24th, 2010.

Ann Higgins believed Alex was still in Spain for his tooth implants but expected him back any time soon. She'd driven from her home in Lurgan to his Belfast apartment block to make sure things were neat and tidy for his return. There was a new warden on duty. He didn't recognise Ann.

'Where are you going?'

'Mr Higgins' flat.'

'I think he's in there.'

'That's funny. He's not due back yet.'

It seems likely that Alex hadn't left his flat since returning from his first trip to Spain a month earlier - a trip which ended catastrophically. The surgeon decided he was too sick for implants. He told Alex to go home, put on some weight and try again at a future date. In reality he knew it wouldn't happen. Alex didn't go back a second time. Nor did he let his sisters know. The warden should have had a clue. Residents are supposed to sign themselves in and out. That was the point of sheltered accommodation.

Alex must have realised the struggle was over. Even if he'd *wanted* to summon his strength for another wild goose chase, it's doubtful he'd have had the energy to get out of bed. Whatever was going through his mind, he hadn't moved out of Belfast since June 27th. It's possible he hadn't moved out of the flat!

Regular drinkers at his daily haunt, the Royal, on the opposite side of the road, are foggy about that missing month. They're not sure whether Alex made an appearance or not. He could well have been lying in bed all that time, too sick to move. Ann hadn't been to visit her brother, believing him to be away.

Nervous now, she caught the lift to the top floor and was alerted by mail on the carpet that something might be wrong. However the radio wasn't playing. He must still be away. Alex always had the radio on.

'Then I got a wee bit of a whiff and I could see one leg sticking out of the bed.' It was the only visible part of his body. She knew without touching that it was cold. In those few seconds when the enormity of life and death banishes rational thought, she half expected Alex to pull the sheet from his face and make one of his usual wisecracks in the hoarse whisper which was now his voice.

Alex always slept with a sheet over his face as though protecting himself from a hostile universe. He was frightened of things that went bump in the night. Hence the all-night radio. At last there was nothing to fear. The sheet stayed where it was.

Ann grabbed his foot and cried: 'Not our Sandy! Not after all he's been through. Dear God, no!' She held her other hand to her nose and staggered out to the lift and down into the courtyard of the small block of flats at the corner of Sandy Row and Donegal Road where her brother spent his last, lonely years. It was two hundred yards from where he grew up.

'I didn't want to go out into the street because the pub smokers were having a fag on the pavement. My panic button was going. I had to get some air. I didn't expect to find him like that. I couldn't take in what my eyes and nose were telling me.'

It was three o'clock in the afternoon. South Belfast went about its usual business while Ann took deep breaths in the courtyard and steadied herself against the wall. She tried to dial Raymond, her husband, but couldn't steady her hands. 'Give me the strength to make a phone call!' She went back to her car and managed to get through: 'I need someone with me, Raymond. I'm sure he's dead. His foot's starting to discolour.'

Pavement smokers at the Royal had detected nothing untoward. It was just another Saturday afternoon down the pub. This had been Alex's milieu. Good guys and losers thrown in together. Guys who wiped the froth from their mouths as early as 7.30 in the morning and existed by and large on liquid diets. Paradoxically, liquid food was all Alex could take now. I'm not referring to Guinness or rum, but to a seemingly inoffensive supplement called Build-Up which Ann bought over the chemist's counter and surreptitiously poured into his tea because she knew he wouldn't bother. His fridge was full of unopened bottles.

Alex's preferred diet was soup or perhaps a small corner of sponge cake crushed with a fork. More often than not he ate nothing at all. It was too difficult without teeth. It's extraordinary to report that in twenty-first century Britain, a former world champion was wasting away like an African famine victim and there was nothing anyone could do to save him.

Three weeks later, adoring crowds lined the streets as Alex's coffin was borne in a horse-drawn gun carriage to Belfast Cathedral. As I stood on the cathedral steps to watch it arrive, I felt the uncomfortable draught of hypocrisy. Maybe I'm being too harsh but where were all those people when he needed them? A five-and-a-half-stone shadow of a human being, who'd been gliding unnoticed between his flat and the Royal for years, was suddenly the subject of a state funeral (give or take the State!).

While Alex was alive they forgot about him. Only when he was dead, did they remember. A pitiful figure had become a national hero overnight. And yet Belfast City Council was indifferent to the whole parade. It declined to be involved. By the way, I include myself in this rebuke. I hadn't spoken to Alex for six or seven years, yet I felt compelled to attend his funeral.

Back at the apartment, Ann was in deep shock as she waited in the summer sunshine for her husband and sister to arrive. Presently Jean turned up. She only lived a couple of blocks away.

'Did you call the ambulance?' she asked.

'No. The number used to be 999 but it's all changed. I don't know what I'm doing, Jeanie.'

Raymond made the call. Ambulance and police cars pulled up fractionally ahead of the press. The family couldn't raise Alex's own doctor, so they had to send for a locum, then the undertaker. Five hours after Ann discovered the body, everything on site had been dealt with.

Ann was still troubled as she looked back to that horrible day: 'It didn't happen the way I thought it would. I thought we'd be in hospital holding his hand like we were with Mummy when she died. We watched our daddy die too. I kept thinking that Sandy might have wanted someone to sit with him those last few hours instead of dying alone. I feel I should have been there.'

Alex had been too weak to use his mobile, so was unable to alert them. In any case, it wasn't his style to keep people informed. 'Our Sandy doesn't tell you anything,' said Jean. 'He'd never say he didn't feel well. He'd rather pretend it wasn't happening and get on with something else.'

The sisters were reassured by the coroner's verdict that death would have come quickly. The report, from the Queen's University of Belfast Department of Justice listed two causes of death:

1(a) Pneumonia, due to (b) Chronic Obstructive Pulmonary Disease.
2 Undernutrition. (Previous Pharyngeal Carcinoma.)

Ann said: 'The coroner's office told us he'd been there a maximum of two days, not ten, as the papers were saying. They said he was probably too exhausted to do anything except collapse into bed. He'd have been too weak to even turn on the radio.'

There's a slight anomaly. Jean noticed that the last copy of the *Racing Post* in Alex's apartment was dated July 10th - two weeks before his body was found. The last message on his mobile was also dated the 10th. Said Jean: 'It was a message he sent to himself. I couldn't possibly repeat it. It was too personal. I can't work out why July 10th was the cut-off point. It's odd.'

Saturday the 24th is etched in Gary Audley's memory. He watched the comings and goings from the Royal. Gary was a boyhood friend. He was born in the next street. They played snooker together as kids. He remembers Alex running away to be a jockey. 'I was a wee boy then, so I was.' Today he's a tiler with no roofs to tile. He spent every day in the pub at Alex's right hand, straining to understand his conversation; rushing his bets down to the bookies before the off and - very occasionally - collecting his winnings.

Gary showed me the seat facing the television set where Alex always sat, pint of Guinness and maybe a bowl of soup on the table, copies of the racing press spilling onto the chairs and floor. Regulars gave the vacant throne a wide berth, almost as if they expected him to reclaim it.

Gary confided: 'I feel lost, big time. We were very close. Days are empty now.'

He fiddled with his mobile. 'I had voice messages from Alex when he could still speak. I wanted to keep them but they must have been erased. Damn!' Despite Alex's fast-deteriorating condition, Gary was stunned by the news. 'I can't believe he's gone. He went through hell but kept going. I never once heard him complain about his illness. He was content to cross the street and sit in the pub. The horses kept him going. That's all he lived for. He was still smoking, but not heavily. I suppose we just thought he'd go on forever. He was a tremendous battler. I visited him in City Hospital a couple of times when he had palate cancer. He was on morphine but still in great pain. He took it all in his stride.

You should have seen him sitting there in his long johns on summer days. His arms and wrists were like matchsticks. People who never saw him in his T-shirt won't believe how skinny he was. I put my arms around him and all I could feel were the bones in his back.'

Craig Cooper, the owner of the Royal, had a ringside seat as events unfolded in Donegal Road the day Alex's body was found. 'I saw the ambulance and police cars pull up and knew it must be Higgy. I felt my stomach churn. Since Easter I'd noticed a big change. It was the worst I'd ever seen him. His face was sunken in. I said: "Higgy, you look terrible," but he just laughed. I wasn't charging him for drinks any more. He went behind the counter and helped himself to rum and coke.'

Conversation had become practically impossible for Alex. He communicated by scribbling notes to his fellow drinkers, some practical, some philosophical. Here's one he wrote to a good friend Valerie McCann when she offered to buy him a pint: 'If I drank every free drink I've been offered, I'd either be dead or a rambling alcoholic. I'm still fighting on and I've got my late mother's spirit inside me giving me inner strength. Says I, Alex.'

Gary Audley reckons he was down to four and half stone towards the end. He showed me the last picture he'd taken with his phone cam. Alex was skeletal but smiling. 'He knew what was happening,' said Gary. 'About six weeks before he died, he gave himself three months to live.'

Craig added: 'He'd fought for too long. He was knackered. We tried many times to talk some sense into him about eating but he was a headstrong guy. He did his own thing. If you wanted him to turn right, you'd ask him to turn left! He came here for peace and quiet and we all looked after him.'

Curious though it might sound, I have a feeling that Alex, agitated soul that he was for most of his professional career, might just have found a small measure of peace once his body was too weak to satisfy the urgent demands of his mind. Nothing approaching an epiphany, but the tranquillity that can descend once you accept your limits. It doesn't get much simpler than walking twenty-five yards to the pub, sitting in a chair all day, studying form, having a bet and walking twenty-five yards home again.

Against that, he was in serious discomfort. Swallowing was difficult. During the final months, he carried a Ventolin inhaler because his breathing was restricted. Lack of flesh meant he was permanently cold. What's more, he was coughing up phlegm every few minutes. It's remarkable in view of those handicaps that he still walked at trotting pace. It was a job to keep up with him. And he was still capable of the grand entrance. He never lost that.

However, it seems inconceivable that someone in his condition – virtually a dead man walking – wasn't under medical supervision. That task fell to his sister, Ann: 'Sandy couldn't be doing with carers and nurses. We had to do it all. He had his disability allowance and he had Jean and me. We just had to get on with it.'

Alex's pathological hatred of doctors and hospitals meant it was impossible to enforce treatment. He insisted on doing his own doctoring. He had an odd collection of remedies. If you don't look for help or refuse to accept it, you don't get any. Alex had ruled himself out.

Ann went to the flat once a fortnight to put two weeks worth of pureed, home-cooked meals in the freezer and do the housework. But she lived twenty-five miles away and had a family of her own to look after. The only other person to visit the flat in those final few weeks was Aaron Tilley, a reporter from the *Belfast Sunday Life*, who recorded the last interview with Alex. Aaron was too young to remember The Hurricane in his prime. To him, Alex Higgins was a wrinkled old man with a shattered larynx. It was early May, 2010. Alex had ten weeks to live:

> When I first knocked on his door, he told me to piss off. He said he didn't trust me. I'd only knife him in the back. I decided to have another go the next day. I bought him some pâté from Tesco. He answered the door fully dressed at about 11.00 am, the time he goes to the Royal each day. He saw the pâté and looked this young reporter straight in the eye: 'Come back in an hour with £1,250 and you can do what you like.'
>
> We came back with £750. He invited us through a dark hallway into his lounge, then made me sign an IOU which promised to pay him the extra £500 by the next day. My editor agreed, though he wasn't happy because we were only a local paper. Higgy called the twenty-four-hour security guard to witness the contract, then he launched off into a soliloquy. He knew exactly what we wanted.
>
> The place was clean and roomy but dull. Like a pensioner's flat. Higgy looked ghoulish with no front teeth. He was just bones. He shuffled about. He took us into the kitchen and showed us bowls of mashed-up carrots and gravy and the protein shakes that bodybuilders use. All I saw him drink was tea. He offered me and the photographer a coke. His lounge table was cluttered with tobacco and piles of racing papers. Higgy was sucking on his pen. He didn't smoke in the flat.

He told me about his victories and defeats and the final he played with a broken ankle. Most of it went over my head. Then he got onto the subject of bribery. He claimed two guys offered him the equivalent of £300,000 to throw a match but he wasn't interested. 'Even though they wear white shirts, they're not clean. I'd rather kill myself than take a bribe.' There was poetry in what he said and how he said it. I noticed that particularly. He had to keep stopping to spit in a bucket he had at his side. He was bright and sparky even though he couldn't speak at normal volume. If he could, he'd probably have told me to piss off again. Why did he want a whippersnapper asking him all these questions?

He said his daily routine didn't vary. He went to the Royal every day at the same time. He'd have two halves of Guinness, two glasses of rum and four cigarettes in the alley at the back. Then he'd place his bets and get home in time to watch *Cash in the Attic*. He seemed to be house proud. His clothes and ties were hanging up neatly. In the spare room there was a wardrobe containing one of Oliver Reed's signed jackets. Higgy put it on. It looked gigantic. He jumped in the air and said: 'Take a picture of me doing this.' He showed us the tuxedos he wore to play snooker. They were all laid out on the bed. On a table nearby was the Irish championship trophy he won in 1989. It was unmounted.

There was a big poster of Audrey Hepburn and pictures of Lauren and Jordan when they were younger. He said in a wheezing whisper: 'I love them dearly.' I could see he was overcome. He said he'd been to see his kids in Manchester recently. Then he looked around the apartment and said: 'I should be living next to Wayne Rooney in a house with marble floors. I used to play billiards in places like that. Now I'm in this wee flat. I've only got myself to blame.'

He blamed his damaged vocal chords on the guy who mugged him in Belfast city centre. His attacker grabbed him around the neck, punched him in the throat and stole his address book. 'Bastard!' he fumed. The subject of suicide came up. He confessed it was in the back of his mind. He realised how ill he was and said he was in quite a lot of pain: 'All I've got now to stop the feelings of loneliness, depression and suicide is my mum's bible.'

For some reason, his mind went back to his first wife, Cara Hasler, the daughter of an Australian racehorse trainer: 'I called her Grievous Bodily Harm because she was very physical. I've never been that highly sexed. I used to sit watching old movies in the living room to keep out of her way! There are no women now. The last one was a former pop star from the sixties. I had a passionate one-night stand with her.'

Before we left, he stood in front of his rumpled bed and, coughing and gasping, said: 'This bed hasn't seen any action for ten years.'

I asked him what he would like as his epitaph. He said he wanted to be remembered as a hurricane which blew around the table making snooker look easy.

The Save Alex Higgins campaign was doomed to failure. Although the concept was laudable, the execution was ragged and the outcome near-fatal. The lesson surely is that medical matters are too important to be left to amateurs, however well-meaning. The fund-raising itself, but especially the fateful trip to Marbella which followed, degenerated into a freak show with Alex playing the freak. To a certain extent he was a willing partner in it, but for the wrong reasons. The money appealed to him more than the implants.

There are signs that Alex knew his days were numbered. Before we examine that regrettable episode, let's focus on the golden years when Higgins was a folk hero. The self-styled People's Champion was feted by the rich and famous, mimicked by impressionists, fancied by women, adored by television executives, appreciated by fellow professionals who grew rich off the back of snooker's growing appeal but dreaded by hotel and restaurant owners the length and breadth of Britain. Few are better placed to shed light on the Alex Higgins mystery than Jimmy White. The Whirlwind was the closest thing he had to a soulmate. He supported Alex to the bitter end.

3

HE WAS MY BEST MATE

'I was in shock for a long time. It still makes me cry when I think about him. I was sad and angry that he'd gone. We lost a great man. I lost my best mate. It didn't have to finish like that. He should be sitting here with me now. We tried everything to save Higgins but he didn't want help. He didn't want pity. He'd tell you to fuck off! The only way I could have done it was to kidnap him, tie him up, lock him in a room and force-feed him. But we don't live in a world like that.'

Note the use of the surname. Jimmy White usually refers to his pal as Higgins. Alex called him James. Although there was fourteen years between them, they were birds of a feather both in style of play and style of life. The public loved their swagger; headline writers loved their antics. As befits young heroes wallowing in wealth, fame and adulation, Alex and Jimmy indulged themselves beyond the limits that most other sportsmen would permit themselves - or indeed be permitted. Snooker, like darts and golf, is more or less self-regulating. There's no code of off-field behaviour. Fitness isn't a prerequisite. Sobriety is - or certainly *was* - optional. The Hurricane and The Whirlwind had carte blanche. They thought it would last forever.

Alex discovered that abusing your mind and body can be fun while it lasts, but it doesn't last long. Jimmy discovered that it cramps your talent. It's a major disappointment to all snooker lovers that he failed to fulfil his immense potential. Jimmy puts it another way: 'I haven't won the world championship *yet*.'

There were essentially two ways of going about your job as a professional snooker player. You either went the respectable way favoured by Steve Davis, Stephen Hendry, Ken Doherty, John Parrott, etc., or you took the road to Sodom and Gomorrah favoured by Alex Higgins, Jimmy White and Kirk Stephens among others. Life's pleasures came to them easily. Alex could afford anything he wanted, though he was adamant he never paid for sex.

As regards close personal relationships, Alex had neither the time nor the commitment. He was too self-focused. He didn't want to be joined at the hip to anyone. Other people's welfare wasn't his concern. Two failed marriages, two bloodstained love affairs and three neglected children bear testimony. Snooker groupies helped him along his picaresque way. Most were forgotten once they'd outlived their brief usefulness. Some genuine friends, like Jeff Lomas who was best man at his second wedding, were ruthlessly cast aside.

Jimmy White escaped rejection. He was a permanent fixture. He was Alex's one true lasting friend. The Leprechaun and the Cockney Sparrer; The Hurricane and The Whirlwind. In the seven-foot portrait he had painted, Alex insisted on giving Jimmy a name check. He had the initials JW added to a pack of cards in his trouser pocket. A small gesture perhaps, but a large one too. It says a lot for Jimmy's stamina that he occupied that exclusive role:

> I must have said twenty times in my life: 'I'll never speak to that bastard again.' I always broke my own rule because I loved him to death. Higgins could be the coldest, most infuriating person in the world, then do the most beautiful things. When his daughter was born, he decided he liked the name Lauren. It wasn't surprising because that was my daughter's name. He told everyone *I'd* copied *him*! He asked me to change my daughter's

name. I humoured him. What he'd forgotten was that *my* Lauren was three months older than his! Classic Higgins. He was from a different planet. Because he was famous, he thought he was extra-terrestrial.

If he came down to earth, he could be a great ally. When I had testicular cancer, he was the first one on the phone. He said he was there for me if I needed him. He meant it. That's when you saw his true colours – the side the public didn't see and probably wouldn't believe. Higgins had a bit of class. He *did* care. He did two exhibitions for me. One was to raise money for the Royal Marsden Hospital where I had my treatment, and the other was for a friend of mine who lost his son in Afghanistan. I knew Higgins would show up, but promoters were usually nervous! Higgins wasn't one to take the lead and organise things. He had enough trouble organising himself, but he was prepared to give his time for nothing when it mattered.

The biggest favour he did for me was being my friend. I could share my problems with him. He listened. I knew it would go no further. It didn't matter how drunk he was or how much dope he'd done – I could guarantee that he wouldn't breathe a word of our conversation to anyone else. He was a hundred per cent solid. We had lots of fun skipping around the country and getting up to mischief. Unfortunately, his way of fun got us booted out of places. It was a shame because before the drink took hold of him, Higgins was hilarious. Sometimes I put a minder on him to stop him abusing people. Then we could all relax.

People say he was mean and selfish but he was generous with me. He always paid his way and often went to the bar first. I remember once meeting him at Manchester Airport for a trip to Canada. We had to buy our own tickets, then get the money refunded with our appearance fee. Before I could get to the flight counter, Higgins had bought my ticket. He refused to let me pay him back. He said I could keep the refund.

Sometimes it takes a funeral to bring home the truth. It gave Tony Meo and me the first chance for ages to reminisce about The Hurricane and the great time he gave us when we were kids. Higgins was our role model. Yes, we were naughty boys and we got up to a lot of skulduggery. We thought we were kings of the universe. Snooker was the biggest show in town and the atmosphere at exhibition matches was electric. Higgins had crowds in the palm of his hand. I was in complete awe of him.

I first met him when I was twelve. He played an exhibition at my dad's club in Balham for the princely sum of £90. It was like a football fan meeting David Beckham. I didn't sleep for a whole week before that event. When I saw him in the flesh I was speechless. Higgins was a god. He had this fantastic thing called charisma which means he was the only thing in the room you noticed. You couldn't stop watching him. There's no-one better than Ronnie O'Sullivan at clearing up with the cue ball but Higgins did it a different way. He played shots we hadn't seen before. He had control of the cue ball but that was too straightforward for him.

Exciting the crowd was more important. He lived off it. That's why I do it. I copied him. Higgins convinced me it was the only way to play. I might never have picked up a cue if it hadn't been for him. Being adventurous cost both of us tournaments we should have won at a canter, but you can't beat that adrenalin rush when the audience gasps because you've played an audacious shot. It's contagious. I only made 300 century breaks. Once I'd reached 70 and the frame was won, I'd start having fun. Higgins and I called it 'controlled flair'.

They used to say Higgins was fast. He wasn't. He ran around the table faster than anyone else but he took his time on the shot. People never knew that because he was so wiry and full of nervous energy. Every part of his face and body was on the move the whole time. But when you look at the statistics, his average shot time was twenty-two seconds. O'Sullivan's is eleven seconds and mine's sixteen. He was faster in his younger days but the name Hurricane gave a false impression.

Having been in awe of him as a teenager, I became his closest pal. In some ways he was a father figure but in others he was a child stumbling about in the dark. The notorious hellraiser *wasn't* at all streetwise. I suppose being a Londoner, used to the night life and the club scene, gave me the advantage but you'd be amazed how naive and helpless Higgins could be. He had no idea about tax or household bills. He didn't bother with shopping or all the other daily chores most people *have* to bother with. He thought the rules didn't apply to him. He got away with it because of who he was. I was twenty and he was thirty-four but I always felt I had to take care of him. Higgins didn't have a clue how to organise his life or his time. It was a mystery how he ever got from A to B. Unfortunately he didn't get a reality check until it was too late. He'd stick his fingers in his ears when you tried to have a sensible conversation. When he finally started to take a look at himself, he didn't like what he saw. I think it frightened him. That's why he got progressively angrier.

His biggest problem was smoking cannabis. It fucked him up. He lost his sense of reality because he smoked it all the time. It wasn't just fags. It was nearly always cannabis. He didn't realise how strong it could be. His life became confused and distorted and he didn't bother to practise. He said he could only perform in front of an audience but when he *got* in front of a big audience at tournaments and exhibitions, he went to pieces because he couldn't deliver the goods. Fear and paranoia set it. That's when the fights started. Things were turning bad. Higgins thought cannabis would make everything okay. The vicious circle carried on turning.

I organised a big exhibition for him in Dublin. We figured the best idea was to book him into the Europa in Belfast, pick him at a reasonable time the next morning and drive him to Dublin. I had a colleague of mine detailed to do it. He gets Higgins up at 9.30 and they set off. They've got all day to get there. At 7.00 that evening, there's still no sign of them. Six hundred people are in the exhibition hall. I've heard nothing from the driver and not a dicky bird from Higgins. It turns out he has done the driver's mobile by using it to place his bets. The battery's dead. He's stopped at every other pub and every betting shop on the way. My colleague's angry and frustrated but helpless. He knows Higgins will be late for the show but he can't let anyone else know. Higgins rescued the event because of his personality but he gave no thought on the anxiety he caused.

You can't blame snooker players for not befriending him. Unless you knew him like I did, you didn't have a hope in hell. People ran when they saw him coming. That included John Virgo – and he'd normally stand up and tell *anyone* what he thought of them. He was chairman of the WPBSA and grew up with Higgins in Manchester, but he couldn't get out of the way fast enough when Higgins lost to Tony Meo in the UK championship. My manager, John Callaghan, saw Virgo running down the path between the venue and the hotel. John chased after him wondering why he was in such a hurry. Back came the reply: 'Alex has just got beat. I'm fucked if I'm hanging around to be slagged off!'

What's it coming to when the chairman of the governing body has to hide in his room terrified? Who better for Higgins to blame than someone who holds the highest position? Virgo didn't give him the chance. Higgins hated everyone on the board, old and new. I told him to change his attitude because most of the blokes who punished him down the years were gone. It didn't matter. To him they were all 'arseholes'. Perhaps they could have done more to help him but they weren't dealing with a normal person. They were dealing with Alex Higgins. In the last few years, even *I* couldn't get near him and I was his best friend! His mates in Ireland couldn't get near him, his sisters couldn't get near him. All he wanted from them was money for gambling.

Some things he did puzzled me. He'd go for months without speaking. I'd miss him and assume I must have done something to upset the guy. I'd be the one suffering. Then he'd ring me and say 'Hello, James', as if nothing had happened. I don't think he knew when he was out of order. It didn't seem to occur to him. He nearly wrecked my moment on *This Is Your Life*. He told me I was going to be on. Higgins said he did it to make sure I was ready for it. Okay, I'll admit I was a bit of a lad at the time, but you don't spoil a surprise like that. I think he was jealous because I was the centre of attention. I still have a problem with it.

It's time to blow the myth of the Great Lover Boy. Higgins was hopeless with women. Although he was a very intelligent man, he couldn't hold a conversation with the opposite sex for more than five minutes. To be honest, he wasn't really interested. My first wife felt safe when I was out with Higgins because she knew he wasn't a womaniser. He only had three or four real girlfriends in his life. Most of his attempted one-night stands ended in drunken failure. His serious relationships ended in tears because he didn't know how to handle them. He was a big-time loner. He had his gambling and his books and he travelled solitary. He didn't like to get close to too many people. I was one of the privileged few.

He called Siobhan the love of his life but that affair looked dodgy from the start. I met her when he began dating her. He invited her to Doncaster where we were hoping to retain our title as world doubles champions. In the final, we were up against 'Dustbin' Danny Fowler, a refuse collector and 'P.C.' Barry West, a policeman. With respect to Danny and Barry, we should have buried them. The reason we didn't was that Higgins was having a running battle with Siobhan throughout the match. He kept leaving his seat to fight with her in the actual arena. Thank God it wasn't televised! He'd miss a shot then start yelling more abuse in her direction. It was crazy. So was the result. We lost 5–4.

He took Siobhan on several of his engagements, which was a good idea in principle. I take my girlfriend to exhibitions at the weekend because I'm determined not to make the same mistakes as before. It helps her to see how tiring it is being on tour – and how much temptation's thrown into your path. There has to be trust.

Trying to balance a professional snooker career with a family life is hard work. When Higgins was going strong in the eighties, his main earnings were on the road, not from tournaments. Once you win a tournament, it sets you up for the *real* money. For Higgins that meant three months travelling the country on top of playing eight or nine tournaments a year. He and Lynn became strangers. So did I and *my* wife. Poor old Higgins had lots of inner battles but with the benefit of hindsight, I can see that all he wanted was a home life. He never really had that. He just couldn't get it right whichever way he played it. Women he left at home grew resentful. Those he brought with him got into even bigger trouble.

I loved his spirit of adventure. He'd go anywhere at any time. That could be in the dead of night if the mood took him. He wanted to *live* life. You never knew where you'd end up and that was the fun. He just said 'Come on, James', and you had to follow. My favourite Higgins story is a classic chapter of accidents nobody could have foreseen, least of all me. Even when you thought you were safe, danger lurked around the corner. I played an exhibition with him at the Mayflower in Southampton, followed by a visit to Stanley's Casino. Apart from gambling away a small fortune, the evening was going okay until we went to the Chinese restaurant on the floor above. Higgins has to go for a joint, so we're in the toilets having a chat. I don't use dope. I'm sitting on the edge of the sink.

All at once, the sink comes away from the wall bringing half the wall down. The pipe's hanging off it. I couldn't believe my eyes. I should have owned up to it but didn't have the bottle. In any case, we'd been on a two-day bender so I wasn't thinking straight. We went back to our table and ordered the meal. The restaurant was packed. I knew sooner or later we'd be getting wet. Water starts spilling into the corner of the room. The waiter notices it. I tell Higgins not to say anything. We'd hardly got enough dosh left for the meal, never mind the plumbing! Higgins doesn't listen. He takes it upon himself to blow our cover. The waiters grab hold of him. My mates jump over the counter to get our cues and we run a gauntlet of waiters to get out of the place. Higgins is hanging back. He doesn't realise we're nearly skint.

Some of the staff try to follow us in their car but we give them the slip. We end up in a shebeen, one of those illegal drinking dens which stay open all night. We decide to stay there. If we thought we were safe, we got a rude awakening the next morning. We stagger out of the shebeen, where the music's still pounding, into the Southampton daylight at around 9.30 am. Bugger me, the police are waiting for us. They've been there for five hours. They can't go into the house because it would look like an official raid and cause a mini riot. Instead, they grab Higgins and me and slam us in a cell. We're allowed to make one call, so I ring a pal in London and ask him to drive down with two hundred readies to pay for the toilet repairs. It's a tense time but they eventually release us. All because Higgins couldn't keep his big mouth shut. It wasn't like him to be so honest.

I planned to tell that story at Higgins' funeral. I thought I had to tell a true tale and not worry about the content. However, funeral day was Realisation Day. I didn't think it was appropriate for me to say anything. I was too emotional. It hurt that I was thousands of miles away when he needed me. I wasn't expecting tragedy. I'd been hoping for good news about his teeth, not that. I asked the Dean if he'd read my story at the cathedral. He said he would.

When Higgins beat the cancer, I met a reporter from the *Daily Express* who wanted to do the 'miracle' story. I put him in touch with Alex and agreed a fee of £15,000 for the exclusive. They arranged to meet him in Belfast but, rather than give them the interview, he said he wanted to show them how to dodge in and out of the city. Christ knows what was going on in his head. He took them to some of his old haunts. The reporter and photographer followed him around for an hour but couldn't get him to sit down and tell them how he cheated death. Higgins broke the agreement. The *Express* published a story anyway and didn't give him a penny for it. Why should they? He was such an idiot. Imagine how I felt.

The last time I saw Higgins was at the fund-raising dinner for his teeth. He wasn't supposed to be there. He was seriously ill with pneumonia but left hospital and flew to Manchester. I was horrified when I saw him. I'd seen him in that state two years earlier at an event in Doncaster. It was the most concerned I'd ever been. Somehow he pulled through that crisis. Now we had another one. He and I chatted like old times. He felt good to be among his mates. He ended up being the star of the show. God knows how he managed to sing and dance! He was excited about the fund and about the future. It was all very upbeat. He said: 'I'll be back with you doing exhibitions next year, James. I'm getting a new cue. I can't wait.'

I had lots of exhibitions in the pipeline for him. John Callaghan and I weren't his agents but we were helping to promote his name again. When people booked me, we told them we could get Alex Higgins as well. Ninety per cent of the time they were thrilled. But although he wanted to do the shows and get back to earning a living, he was too weak. I didn't know what to say to him. At just over six stone, he had no strength to play the shots. We made him top of the bill on the Snooker Legends tour but the first show he did was the last. It was disastrous. He played Cliff Thorburn. Both of them were out of touch so the game took forever. They only completed two frames in four hours. Nobody was going to pay to see that rubbish! Higgins was in denial. He didn't accept the truth that was staring at him. He said he'd be raring to go once he'd got his tooth implants and built up his strength.

John Callaghan and I worked on the Save Alex Higgins Fund. We booked the celebrities and did a lot of the organising. I did it out of friendship. I'd do anything for Higgins and I know he'd have done anything for me. Ronnie Wood offered one of his guitars for auction at the dinner. He joked that he'd be the proud owner of Higgins' bottom teeth!

It was Catch 22 with his teeth and bulking up. He couldn't eat till he got his teeth and he couldn't get his teeth until he ate. I'm not being funny but Higgins wouldn't take any advice. The doctors were wrong, his sisters were wrong and I was wrong.

Only Higgins was right. When you're that ill you should stop being stubborn and do what they tell you. He played around with the things they prescribed for him. Because he was a bright bloke he read alternative medical books and came up with his own treatments. He got hold of the ingredients, then he couldn't be bothered to take them. Higgins couldn't his win his battle because he didn't like food. He never did and he never would.

There were times when he got really low and said he'd rather die then keep fighting. He was depressed about what his life had become and the money he'd wasted on gambling. It made him feel wretched. He wouldn't do anything to change it, though. That's what makes me so angry. At the funeral, the singer Doug James, who was one of the fund trustees, said he wished we'd just given Higgins the fund to spend as he saw fit. Spending it to bury him wasn't the plan. Of course, we all knew bookmakers would be the beneficiaries if we had given him the money. Higgins even suggested it himself at the dinner. He said Goodwood Races were on the following week, so could he have the £20,000 now because he might not be around afterwards!

I went to Thailand and China while Higgins went to Marbella for his implants. I was very worried about the guy but thought he'd seen sense at last. I hoped for a minor miracle. Then I got the news that he was dead. It was a fucking liberty! Higgins could have had a nice life. He was such a superstar. There was still a good chance of earning a decent living and getting the respect he deserved. He couldn't get it out of his head that everyone was against him. People who came to see him weren't against him. Nor were promoters. They saw him as a money spinner. They'd book Sadam Hussein if it filled the snooker club!

If he was here now I'd say this: why did you insist on doing everything the Higgins way and ignoring what everyone told you? What was it that stopped you saving your own life? I told you I'd give you a driver and find you somewhere to live in Epsom close to me. I told you there was money to be made on the Question and Answer circuit. You'd have been brilliant at that. People like provocative answers. They like to be insulted. You wouldn't have let them down.

Thanks for all the good times, my friend. You were a fantastic bloke. You changed my life. I won't get over this quickly.

4

HE WAS A FREAK SHOW

It was a blisteringly hot June in Marbella. Much of Spain was cemented to the television screen as their team came closer and closer to winning the 2010 World Cup. Charlie Hawley, a long time friend of Alex, was watching the football in his luxury apartment when the phone rang. It was the man at the supermarket.

'Your mate's here, Chas.'

'Who's my mate?'

'Alex Higgins. He's in a bad way. Says he wants to see you.'

'What the hell's *he* doing here? Tell him I'm on my way.'

They met in Julie's Bar on the seafront. Charlie's heart sank when he saw Alex. They hugged each other for several minutes. Alex couldn't or wouldn't let go. As the temperature hovered in the mid-30s, he stood there in a jumper, jacket, overcoat and hat – shivering. He couldn't speak so he wrote Charlie a note.

'I've come to get my teeth sorted.'

'What – on your own?' asked Charlie.

Alex nodded.

'Where are you staying?'

He shrugged his shoulders.

'Right, you're coming with me.'

So began a degrading episode which would have broken anyone's resolve. It almost certainly broke Alex's but he didn't let it show. Put it down to pride. Charlie couldn't figure out why such a sick man, incapable of speech and barely able to walk, had been sent unaccompanied on a flight to Spain - and with nowhere to stay when he arrived. How crazy did it get?

The pair set off for Charlie's apartment complex in Cabopino where Alex had stayed a few times before. The short car journey passed more or less in silence. Alex was sucking a Fisherman's Friend to ease the soreness in his throat. He got through packets of them. Charlie handed him one of his old army notebooks to scribble on. The name Will Robinson appeared. Charlie hadn't heard of him. Gradually, a confused and rather desperate story began to emerge.

Alex wrote that he'd signed a deal with a production company to film his tooth implants. The figure quoted was £20,000. However, he'd also been approached by a representative of another company who offered him £5,000 for a thirty-minute documentary they'd apparently been commissioned to make for Channel 4. Alex's scribbled messages were accompanied by growled abuse, seemingly aimed at all and sundry. That was all Charlie could glean.

The next morning, he got a call from Eileen Knight, a PR woman who worked for Mills and Mills, a cosmetic dental practice in Marbella. She confirmed that Alex had been sent from Manchester to get his teeth done. The man behind it was a musical agent called Will Robinson. That name again. Charlie was aghast.

'Have you seen the state of him?'

'Not yet.'

'You're in for a shock. Listen, I'm a good friend of Alex, why wasn't I in the loop?'

'I don't know.'

'We're toying with a man's life here, Eileen. I don't like this cloak and dagger stuff.'

Eileen explained the background. It began with a *News of the World* 'exclusive' that Alex was dying of starvation because his teeth and gums had been blitzed by radiotherapy. Eileen saw the accompanying photograph and was stung into action. As a snooker fan when Alex was in his pomp, Eileen she was horrified by what she saw and read. It reminded her of her father who had died of cancer after wasting away in similar fashion. With the consent of the clinic's owners, she got in touch with the *News of the World* and, through them, offered Alex £20,000-worth of state-of-the-art dental treatment *free of charge*. She was unaware that another interested party had read the same story and also decided to act.

Eileen told me: 'I loved Alex. I used to think he was quite dishy. It was awful to see him so emaciated. I'd have done anything to help him. We thought we might be able to save his life. A successful implant would obviously have been good publicity for us so there was no question of him having to pay.'

The *News of the World* story also brought tears to the eyes of Will Robinson who was on holiday in Antigua at the time. Will had known Alex since the early 1980s and acted as his driver and minder for a period. He explained: 'I hadn't seen Alex for years. It shocked me to the core. I had no idea he was in such a state. No-one, to my knowledge, was doing anything to help. *Someone* had to get those teeth for him. He should have had more help from the WPBSA but his relationship with them was always fraught. Those implants could have been done ten years ago. I couldn't believe his doctor or surgeon hadn't recommended it. Alex might still be here today. I decided I could sort it but it was going to be a sweat.'

Things began to accelerate when Will and Eileen were put in touch with each other. Within three weeks, Alex had his first consultation with Dr Bart Van der Ven, a facial reconstructive surgeon in Harley Street, although, as we shall hear, getting him there was a task and a half. To most people's surprise the surgeon gave Alex's gums a clean bill of health. He'd been applying a special substance to protect them during radiotherapy. Dr Van der Ven's verdict: 'He's ready for the pre-op.'

Will decided a fund-raising scheme was urgent, despite the fact that the treatment was being offered free. Lauren's extremely suspicious about this. She can't understand why so many people donated hard-earned money when it wasn't necessary. Lauren's also mystified by the way urgent treatment was delayed for a rather pointless fundraising exercise. He said there'd be planes, hotels and phone calls to underwrite. Will got hold of Alex's sister, Jean. Could she let Alex know that he was inviting donations to send him to Spain?

Alex got the message and left a croaky reply on Will's mobile: 'Mr Robinson. Bubbles. Alex the Hurricane here. Thanks for everything you're trying to do. I love you. I'll always love you. Call me. Alex. I love you. I love you.'

Said Will: 'He always repeated that at the end of his messages. He kicked me around when I was a teenager but I've got a good business head now and he respected that.'

The musical agent discovered that Alex had tried different sets of dentures but complained that they kept coming loose. Some people can't get used to dentures. Unfortunately, Alex was one of them. So he gave up. His sisters were at a loss to know what to do next, other than provide him with pureed food and vitamin supplements.

Alex and Will had first met at Mere Golf and Country Club in the Cheshire stockbroker belt when Will was fifteen years old. He caddied for Frank Carson and played in a junior card school: 'I was gobsmacked when Alex walked in. The world snooker champion asked if he could join our card school. It was only a pound pot till he arrived. He pulled out a pile of change – fivers and tenners – and the pot became a lot bigger. I was sitting on aces. I knew he only had threes. He raised the pot by £10 so I put in all my caddying money plus an extra £50. Alex's eyes rolled. He couldn't believe a fifteen-year-old would outdo him but I did! We went for a drink at the bar. He christened me "Bubbles" because he said I had a nice, smiley face. He asked if I'd caddy for him. He gave me his mobile number and offered to let me practise snooker at his house if my dad would drop me round.'

Will's dad was Noel Robinson, once the all-England amateur snooker champion. Alex was managed - he would say mismanaged - by Howard Kruger. He wanted Kruger to engage Will as his personal assistant and Kruger went along with it. It was a very loose arrangement. Alex would ask 'Bubbles' how many hours he'd done, then slap a few £20 notes on the table and say: 'Double or quits.' Will had to beat him at cards to save his salary.

For reasons best known to himself, Will pressed on with his fund-raising. He was supported by Jimmy White, Tony Knowles, John Virgo, a number of *Coronation Street* actors and singers from Will's client list. Also included was Raymond Chan, the owner of Alex's favourite Chinese restaurant in Manchester. Alex himself wasn't expected at the fund-raising dinner. He'd been ordered not to leave his hospital bed. He tried secretly to get Jean to escort him out of hospital but she refused and the two had a blazing row. Jean told him: 'I'm not taking you out to die! Stay where you are.'

To Jean's fury, Alex discharged himself and made his way to Manchester. No hospital can keep a patient against his or her wishes. Alex's reckless behaviour did untold damage. He'd been admitted with pneumonia. The prognosis was bad. Small quantities of food were making their way into his lungs, turning dark and coming back up again. That was potentially fatal.

'Obviously we'd have loved Alex to be at the dinner,' Will said, 'but I wasn't going to push him.'

He arranged for Jean to represent him. That wouldn't go down well with Alex. Then Will's phone rang. Alex was doing his best to speak. It was hard to understand him: 'Bubbles, the flights are terrible. Get me on the ferry.'

'What flights, Alex? You're sick. Stay where you are.'

'Don't make me angry.'

A cloud of volcanic ash from Iceland had delayed flights in and out of Ireland but air traffic was now back to normal. Still Alex insisted on sailing over.

'Get me on that ferry.'

'Don't be silly. You're not coming by boat. It takes eight hours.'

'Don't make me angry, Bubbles!'

'I've checked the ferry. There aren't any berths left.'

'It's okay. I'll sit on a bench.'

The prospect of a pneumonia victim spending eight hours on a bench while crossing the Irish Sea made Will shudder. He logged onto the Ryanair website to double check that flights from Belfast were leaving on time. They were. He called Alex back: 'The flights are okay. If you *must* come, that's the best way.'

'Listen to me, Bubbles. I'm in Belfast and you're in Manchester. There are no flights.'

'Go to City Airport. I've booked you on the Manchester flight. If there's a problem, go to the ferry port. End of story.'

Miraculously, Alex got to the venue – by air. The reason he was so determined to go against doctor's and Jean's advice is that he longed for the company of friends. He hadn't seen Jimmy White, John Virgo or Tony Knowles for a long time. He needed some TLC and Alex also relished the big event. He was a performer and there wouldn't be many more red-letter days on his calendar. Indeed, this could be the last.

Said Will: 'We were over the moon to see him. His stamina amazed me. Alex didn't get off his deathbed just to put in an appearance. He was the star of the show.'

The highlights of the evening are on YouTube. They show Alex centre stage dancing with guests, then seizing the microphone to sing 'Bridge Over Troubled Water' and 'My Girl' as best he could.

Several guests filmed it on their mobiles. The footage is every bit as touching as his famous Crucible celebration with Lynn and Lauren. His doctor wouldn't have believed it.

Alex was as surprised to see Jean at the dinner as she was to see him. He cast her a withering glance: 'I'll deal with you later!'

The evening raised £15,000. It included £5,000 for one of Ronnie Wood's guitars in the raffle and another £4,500 for a signed photograph of Alex. Will Robinson was ecstatic: 'What a fantastic night! We were worried sick about him but watching him do his Hurricane dance made us realise that, if nothing else, the evening had raised his spirits.'

When the party died down, Alex was left to choose between three dentists who'd offered the implant treatment. Apart from the Spanish option, there was an invitation from Cheshire and another from Belfast. Eileen Knight was bewildered when he plumped for Belfast. Her clinic boasted such luminaries as Ronaldinho and Wayne Rooney among its satisfied customers.

Matters begin to deteriorate when Will Robinson agreed to meet Alex in Belfast and pursue the Irish option. At any rate Will presumed that was the purpose of his trip as he stepped apprehensively off of the plane at George Best Airport. Managing Alex at the best of times put years on you. At the worst of times you could end up in physical danger.

After checking into the Europa Hotel, Will soon found himself in Alex's natural habitat – a betting shop. He went with the flow. The absent-without-leave pneumonia patient commanded: 'Have twenty quid on this one, Bubbles.'

Will did as he was told. It yielded nothing. Then Alex made a rare declaration. He was hungry. A voice croaked from somewhere inside his body: 'I'll have a bowl of soup.'

'I fancy something more substantial, Alex. I haven't had anything all day.'

'Bubbles, you need to lose weight. Have a chowder. It's good. I'm going to the bookies. Back in five. Wait here.'

He was speaking in shorthand. Will saw the funny side. An hour and fish chowder later, Alex returned, only to find that he couldn't get into the restaurant bar. It was a Catholic establishment. He and Will left smartly. Alex insisted on showing Will the shopping centre where he was mugged. Alex claimed his throat problems started when a thief struck him a heavy blow in the Adam's apple.

Said Will: 'These were delaying tactics. He didn't actually want to see the dentist. He didn't want to discuss the point of my visit – his teeth. He thought I wanted a sightseeing tour!'

The pair jumped into a taxi and headed for Robinson's (no connection), a long established hostelry opposite the Europa. Will was conscious of time slipping by. He tried again to bring up the subject of tooth implants: 'Look, Alex, I've got this amazing DVD showing how the implants are done. We'll go to my room and I can let you see it.'

'No, you're staying with me, Bubbles. Check out of the hotel.'

'No Alex, I've got a deal at the Europa. I'm staying there. Come and watch this video. It's brilliant.'

Alex put his hands over Will's ears and croaked in his face: 'You don't listen to me. Are you deaf?'

Will despaired. Alex's whistle-stop tour included a detour at his favourite bookies to watch the night racing. He loved night racing. Will drummed his fingers on the table until 9.00 pm wondering how to get Alex focused. Once the racing was over, Alex said he wanted to go to the Royal: 'A guy there owes me money. I need it badly. Come on, babes.'

'Listen, Alex, I've been here for five hours and still haven't had a chance to show you the video. This is why we raised the money. This is why I'm here. It's your only chance of a life. Can't you see that? Come on, we're going back to the Europa.'

'Do as you're told, Bubbles. You're staying with me.'

'No, Alex. And I'm not going to the Royal to have an argument with a drunk.'

'Whatever.'

Will strode off towards his hotel. Alex went in the direction of his favourite pub. Halfway down the street, he stopped and tried to call his friend back. He was crying. It was the first time Will had seen him so upset. He waved his arms, trying to shout: 'Bubbles, I love you. We'll go to the hotel.'

At long last, Will was able to plug in his laptop and show Alex the video. He watched silently. Will replayed it. Alex became excited then burst into tears again. Will showed him the 'Save Alex Higgins' website with comments from supporters and friends. Had it registered at last? Sadly not. Alex looked at his watch, jumped up out of his chair and wheezed: 'Bubbles, you've had two hours of my time and I've had five hours of yours. It's time to go!'

Will swore under his breath: 'Ungrateful bastard! I've only come here for your sake.'

He ignored Alex's instructions to meet at his apartment the next morning. He'd had enough. He abandoned Alex and caught the return flight to Manchester. Nothing had been resolved about the implants. The Belfast idea seemed to have vanished into thin air. Alex was never serious about it. The trip was a costly waste of time.

Back in Marbella, Eileen was also in the dark. Was anyone taking her offer seriously? Was there another agenda here? Who was pulling the strings? Several days passed before Alex agreed that he was ready to visit the Harley Street surgeon, Dr Bart Van der Ven, before going to Spain for his implants. Hallelujah! Alex asked Will to book him a flight to London but makes one stipulation – the plane had to land at Gatwick not Heathrow because there was a bookmaker at Victoria Station where the Gatwick train pulls into London. He said he needed to pick up some money on the way through.

Will thought to himself: 'Here we go again!'

He couldn't get Alex out of the Victoria Station betting shop till 6.00 pm. He'd been there for two hours. The Harley Street appointment was at 6.00 pm. They grabbed a taxi and made it to the surgery twenty minutes late. Once more, Alex's health had come a poor second to the horses. He and Will had hardly sat down in the waiting room when Alex began to twitch and moan.

'Bubbles, we've been here five minutes. What's going on, babes?'

'Alex, forget about night racing. This is more important.'

'My time's precious.'

'You're exasperating. Why don't you relax and read the paper.'

Alex went one better and tackled a difficult-grade Sudoku which he completed in record time. Years of travelling by train had honed his crossword and Sudoku skills. He had that type of brain anyway. Eventually they were shown into the consulting room, whereupon Alex did a U-turn. He won't go to Spain for the operation after all. He'll get it done here in London. Dr Van der Ven says it can't be done in Harley Street for two weeks. He thinks Brussels might be a possibility. Alex's eyes light up. They leave the surgery and stop for a drink. Alex is warming to the Brussels option.

'I won a tournament in Brussels. They know me. We'll go to Brussels.'

Will's losing patience: 'Why bother with that? Eileen's waiting for you in Spain. What's your problem?'

There was no reply. The evening drags on. Will's tearing his hair out. Alex changes the subject. He wants to go to the Groucho Club, but first he wants to get a copy of the *Racing Post* from a stand in Leicester Square. It almost 2.00 am!

Will tells him: 'The papers won't be there yet.'

'You don't know London.'

'Oh yes, I do. I collected the papers for my dad when I was a kid. They're not out till five o'clock.'

There followed a forty-eight-hour bender which might have wrecked a *healthy* man. How Alex came through it is another of those Higgins mysteries. He very nearly didn't. The unfortunate Will, trying to put together a plan to get Alex to Marbella, found himself walking the streets of London for the next two hours so that Alex could buy the racing papers. Never one to miss an opportunity, Alex signed autographed pictures at £20 a time for half a dozen fans still on the town at that time of night.

'We're having a night out, Bubbles,' he thrilled.

'I can't believe your energy.'

They rocked up at the Holiday Inn, Mayfair, at 7.00 am, much the worse for wear. Alex immediately settled down in front of *Morning Line* on television, while Will escaped to his room for some shut-eye. When he got up around lunchtime, Alex had left a message with the concierge: 'Gone to Ladbrokes to check odds. Meet me in Soho at nine tonight.'

He also insisted that Will get hold of a violinist called Jenny who played at his fund-raising dinner. She lived in London. The three of them met up at yet another bookmakers in Soho. Alex blew £1,500 on the horses but recouped some of that by selling more pictures. He carried a bunch of signed photographs in his shoulder bag and dispensed them like a street vendor. During the evening he phoned his friend, the singer Dougie James, with a tip, telling him: 'Get the bet on quickly. I'll be dead in a week!'

Will didn't think he was joking. Alex, Will and Jenny moved on from the betting shop to a backstreet pub full of Millwall fans. The music was too noisy, so they deferred to the Groucho Club where Alex racked up the balls on a snooker table upstairs. Jenny saw her chance and left before it turned ugly. Alex was in his element on a table he knew well. Who should walk in but the comedian and television presenter, Rowland Rivron.

'Fancy a game, Alex? Let's see how good you are.'

Alex, naturally accepted. Will was apprehensive: 'It was pitiful to watch. Alex could only get breaks of 10–15. Rowland was relaxed but Alex was deadly serious with every shot he played. He was so weak he could only roll the balls towards the hole. Rowland kept telling him he was rubbish. Alex tried to punch him but barely had the strength to stand up. He began swearing at Rowland's wife, then hit him with his snooker cue. The Rivrons departed.'

Will, exhausted, hungry and embarrassed, went back to his hotel at 1.00 am. Alex said he was going out on the town. Will was past caring. He was awoken the next morning by Alex beating on his door. Will ignored it. The banging grew louder.

'Bubbles, it's Alex. Open the fucking door!'

'Go away.'

'I'll break every bone in my body until this door's off its hinges. Open up!'

Will wrapped a towel around himself and answered the door. Alex came up with the most unexpected announcement: 'I feel great today. I've just had breakfast.'

'Fantastic, Alex.'

'Now we need to discuss a plan of action.'

'Get some sleep first, Alex. You've been on the go for forty-eight hours. You'll kill yourself.'

'Wake me at 11.00 then. Don't leave without me.'

'I have to go back to Manchester. *You're* going back to Belfast.'

'No, we need to talk.'

Will ignored him. Once Alex had gone to bed, he went to Euston and caught the train home. It was approaching Crewe when his mobile rang. 'Mr Robinson, it's the manager of the Holiday Inn in Mayfair. Mr Higgins is very ill.'

'I'm on the train. I can't do much about it.'

'Can we call an ambulance?'

'Of course. Go ahead.'

They thought he was dead. Against the odds, Alex pulled round after four days rest at the hotel, but was critically ill. Few would punish their body like Alex did - constantly. Somehow he got himself back to Belfast. It was like witnessing a resurrection. The following day, he was back on the tooth implants case as if nothing had happened in between. It was a classic slice of Higgins behaviour.

'Bubbles, forget Brussels. I want to go to Spain. Spain, Bubbles, Spain. Book the flights now and tell me the details.'

Will arranged it but decided to fly separately to Malaga because Alex was out of control. Before the flight, he had another crisis to deal with. Alex wanted to settle a gambling debt: 'I need some money, Bubbles. Do you hear me?'

'I'll put a couple of hundred in your bank account.'

'That's no good. I need £2,000. Take it from the fund.'

'I'm not touching the fund. If I do that, what does it make me? Every penny's accounted for.'

'Don't make me angry. You're putting obstacles in my way, cunt.'

'Don't you understand, people have donated money for your teeth, not to fund your betting?'

'I'll fucking kill you. Fuck off. Fuck off.'

Talking on the phone left him exhausted. The conversation was interrupted by constant bouts of coughing as Alex struggled with the congestion on his chest and in his throat.

Will said: 'He was going mad. I'd never seen him that bad. I rang Jimmy White and asked his advice. He said: 'Don't for Christ's sake give him the money. Get those teeth done now or it's never gonna happen!' I was under a lot of pressure. I didn't know how to handle the guy. He called me all the names under the sun, then asked what deals I could do for him. Weren't we doing enough? It was my idea to make a television feature of his teeth. We had £10,000 promised for a thirty-minute documentary and £17,000 if it made an hour. *The Sun* agreed to pay £5,000 for the story and *Cutting Edge* were interested. But because I wouldn't give Alex the £2,000, he rejected them all.'

With a huge sense of foreboding, Will telephoned Eileen Knight to say Alex was on his way to Malaga. On no account was she to meet him at the airport because he was in a foul mood. Will left strict instructions for a driver to take Alex straight to the El Rincon Hotel in Marbella. In hindsight, this was a red rag to a bull. Alex never wanted to go 'straight' anywhere and was likely to take a dim view of anyone who forced the issue.

Only a couple of weeks earlier, Rosie, a former Chinese restaurant owner and long time friend of his from Manchester, felt the full force of his fury when she was detailed to chauffeur him to the airport after the fund-raising event. She too had been under strict instructions not to stop on the way.

'He wasn't interested in the flight. He just wanted to me to drop him off at a betting shop. I refused but he kept on and on. Then he whacked me on the hand while I was driving. I told him to behave and went into the fast lane so we couldn't stop. He was seething but I wished him all the best when we got to the airport. Instead of thanking me for the lift, he accused me of losing him money and said he'd have to pay for a taxi to take him back to the bookies.'

Predictably, Alex gave the Spanish chauffeur hell. He didn't want to go to El Rincon where he had a room reserved for him. He told the driver that if he didn't take him to Julie's Bar in Cabopino, he'd be stabbed! Alex was behaving like a caged animal. He desperately needed someone he could trust and decided Charlie Hawley was the man. Trust had all but vanished from Alex's vocabulary.

Most of his professional life was soured by a deep-lying *mistrust* of those around him. His paranoia was largely self-induced, although it's true that snooker's old guard was both envious and resentful of his talent. Turkeys don't like peacocks.

And so this husk of a man found himself at Charlie's apartment while his friend tried to work out what to do for the best.

'The longer it went on, the more farcical it became. Eileen seemed a friendly, genuine person but Alex treated her like shit. She took him to the clinic for an introductory meeting but he told her on the way that she was the ugliest PR lady he'd ever clapped eyes on and hadn't a clue what she was doing. When he got back, he whispered to me: "I don't trust that woman. Get rid." He'd fallen out with Will Robinson and thought Eileen was part of the same conspiracy.'

In the meantime, Alex was emailed by Amanda Stocks from an independent television company called Daisybeck. She said they were pitching a documentary idea to the TV channels and wanted an update on his condition. Alex sent a handwritten reply:

> Dear Amanda.
>
> I had two tests on Tuesday. Passed A1. Go this afternoon for blood tests. If I'm ok I will have the dental implants put in 2 to 2 ½ weeks. Don't worry I will deal with Eileen. Get the best deals. I have taken 4 pictures of my emaciated self for a very good friend called Chas Hawley. Very trustworthy. You can rely on Chas.
>
> Yours
>
> Alexander Gordon Higgins

Charlie left a message for Will Robinson to contact him. He heard that Will was in Marbella: 'I didn't know the fellah. To be fair, he didn't know me either. He called Jimmy White to check me out and was told: "Don't worry, Charlie's a good mate." Robinson never showed up. He didn't ring back either. This farce was becoming a pantomime. I wasn't sure whether *I* was the back end of the horse or whether it was Alex.'

Alex stayed for ten days. It was a mountainous job getting him back to the clinic. Charlie agreed to go with him on the second visit. He was dreading the experience.

'To see Alex stripped off having all those wires attached to him for the ECG was the saddest thing I'd seen in my life. They couldn't find a vein for the injection. He was skin and bone. If he'd been a dog they'd have put him down. There was no dignity for him. No-one was there to fight his corner except Eileen and me - and for some reason he didn't want Eileen. It was very unfair on the girl. Thank God I was in Spain when he arrived.'

Eileen knew instantly that raising everyone's hopes had been a mistake.

'I was embarrassed to take Alex into the clinic. I didn't think he'd survive the thirty-minute car journey! I forewarned Dr Simon that implants would be impossible. Alex was terrified. He looked lost. I hadn't seen someone so ill, not even my father. I found it very upsetting. I was angry that anyone could have seen fit to send him over alone in that condition. On top of that, it hurt that he was suspicious of me after all I'd done. I contacted Will and told him the situation was hopeless.'

Will's dilemma was that he'd blown trumpets to raise £15,000 for the operation and now had to accept that it was too late. He kept his distance. Eileen continued: 'Everyone at the clinic was shocked at Alex's condition and his attitude. He kept swearing, hitting me with newspapers. The he wrote me the most hideous messages in his notebook. I replied that he was the most horrible person I'd ever met. It was true but I wished I could have cut my tongue out afterwards. I use to idolise the guy. He was still smartly dressed but his clothes were dirty. He'd brought them in holdall with some photographs of himself winning the world title. It was extremely sad. I'm a hundred per cent convinced he knew he was dying. He was just going through the motions. His only pleasure was betting on the horses and he did it every single day he was here.'

The outcome, as Eileen had foreseen, *was* hopeless. Dr Daniel Simon studied the results of his blood test and likened his immune system to that of an Aids sufferer. In other words, it was shot to pieces. Officially, Alex was told that he was too weak for the implants but that if he built up his strength, there might be another chance in the future. This is the letter Dr Simon sent to Eileen:

> I am writing to inform you that after evaluating Mr Alex Higgins together with my team, we have decided it is not possible to perform surgery. Our intention was to perform Oral Rehabilitation surgery with placement of dental implants and immediate placement of fixed bridges under general anaesthesia.
>
> Because of the nature of Mr Higgins and his fragile health, despite our desire to help him, we cannot risk his life for a procedure that can be done in the future if that is what he would wish.
>
> We strongly recommend that he is followed up by his medical team in Ireland to assess his situation and take the necessary measures to improve his condition immediately.
>
> Greetings,
>
> Dr Daniel Simon

Eileen passed it on to Will Robinson with her own thoughts: 'I'm very saddened to think we're unable to help Alex. He is obviously very ill and needs immediate medical attention. It's such a shame because all our best intentions for him have not come to fruition. I hope Alex gets the medical help he needs soon.'

The episode left a bitter taste in Eileen's mouth: 'It was nothing more than a money spinning exercise as far as I could see. A publicity stunt. Alex's welfare was no longer the priority.' Charlie was incensed by it: 'We had all that bullshit about television deals yet no-one filmed a bloody thing. I never saw a cameraman. A man's life was hanging by a thread and no-one gave a toss.'

Will Robinson denies that. The reason he didn't supervise the pre-op was that, having fallen out with Alex after his traumatic time in London and Belfast, he didn't want to aggravate matters by accompanying him to Spain: 'Alex's mental condition had deteriorated rapidly. He was very difficult to be with. That's why I warned Eileen not to get too close. I was shattered when they said they couldn't perform the operation because we'd thrown the kitchen sink at it. When he missed two appointments I rang his sisters and Jimmy White for suggestions. They sent him emails basically saying "Get your arse over there, Alex." '

It's hard to know how Alex took the consultant's verdict. Drinking pals in Belfast say they'd never seen him so low when he got back. Others say Alex didn't even reappear at the Royal. Charlie, who was closest to the action in Marbella, is convinced the survival instinct was still burning: 'Alex didn't take the news as a death warrant. Quite the opposite. He seemed very positive. He told me he was looking forward to putting on weight, having the implants, then getting back to the snooker table.'

Charlie booked Alex's return flight to Belfast, then had the unenviable job of looking after him for the next few days. Alex had only four weeks to live. In spite of the bravado, he must have known the end was near. Charlie knew it too. Effectively, he was the last person to spend quality time with The Hurricane.

'English people in Cabopino kept asking me whether it was Alex Higgins or not. They didn't recognise the guy. They were very kind to him at Julie's Bar. Regulars fetched the racing papers for him.

He placed his bets over the phone. One day he came very close to winning a decent amount of money, but the horse faded and Alex missed his chance as gamblers do. He tried to drink Guinness but kept having to spit in another glass. It was pitiful. In my heart of hearts, I knew he wouldn't see Christmas.'

The last day they spent together was difficult *and* hilarious.

> I got him dressed the morning after the verdict. All I could see in his bedroom was a head on the pillow. There was hardly anything left of the body. I looked at his belongings. This was a guy I'd know for twenty-two years and the highlights of his life were scattered around the room like flotsam and jetsam. Trophies with bits missing; a presentation set of golf clubs which should never have been used but were; his holdall with those famous pictures from 1982 of Alex in his green shirt with red collar. He was selling them on eBay for a tenner.
>
> He limped about in his pyjamas, still rolling joints. I made him a cup of tea and he told me off because the tea wasn't hot enough. My heart went out to him. He hardly had the strength to hold the cup and could easily have scalded himself. The radio was still on from last night. Each night he asked me to tune into *Talk Sport.* He needed to hear voices. I put his trousers on top of his long johns. Then he wore a T-shirt with a shirt over the top, followed by a pullover, a blazer and a leather coat. This was June. The heat was unbearable.
>
> He ate a tiny piece of sponge cake and was adamant about putting on weight. I picked up his bible. It was from his mum. I read out the dedication. Alex was choked. He gave me a hug. The smell of cannabis hung in the air. It was nearly time to go to the airport. I sat outside to wait for the taxi. Alex came down half an hour later carrying two frozen cottage pies the size of dinner plates. He'd asked me to buy some more at the

supermarket. He liked to suck on the gravy, bless him. It soothed his throat.

I'd left them in the freezer because they were too big to fit into his bag – and he wouldn't be allowed to take them on a Ryanair flight anyway.

He wouldn't take no for an answer: 'I want the pies, Chas. They'll keep me alive!'

'For God's sake, Alex, you'll never get away with it.'

'Don't worry, babes, it'll be okay.'

Charlie tried to cram the frozen pies into Alex's shoulder bag. The zip broke. They were both getting agitated. Charlie continues the story.

'I told him to get in the taxi or we'd miss the flight. I was sweating like a trooper because Alex wouldn't allow the air conditioning to be switched on. It felt as hot as hell! We got to Malaga airport but I couldn't get the flaming pies in the bag. We both started laughing. Then he pushed a young lad out of the way so he could sit down in the airport lounge. I had to apologise to the lad's father. They'd no idea who he was.

We spent twenty minutes trying to repair the zip and finally squeezed the meat pies home. I asked one of the ground crew for a wheelchair for Alex. He was completely exhausted by now. I gave him lots of hugs and kisses and off he went in the wheelchair. The pies were removed at the first checkpoint and handed back to me. I threw them in the bin. That was the last I saw of my friend. A month later I get a call from Jimmy White's agent, John, to say Alex had died.

He was a fighter but even if you'd managed to feed him egg and chips every day, his body couldn't have kept it down. The efforts to save him came at least five years too late. I thought he'd be dead by Christmas. He'd gone too long without proper treatment.

By sheer coincidence, a former business acquaintance of Ann Higgins' was on the same flight home from Malaga. And by another coincidence, her son was being treated for cancer in the same Belfast hospital where Alex received his radiotherapy. She did a double take when she saw him pushed to his seat in a wheelchair. His ghostly image upset her so much that she couldn't face her usual glass of wine on the plane and sobbed most of the way home. It says an awful lot for Alex's courage and determination that he got himself off the plane in Belfast, hailed a taxi to Sandy Row, managed to unlock the door with hands too weak to operate his mobile and climbed into bed.

The final four weeks were spent mostly with his own thoughts. There was no contact with Charlie, Will, his sisters or his son and daughter. It's not true to say that he ended his life friendless. He still had a few of those. Did he end it bitter and twisted, as Charlie had forecasted many years before? Or had Alex come to terms with the prospect of dying? We'll never know.

5

HE WAS MY SON

Alex Higgins hurried out of his mother's womb as fast as his frail little body would allow, but missed St Patrick's Day by a whisker. Wasn't that just like a Protestant? Fortunately, there was no-one from the WPBSA to dock him points for being late.

Perhaps he knew instinctively that St Patrick's Day that year would be a damp squib. Speaking at Westminster, Sir Hugh O'Neill, the MP for Antrim, put it like this: 'There's no cause for hilarity. The south has broken its last ties with the Crown, and that's a tragedy.' For the first time in history, St Patrick's Day was celebrated with Eire outside the Commonwealth.

Prostrate in Belfast's Jubilee Hospital, Elizabeth Higgins couldn't give a fig. Catholic, Protestant – it was all the same to her. Mrs Higgins had more pressing things on her mind. While overjoyed to give birth to her first and only son, she was wrong-footed by the speed of Alexander Gordon's arrival.

He was born, as he died, prematurely. At four pounds six ounces, he fitted snugly into a shoe box. The date was Friday, March 18th, 1949, and times were hard. Though the Second World War had been over for the best part of four years, Belfast was experiencing severe austerity punctuated only by occasional shafts of brightness. If Mrs Higgins had had the time or the inclination to pick up the *Belfast Telegraph* that epic day, she might have noticed that *The Vic Oliver Show* was playing at Belfast's Royal Hippodrome (seats one guinea or two guineas). Elizabeth loved Variety. Her husband, Alexander senior, couldn't read so he'd have missed the announcement that James Department Store in Lombard Street was offering suits 'with blue-stripe effect' for £6.12.6d. It would have appealed to Mr Higgins, a dapper little chap with sartorial taste above his status and beyond his earning capacity.

Alex's dad was partial to horseracing too. It may not have occurred to him at that precise moment but fathering a son after two daughters opened up new possibilities. He'd have Alex junior taking his betting slips to the bookies before the lad was out of nappies! The big sporting news was that Gordon Richards - as yet unknighted - rode the favourite, Psychology, through driving rain at Lincoln to record his first success of the season. Mr Higgins may even have backed Psychology. Gambling was one of the more troublesome interests he passed onto his son. Love of smart clothes was a relatively harmless one.

On a more whimsical note, this front page advert in *The Times* on March 18th, 1949, would have tickled Alex's fancy: 'Join the chain of Biro enthusiasts! Why hold fast to out-of-date writing methods in this modern age? No blotting paper required. Ten thousand biro agents in Britain. A boom to the left-handed. A pen for your thoughts.' Alex always preferred a notebook and pen to electronic communication. He wasn't a great one for texting or emailing and Facebook was out of his league. In the final years, handwritten messages were his only way of holding a conversation.

In 1949, television still belonged to science fiction. Radio was king. The BBC Home Service began the day with Alistair Cooke's *Letter From America*, to be followed at lunchtime by *Workers' Playtime* and in the evening by *Much Binding in the Marsh*. Welcome to the human race, Alex! Sorry that the birth of a legend didn't merit a paragraph or a sound bite anywhere. The immediate concern at the Jubilee was keeping you alive. I'm pleased to report that staff on the maternity ward nursed you well. With the help of an incubator, Alex Gordon Higgins survived. It was a template for his life.

Meanwhile, out on the spartan streets of Britain, snooker was growing in popularity. What began as a gentleman's pastime for senior officers of the British Armed Forces in India was metamorphosing into a game everyone could play, especially the unemployed. It became their saviour; their shelter from the storm. Billiard halls sprang up all over the country and while the original cue game remained a favourite with the older generation, its more colourful brother was coming on in the outside track.

The untrained eye would have struggled to make out which of the disciplines was being observed in some of the seedier joints. Cigarette smoke hung as thick as gravy around dim, overhead lights. Men with time to kill and nothing else to absorb their energy floated through the clouds like fishing boats in a foggy harbour.

Alex spent much of his twenties in the back-to-back streets of Lancashire where many of the country's best players were building up a storm. A far cry from colonial India. His future sidekick, Jim Meadowcroft, described it well.

> Snooker got its misspent youth image because the halls were full of depressed, lonely and unemployed men trying to get out of the cold. Billiard halls were nearly always temperance buildings with a Robin Hood boiler in the cellar. You were guaranteed a cup of tea and a warm. Don't forget, a lot of these guys couldn't afford to keep the home fires burning. Winter was grim.
>
> The only way many of them could make a few shillings was by pinching things. Hardware, clothing, lamps, plates and cups – the sort of stuff a rag-and-bone man might have on his barrow. Thieving was a national pastime. Billiard halls were the obvious place to exchange your ill-gotten gains. The wheeling and dealing was as lively as the snooker. Young Teddy Boys would

> turn up in drain pipes and blue suede shoes, play team matches, then head for the pub to spend the bets they'd won or a couple of florins they'd made in the illicit market place.

Several years later, the twenty-one-year-old Willy Thorne was still experiencing the fallout of this shady tradition in his native Leicester. Willy had graduated from the relative sobriety of Anstey Conservative Club in the fashionable Charnwood Forest area of the county to the rather less salubrious Osbourne's in the middle of town. He needed stiffer competition to improve his game.

Says Willy: 'Suddenly I was mixing with thieves and vagabonds. People who didn't work but could get anything you wanteds. One of the lads specialised in nicking Crombie overcoats from Fenwicks. He stole them one-by-one over a period of months until he had a collection better than Fenwicks itself! I can't think why the shop never caught on. He used to ask: "What size would you like?" He had the whole range. We could all have been done for receiving.'

The newly born Alex Higgins – Sandy as he was known in the family – had only nine years to wait before snooker would ensnare him, before the sleepless rhythm of its twilight beat would shape his future and before this spotty-faced kid would teach the plodding down-and-outs of this demi-monde that snooker could be played on the hoof and new shots were waiting to be invented. Elizabeth was lucky to be spared a crystal ball as she held the infant to her breast in that hospital bed. If she'd had any inkling of what was to come, she'd have been calling for extra supplies of gas and air.

The little chap she kept in a wardrobe drawer until he gathered strength was destined to enthral millions, create turmoil at every turn and eventually drive her to drink. At least she'd be spared the grisly denouement. Elizabeth died before Alex was diagnosed with cancer. Thankfully, she never saw him suffer. She never witnessed the toothless, directionless stick of a man who clung to life in a sheltered flat only a stone's throw from the street where he grew up.

She never heard the barely audible rasp which replaced his famous Belfast-cum-mid-Atlantic twang. Sure, the twinkle in his eye and the sharpness of his brain remained undiminished, but that mischievous, forgive-me-everything smile had gone for good. Alex was sixty-one going on eighty. His mum couldn't have coped with that.

There were many times during that bleak last decade when Alex wished he could crawl under a stone. He dreamed of checking into the well-publicised euthanasia clinic in Switzerland, taking a pill and slipping painlessly away. He considered suicide but confessed he had neither the courage to do it nor the selfishness to distress others by taking 'a cowardly way out'. In truth, the people who mattered would have sanctioned any escape route from the mental and physical prison which increasingly pressed in on him.

Alex had been flirting with danger since throat and palate tumours were first detected. He actually conquered cancer, but at a price. Most of us were surprised that he lasted as long as he did. None of us wanted to see such a miserable, protracted end. He'd pushed life and people to the limit. Life or someone was bound to bite back.

In Belfast on an overcast spring day, Alex joined several thousand other baby-boomers at a time when food rationing kept the pantry empty and Ulstermen had to seek work wherever they could find it. In the case of his unassuming father, it meant long periods away from the family's council house while he queued for labouring jobs in England.

At least the religious temperature in Ireland was cool between 1949 and 1969 when Ian Paisley began to raise it. However, it paid not to underestimate the depth of feeling or overestimate the fragility of a peaceful veneer. Without consciously setting out to be so, Alex Higgins became a unifying force across the religious divide. Perhaps more so than George Best and certainly on a par with Barry McGuigan. If anything, he enjoyed greater support in the Republic than he did in Northern Ireland. That was some achievement. He was carefree about the sectarian divide and ambivalent about religion. This remark in the mid-eighties seems out of context with his freewheeling lifestyle: 'God has been an influence in my life. That might surprise some people. They don't know me. Our family is Church of Ireland. It doesn't mean I go to church. I don't. I probably never will. A prayer in church is no different from a prayer in the garage. I've prayed for help at the snooker table. I've sometimes cursed myself for expecting too much from God.'

And yet, as his detractors will rush to point out, he frequently displayed the moral rectitude of an amoeba and the goodwill of an AK49. On the positive side, this was the same chap who posted money to his mum and dad every week and kept a bible in his travelling bag until the day he died. The book was presented to him by his mother when he left home at the age of fifteen. She wrote on the inside cover: 'To Sandy from Mam with all my love and best wishes. May God protect you and keep you safe always, no matter where you are.'

As Alex's sister Ann and I were leafing through it after Alex had died, we came across a dried leaf from his father's wreath and another from Oliver Reed's. A few years back Alex told me: 'This bible's travelled everywhere with me. It's still in good nick after forty years on the road.'

He grew up at number 16 Abington Street in a close, loving household dominated by females. There were two older sisters, Isobel and Ann. Jean came later. The nominal head of the household, Alexander has been handicapped by a serious accident as a boy. He was hit by a lorry, leaving him with a fractured skull and residual brain damage. Mr Higgins was unable to read or write until his wife taught him to scratch his own name. Isobel, the oldest child, admits: 'Mummy took on a big job with Daddy handicapped like that. But he was a good looking man – very handsome.'

Alex was angry about the way his father's injury was disregarded. He said: 'These days Dad would have got three quarters of a million pounds compensation. He didn't get a penny.'

For Mr Higgins, the jobs market in Belfast was more or less dead. He'd catch the ferry to Birkenhead and stay with an aunt in England while he searched for a day's pay. If successful, he'd sometimes be gone for months. When he came back, he might be lucky enough to pick up a few days' work on the railway. The kids were always delighted to see him home again, even though it usually meant the family had to fall back on Elizabeth's meagre income.

As well as bringing up four children, Mrs Higgins worked as a cleaner in the cinemas and doctors' surgeries of south Belfast. She supplemented that in spring and autumn by getting up at 6.00 am to pick potatoes. Alex admired his mother: 'Great lady. She had to deal with the grief of a father who died at sea and a mother who died at thirty-four. She brought up several brothers and sisters on her own. That's where I get my survival instinct from. Mum was afraid of nothing or no-one.'

The last bit isn't *quite* true, Alex. Elizabeth was afraid of *you*! More precisely, she was afraid to pick up a newspaper in case it contained another lurid chapter about your wild escapades, your drunken brawls, your fines and your inadequacies as a husband and father. Alcohol was her escape and ultimately her illness. Until her son became a running saga in the red tops, drinking was confined to Saturday nights when she and her husband enjoyed a gin and tonic at the bingo hall. Through the week, she had neither the wherewithal nor the desire, though Mr Higgins couldn't wait until the weekend for his tipple.

When Alex was at the peak of his notoriety, Elizabeth hid bottles of gin around the house. Says Ann: 'Dad would have been furious if he'd known. Mum was so upset by the newspaper stories that drink was her only way out. She had a few nasty falls then she'd take it out on our daddy. He couldn't read the stories by himself so he came in for even more stick. They had awful rows. My mummy's nerves were frayed. She'd start crying about Sandy: "They'll send him home in a box, Ann, I know they will. Them referees don't like him. They want to get rid of our Sandy. The whole of snooker wants to get rid of him." '

To give Elizabeth her due, she never stood in Alex's way, neither while he was bunking off school to keep score at the Jampot, nor when he set off for Berkshire one midsummer morning to become a jockey. Alex's parents might have taken a stricter line after the school inspector knocked on their door to complain that their son had been marked absent thirty-four times in the school year. 'Instead, Mummy pretended he was sick in bed and prayed that the inspector wouldn't go upstairs to check. She got her wish. My mummy also suspected that dressing him up for Sunday school was pointless. For Alex that meant long trousers, collar and tie and shiny shoes. It was obvious when he came back tieless with scuffed shoes and a hole in his trousers that he hadn't been to Sunday school at all.

Alex knew he got off lightly. Not to put too fine a point on it, he was spoiled. By his own admission: 'Mum was too soft-hearted to crack the whip. Neither she nor Dad ever tried to stop me playing snooker. They must have realised there wasn't much else on offer for a young lad growing up in Belfast. It had to be better than hanging around on street corners vandalising tower blocks.'

The Jampot was tucked away behind a row of terraced houses off Donegal Road – literally around the corner from Abington

Street, and – much worse – on the way to Kelvin School. Needless to say, Alex found it difficult to complete the journey. On the few occasions he did, he returned to the Jampot in the lunch hour. He wasn't by any means the only Kelvin School pupil heading for a misspent youth, just the cheekiest and most talented. Elizabeth once heard two older pupils chatting in the street. One said he was going to the Jampot; the other warned him to stay away. 'Higgins is there he's a shark, he'll swallow you up!'

Elizabeth figured that the Jampot kept Alex out of trouble. Belfast wasn't a place where parents could relax while their kids played outdoors. She believed that Alex's time at the snooker hall taught him independence at a tender age and gave him the chance to earn some money. The prevailing view on their council estate was that education was of marginal significance in a society which offered few outlets unless you were talented enough to qualify as a lawyer, doctor or priest.

Alex was clever enough but committed only to the green baize. Academia, which might involve sitting still for more than five minutes, was anathema to this jitterbug of a boy. His mum called it the 'Higgins Twitch' – a nervous disposition which afflicted her husband and Ann as well. Alex turned it to his considerable advantage around the snooker table but socially he was a landmine waiting to be trodden on. Alex was wired into several different sound and vision sources at the same time. Whichever one played louder or shone more brightly took his attention. He was either exhausting or fascinating to be with, depending on your point of view.

Ann also put her twitch to good use. She worked in the equally heady atmosphere of a hairdressing salon. She did heads as fast as Alex potted snooker balls. Said Ann: 'Customers called *me* The Hurricane. In my younger days I did thirty-three sets a day, in between perms and highlights. The rollers flew in and out like a fiddler's elbow. I just couldn't relax. Still can't for that matter.'

Alex's mum gave him five shillings a week for his school dinners, little realising that most of it subsidised his snooker. He bought a single dinner ticket – for Fridays – on the basis that he'd be skint by the end of the week and in need of a square meal. Impressive thinking for a nine-year-old. For the rest of the time, dinner was a Mars bar and a coke. This unhealthy regime was the start of a lifetime's malnutrition. There were very few occasions when he ate well, if indeed he ate at all. Even if, by some miracle, surgeons had managed to implant a set of teeth in his chemo-ravaged gums, he still wouldn't have eaten. They couldn't implant an appetite.

Spare a thought for Stewart Love, Alex's maths teacher. He tried to instil a fascination for trigonometry in kids who wanted to be somewhere else. It was the pedagogic equivalent of trying to pick a lock with a piece of wet string! Mr Love repeatedly warned Alex that snooker would be the ruin of him. You can imagine the response. In a way, the teacher was right. Alex *did* end up in ruins. This was his recollection of Mr Love: 'I felt sorry for him. He paced up and down the room biting his fingernails, wondering where to turn next. He took an interest in me despite, or maybe because of, my waywardness. I wasn't exactly teacher's pet, but I was different from the rest of the herd.'

Mr and Mrs Higgins put in the occasional appearance at parents' evening but scraping together enough money to feed and clothe a family of four took precedence over schooling. If Alex managed to win sixpence behind everyone's back at the Jampot, good on him – as long as he gave his mum a cut, which he usually did.

Elizabeth lost three vital shillings one day when a gypsy fortune teller knocked at number 16. She'd drummed into the kids that you should never turn a gypsy away or you'd be cursed. Mrs Higgins was beside himself when the scruffy clairvoyant put down her bag of clothes pegs and told her she had a star in the family. 'That'll be our Ann,' replied Elizabeth, referring to her daughter's fledgling career as a teenage songster at local theatres and community centres.

'No, it's a boy,' replied the gypsy. Alex's mum was flummoxed. 'I've only got one boy,' she thought to herself. 'What could Sandy possibly do that would make him a star?'

While embracing that conundrum, she was hit by another surprise. Her Sandy decided there was no point staying on at school, even though his report indicated that he was more than useful at English, Geography and Woodwork. Neither did he fancy the Belfast shipyards. So, at the tender age of fifteen, he left home to seek his fortune as a jockey. Was this what the gypsy had in mind?

His destination was Eddie Reavey's stables at Wantage in Berkshire. Eddie was an Ulsterman so he went out of his way to recruit Belfast lads, Catholic or Protestant. He said: 'Let's get them out of that dreadful place before they become gangsters.' Alex answered an advert in the *Belfast Telegraph* for a stable lad and was accepted on a month's trial.

He said: 'It was a big blow to Mum and Dad. Mum was never happy to let me out of her sight. I was her son and she took that very seriously.' Both parents were fighting to hold back the tears as they waved him goodbye on the Liverpool ferry. Elizabeth told me years ago: 'I was saying goodbye to my only son. I knew he'd never come home again. After he'd gone, his daddy and I cracked up. But I knew it would be good for him to get a trade.' Not many parents would be as understanding about a fifteen-year-old undertaking a journey like that. After arriving at Liverpool, Alex faced a long overland trek to Berkshire across a country he'd only read about. If he'd known what was coming, he'd have been crying himself.

He was sacked six times in the first month for shirking. Horses were a romantic notion to him. He loved the synergy of man and animal in athletic pursuit, but wasn't so enamoured with mucking out. Why did he have to get up at five o'clock in the morning for a trifling 35 shillings a week? For the first and only time in his life, he became a trencherman, getting into the breakfast habit big time - or, to put it another way, becoming half normal. Mrs Hillier, the stable cook, piled on the sausages, bacon, eggs, tomatoes and fried bread and Alex piled on the weight. He shot up to ten stone - far too heavy for a jockey. Somehow, he hung on for two years before it became screamingly obvious that life in the saddle wasn't for him.

Elizabeth bought socks, handkerchiefs and pants from a nearby outfitters in Donegal Road and sent weekly packages to Wantage. She packed the parcels so tight, Alex could hardly get them open. 'Mum was on the phone regularly to see how I was getting on. She wanted to know if I was eating properly. She wanted me to stick at being a jockey but there was no point.'

If she'd read her son's end-of-term report from Jocelyn Reavey, the trainer's wife, she'd have agreed. It said: 'Alex is a nice lad underneath but every time you leave him to do a job, he disappears to the bookies. Apart from anything else, it's illegal for a fifteen-year-old. He has a certain ability as a horseman but no staying power. As a worker, he's well nigh hopeless.' QED.

His mum beseeched him to come home but having tasted life on the outside, he was unlikely to find Belfast big enough to contain his ego. For all that, The Hurricane was always her little boy. She carried on sending clothes parcels until the day she died. It always made him smile: 'Oh no, Mum, not another pullover! Where am I supposed to keep them all?'

Elizabeth was no different from a million wives and mothers in the 1950s. She worked part-time to help with the family budget but caring for the children, especially the prodigal son, was her raison d'etre. In her latter years she'd say to Ann: 'Please make sure my Sandy's all right. Look after him for me.' He was undoubtedly her blue-eyed boy. She was probably over-fussy but recognised a neediness which helped to turn Alex into the tormented person he became. He needed to be loved and he needed to be tutored in the art of everyday living. Elizabeth was an alcoholic when she died of a stroke, aged seventy-two.

That is the background against which Alex Gordon Higgins grew up. A bright lad with an appetite for learning but no stomach for school. A Protestant kid with no interest in religious doctrine and no fear of wandering into Catholic areas of what would become one of the most lawless cities in Europe. Was he a child in a man's world, a child who grew up too fast or a child who didn't grow up at all?

6

HE WAS ONE OF US

There were numerous hangers-on in Alex Higgins' life. There are dozens of people who still call themselves friends of Alex Higgins. Perhaps for a while they were. Alex kept friends like a marathon runner keeps bottles of water at strategic points along the route. His little black book is crammed with phone numbers from Sydney to Bangkok; from Toronto to Dubai. These were generally people who could help him. Someone to call if he needed a favour - a place to hang his hat; a lift to the airport; a few readies to fund his gambling or a pal to take to the dog track.

Then there were the people who knew and loved him all his life. Men like his boyhood chum Tommy McCloughlin who fidgeted in the same classroom at Kelvin School. Tommy jokes about Alex's doomed chat-up lines with the maidens of Belfast: the conversation would invariably go like this:

'Do you know who I am?'

'No. Who are yous?'

'I'm the Amateur Snooker Champion of Northern Ireland!'

'So what?'

Tommy laughs: 'It failed to impress every time. They looked at him as though he had two heads.'

Because Alex died relatively young, there are plenty of his contemporaries in south Belfast. They're not the fittest specimens I've ever seen. Too many have been aged by drink, smoke and the stresses of Ireland's recent history. Some are alcoholics. Few know what it means to jog around the park or stick to a healthy diet.

They'll argue, with some justification, that Belfast wasn't tuned into that way of life when they were young men. Staying alive during the shootings and bombings was priority number one. If you didn't work at the shipyards, where jobs were hard to come by, you were lucky to get anything. Drink masked the fear and uncertainty. Snooker soaked up the time.

Some of Alex's buddies are to be found at the Rangers Supporters Club; others at the Royal which was his regular haunt during that harrowing last decade. They've painted a street mural in his honour. Tourists will come to admire it many years into the future. All of Alex's drinking pals speak warmly of the friend they've lost. One of them is Joe Nellins, a tour-bus operator of the same vintage who toughed it out in Belfast while Alex went off on his adventures. Joe was still there when he came back.

I remember when Higgy was making a name for himself at the Jampot and the Shaftesbury. I watched him make 100 breaks. We all did. He was a phenomenon in short trousers. No-one saw him for years when he went to England and turned pro. We didn't expect to see him again. It's funny how things work out. Suddenly he's back in Sandy Row where he started. In the last three or four years I saw him nearly every day. He always did the same – order a pint of Guinness then read the racing papers and get people to run his bets for him. Usually it was Gary Audley. Occasionally Alex would go with him. Gary had a job keeping up. Alex was a quick walker even when he was dying.

I never saw him eat so much as a crisp. For the last six months he could hardly talk at all. He left small notes. He did a lot of writing. It was funny watching him try to talk with two people at the same time! We saw the weight drop off him every day. He looked like a wizened old man. He started wearing two jumpers and T-shirts to disguise his appearance. The hat never came off. Everyone recognised him from the hat.

It troubled him when people introduced themselves and wanted to shake his hand. His hands were so bony it hurt. People thought he was being ignorant. We tried to protect him. He was embarrassed about his teeth. That's one of the reasons he didn't try to talk. It was a great shame because Higgy loved a conversation.

However ill, he was constantly thinking of ways to make a few bob. When the Scots came over on July 12th, the start of the Orange marching season, Alex had his signed photographs arranged around the Royal – £10 or £20 each depending on the size. Because he was running out of photographs, he had sketches done of them. He rarely missed a trick. I'm not sure what the Scottish visitors made of him in that state. It must have been a shock to them.

His sisters popped into the pub to keep an eye on him. They didn't want people to think he was disabled. Not so long ago, he had a big, fancy apartment. He didn't have to stay in sheltered accommodation. I don't know why he did. It must have been humiliating. A superstar like him should have been living in the big house on the hill, not in Donegal Road. If he'd asked the right people for a house, he'd have got one. He was too proud to ask.

He got his betting money from his disability allowance, but he was still playing the odd snooker match for a few hundred quid. I actually saw him having a go at someone over a bet. His thin little arms were flailing against a guy about eight stone heavier. Higgy couldn't have bruised a fly! It was like watching a fight in slow motion. The he settled down again with his Guinness and papers as though nothing had happened.

Everyone in the Royal looked after him. If he'd been short of anything we'd have helped him out. He hadn't been in for a while before he died, but we didn't think there was anything odd about it. We assumed he'd gone back to Spain for the tooth implants. He didn't always tell us where he was going.

People accuse of him being arrogant but he wasn't with us. He was among his own people here. We loved him. We knew he was going to die but it was still upsetting when it happened. I think Higgy thought he'd get through it. He didn't behave like someone who was dying. He just got on with his routine.

His only regret was that he didn't see enough of his kids. He loved those kids. The Royal seems empty now. Belfast seems empty. I'll always think fondly of old Higgy. He never did or said anything wrong for me. He was our hero. He came from Sandy Row and made it to the top. He was one of us.

Shane Hamilton is Joe's office manager. His view is less rose-tinted but just as affectionate. The most enduring memory is of a three-carat diamond he once owned. Alex took a fancy to it.

We'd gone to Dublin to support Higgy in an exhibition match at the Red Cow. He heard about my ring and kept asking to see it. He was a real magpie with anything that glittered. He was a wheeler-dealer too. He knew the value of most things, especially antiques and jewellery. There was a carbon flaw in the ring otherwise it would have been worth £20,000 instead of about £4,000. Higgy begged me to sell it. We agreed a price. He played the exhibition with the ring on his little finger and got hammered. Once he'd got his appearance money, he paid in £50 notes. Then he started drinking and got into a ruck with some young guys. He was wild. They locked him in a cupboard. We had to call security guards to get him out. Luckily the ring was safe.

After that, he went to Australia to stay with Isobel. She asked if she could borrow the ring. They all got drunk one night. When he asked Isobel for the ring back, his sister couldn't find it. We never knew what happened to it. Nothing more was said for twenty-odd years. Then, in the last few months of Higgy's life, he brought it up again. He started accusing Isobel of running off with his diamond. It was still bugging him when he died.

The man was totally crazy. He had an incredibly fast metabolism. He was permanently hyper. He never stopped twitching. Hurricane was the perfect name. He went around the pubs of Belfast as if he owned them. He got away with murder. I took him newspapers and cakes in hospital when he had his cancer operation. He sucked food through a straw. Not once did I hear him talk about dying. He was always fighting. His body gave up but his mind was alive. A lot of people thought they knew Alex Higgins but you had to see him day to day to understand the guy. I'll admit his attitude to people sometimes wasn't the nicest. Underneath it though, he had a good heart.

Gary Audley called me before Christmas 2011 with a hint of glee in his voice. It was a good to hear. Gary had been missing Alex more than most because his daily routine had been taken away. Gary was much more than Alex's labrador. He was he prop and staff.

He was happy because a trainer from Lambourn who wrote some months earlier for permission to name one of his two-year-olds Hurricane Higgins had just seen the horse win its first race. Gary's excitement had an undercurrent of sorrow. He knew how much Alex had been looking forward to seeing the horse, Hurricane Higgins in action. To compound his frustration, Gary had forgotten to place a bet!

Each time I cross Belfast's rebuilt waterfront where the Titanic was built but Harland and Wolfe are now just a faded memory, I think of Cecil Mason and the boys from the Jampot playing ghostly games along the river Lagan at night. Cecil's an avuncular seventy-year-old who first met Higgy at the now infamous snooker hall, then decided to buy it. Cecil recalled their nocturnal adventures.

> The river meanders down from Lurgan in big, wide sweeps. Four or five of us would go for walks to get a break from the smoky Jampot. Higgy liked to tag along. There was only a narrow footpath with a swamp on the other side. One false step and you were in the water. There were no lights, only the glow of cigarettes. It was spooky. We'd tell ghost stories, then spin around as if we'd heard a cry from the rushes. We pretended to catch a glimpse of a giant in a black cape and started to run away. Higgy would be a few yards behind us because the path was too narrow to walk four abreast. He'd start running too. He was frightened but he loved it. He used to beg me: 'Please can we go down the Lagan again.'
>
> In those days young fellahs made their own entertainment. There wasn't much life outside the Jampot. There was no Kentucky Fried Chicken. We didn't have video games or mobile phones. Now I see cats and dogs running around with mobiles!

Fifty years after he first took Higgy under his wing as a precocious schoolboy, Cecil kept a nightly vigil while Alex tossed and turned on the sofa of his council bungalow. Sleep for the ailing Hurricane was at a premium. Breathing became more and more difficult as his lungs clouded up. Neither of them could have imagined it would come to this. Closer than anyone outside Alex's immediate family, Cecil witnessed the rise and fall of a genius. Being a wordsmith, he wanted to pen his own tribute. Here it is.

What the Beatles did for the Cavern, Higgy did for the Jampot. Thanks to him, it became the most famous snooker hall in the world. I'm in the privileged position as a one-time regular and former owner to say I was there. Alex was just another one of the boys but he was taking his first steps to being the greatest, most exciting, most talented snooker player there's ever been – a genius. He's up there with Tiger, Geordie Best, Maradona, Ali and Lester.

Harry McMullen liked to see the youngsters playing snooker. Alex was the artful dodger straight out of Dickens' novel – a cheeky kid with great natural ability and speed. He had to be fast to get away from the grown men he beat. He was *very* fast. Kids were given tables 6 and 7 or 13 and 14. They mustn't stray. Alex sat under the clock looking up the full length of the hall. He was the sparrowhawk surveying his domain, waiting to see where he could swoop. He had a habit of chewing his fingernails down to the quick until they bled.

He'd tell me he had eight pence in his pocket. Could I give him the fourpence he needed to make a shilling and get onto table 8? I usually obliged. Table 8 was where you'd find the best players. Four of us played a shilling a stick. You threw to see who would play first, second, third and fourth. The highest scorer won the stick and took four bob.

Higgy was accepted because he was good. Everyone loved the artful dodger, even if he beat them, which was often. The pockets were tight and the balls were heavy. A break of 25–30 was good. Nobody did a 147. Soon Higgy was doing the century breaks that Davis and Hendry had to wait until their twenties to achieve. We couldn't believe it. As soon as he could do everything clockwise, he wanted to do it anti-clockwise, the way other players couldn't. In between games, he had one ear on the dogs at Hackney Wick, White City and Haringey. He's one of only

> three people I ever met who could fill in a crossword, watch television, listen to the radio and hold a conversation at the same time without missing a trick. When Ann came to fetch him for dinner, he hid under the table and told us to say he wasn't there.
>
> To us the Jampot was the Stardust Casino of Las Vegas in the fifties, where Rat Pack wanabees drank Manhattans and smoked through the night. *Everybody* smoked down Sandy Row. Players passed fag ends around until their fingers were black. There were no Manhattans – just Mars bars, Milky Way and Tizer. That was some diet! We didn't care. It was the greatest place on earth.

The Stardust Casino Cecil mentioned, was run by a sports bookie called Frank 'Lefty' Rosenthal, fictionalised by Robert de Niro in Scorcese's film, *Casino*. They might not have had a 'Lefty' at the Jampot, but they had a bigger cast list than *Coronation Street*. Cecil gives us the rundown of Alex's contemporaries in that smouldering snooker nursery. It's no wonder these imprints stayed in Alex's mind. It's no wonder the spirit of the hustler stayed with him:

> Geordie 'The Bug' McClatchie was probably the best player in Belfast; Billy 'Maxi' Maxwell wasn't far behind him. He was a great comedian from a big family and was usually unemployed. He needed the cash therefore he was hard to beat. Buster 'The Hat' McHarry was a small-time loan shark. He'd go through the pockets of a dead man if he owed money. By contrast, Ivor Hayes was a good player but too honest to survive. Harry Goldfinger got his name by throwing his money away against better players. He worked in a shop. He thought he owned it and thought he could play. He was wrong on both counts. Wesley 'the Side King' Johnson could play wrong side, top side, bottom side, horror side – you name it, 'the Side King' could do

it. Bobby 'the Lumberjack' Fraser smoked cigars and broke cues – usually when trying to hit young Alex over the head. He didn't succeed. Porky Wilson fell in love with every girl who spoke to him. And then there was me – a player in the top ten, a good card player and a failed entrepreneur. Welcome to the human race!

The Jampot taught us 'A' level mathematics. Without it you couldn't play five-card stud, seven-card stud, Southern Cross, Railroad, Pontoon or count six doubles and four trebles in a quad. That is, not unless you came from another solar system. We were called the Loonvilles, the Rabbits, the Teds, the Celebs or the Con-Artists. Sometimes local thieves would drop in to disperse their ill-gotten gains.

Generally speaking, though, theft wasn't a big problem in those days. It's not that people had better morals – just that in there was nothing worth stealing. Certainly not in the working-class district surrounding the Jampot. We had the odd break-in where the stock would be quietly 'transferred' to a new owner in the small hours. After one such raid, Maxi the comedian walked though the door to see the place turned over. He said to the owner:

'Another robbery, Harry?'

'Yes. This time the thieves left their footprints behind. There was a heavy dew on the roof last night.'

'Well you know who it was then.'

'No.'

'McHarry the money lender. He's a heavy Jew!'

One spring day, we witnessed a minor miracle. Several of the players were wondering where they'd get the money to buy Easter eggs for the kids. They'd either be unemployed or earning a measly seven to eight pounds a week. As if by magic, a well-dressed stranger walked in off the street and asked if anyone would like to challenge him 'for a small wager'. Johnny 'Easter Egg' was a saint amongst sinners. He got pleasure from spreading a little brightness into other people's darkness. Four games and £20 later he'd done just that.

Although it cost him, that was the start of Johnny's love affair with the Jampot. Some said his father owned a bank. Some said Johnny managed a bank. Others said he must have *robbed* a bank! He was sorely missed when he had to leave after a misunderstanding with the management. Many small but well-fed children had good cause to thank Johnny 'Easter Egg'.

Higgy went from strength to strength. He was very sharp, very observant. He could see the smallest leaf on the tallest tree. He could spot a phoney a mile away. That stood him in good stead throughout his career. We all knew he was more interested in gambling than riding horses. He sent telegrams home to his mum and racing tips to the boys at the Jampot. Shall I just say tipping wasn't one of his talents?

When he came back to Belfast, he was too good for the Jampot. I used to go with him to the Shaftesbury instead. It was only 400 yards away but very different. If you dropped a pen you'd be making a noise. It was more like a library. Spectators sat down. So did players when they weren't at the table. In the Jampot you'd have ten people standing around the table. It didn't bother us.

I'm in the rare position of saying I knew Alex Higgins from the beginning to the end of his life. In some ways I was the snooker equivalent of Gazza's pal, Jimmy 'Five Bellies'. Higgy and I travelled many roads. I was on *This Is Your Life* with him. I went to most of his big matches. I knocked about with him in London. I even went with him to Oliver Reed's funeral. He could be mean, selfish and cruel but, my goodness, we miss him. There'll never be another entertainer like him.

After his pneumonia attack, I kept a nightly vigil. He did a lot of hallucinating. He thought the 'Yardies' from Moss Side were after him. The last time I saw him was four weeks before he died. We were in his flat having a chat about old times. He got up and announced:

'I'm gonna make you something to eat, Cecil, and you're gonna love it.'

He nipped out of the flat, down to the bakers in Sandy Row and came back with two scones. He cut them in half, put on the butter and the jam, then poured fresh cream over the jam. He looked at me proudly and said:

'What do you think of that?'

'Wow!'

'Do you know what it is?'

'A cream bun.'

'You haven't a clue, Cecil. It's a Devon clotted-cream scone.'

We had big mugs of tea to swill it down. Not only did he eat his own half, he ate most of mine too. I was amazed. Then Higgy started to laugh. We'd gone from the Jampot to the jam scone.

7

HE WAS MY FELLOW MUSKETEER

Jim Meadowcroft was one of snooker's pioneers as the game struggled to make the graduation from idle pursuit to sensible occupation. There was little ennobling about a game played for money among hard-drinking, heavy-smoking millworkers in seedy Lancashire clubs. Who who'd want a son of theirs growing up in that environment? Jim's dad tried to keep him out of the snooker halls of Bacup and Oswaldtwistle and persuade him to get an apprenticeship and learn a trade. Jim tried to explain: 'I know what you're saying, Dad, but it's a drug.'

In order to close the case, Meadowcroft senior challenged his son to a game. This would be the decider. If Jim won, he could follow the snooker route. If Dad won, snooker went on the back burner. Jim thrashed the old man and went on to become a well-paid professional and a television commentator.

But a less conspicuous start is hard to imagine among the factory chimneys and terraced streets of the industrial north. Jim was in league with Dennis Taylor who'd made the bold gamble of leaving County Tyrone to live with relatives in Lancashire. He was equally determined to carve a living from this addictive pastime. Neither player had reason to believe there was a lucrative future in the offing. They were just a couple of freelances chancing their arm while John Spencer was snooker's Mr Big, not just in his native Bolton, but throughout the northern half of England.

In the mid-sixties, booking agents and wannabe managers circled around the clubs like moths around a light bulb. Cigarette companies cottoned on to snooker's advertising potential. Holiday camps contracted the six-times world champion, John Pulman, and, later, Jim Meadowcroft for a summer season. The *Lancashire Evening Telegraph* ran a 'Find a Champion' competition in which Spencer toured the county challenging the best young talent. Little by little, the game was developing.

Into this environment walked an Irish ragamuffin with hunger in his eyes – Alex Higgins. Jim had met him briefly at a national team championship in Bolton but was surprised when he turned up at the Benarth Club, next to Blackburn Post Office. This was Jim's home ground. Of all the gin joints in all the world . . .

> I don't know why Alex chose the Benarth but I was glad he did. He stood there surrounded by all his worldly possessions – a plastic carrier bag with a few personal effects and a battered cue case he had to hold at one end to stop the cue falling out. Alex Higgins had miraculously arrived on our doorstep and life would never be the same again.
>
> Although he made enemies because of his outbursts and mood swings, I liked him immensely, right from the start. He was driven by a force he couldn't control. If you could accept that, Alex was a loveable bloke underneath. He was like any mother's son. He showed his emotions. He wasn't ashamed to cry. You could wrap him in ermine robes and he'd still be old Higgy. Tetchy and aggressive at times, occasionally vindictive – but millions loved him for what he was. People turned a blind eye to his faults because they were seeing something rare – a true genius at work.
>
> Blackburn wasn't my first sighting of Alex. I'd seen him a few weeks earlier in the Players No.6 UK Team Trophy final in Bolton. His reputation had preceded him but it didn't prepare me for what was to come. I witnessed the most amazing snooker

I'd ever seen. I knew instantly that Alex Higgins was destined for greatness.

After his abortive attempts to become a jockey, then a brief period at an East End paper mill, Alex had drifted back to his roots. He couldn't find a job in Belfast, so he decided to leave home for a second time and establish a base camp in Blackburn. He rented a small flat above a newsagent's close to the Benarth.

Pretty soon, a couple of local entrepreneurs, Jack Leeming and John McLaughlin, signed him up and handed out cards advertising the services of 'Hurricane' Higgins. It was John and Jack who coined the name. Alex would have preferred 'Alexander the Great' because he conquered half the world. His antennae told him the northwest circuit was the place to be. Apart from being first stop on the ferry from Belfast, this is where several like-minded souls were gathering. He knew Dennis from his Northern Ireland days. He didn't like the cut of his gib. The pair would become mortal enemies, but for now the three young men, Higgins, Taylor and Meadowcroft, metaphorically nicked a vein in their arms and swapped blood. Says Jim: 'They called us the Three Musketeers. We went hunting together.'

Both Dennis and Jim had families to go home to. Alex only had a dowdy little flat. In fact he kept edging his way up the street as, one by one, the houses were demolished. This had all the makings of a rags-to-riches saga. You can see the sepia filter, hear the adagio horn concerto. Jim was concerned about his mercurial friend.

He was a human dynamo when he got going, but he'd sleep all day if you let him. He was a cross between a man and a boy. His socks and underpants were strung out on a line across the bedsit. It was funny but sad. Alex made an effort but he was ruled by the moon.

Leeming and McLaughlin sent him to the hairdressers and kitted him out in decent threads. They said he needed to impose his image.

Alex's mum and dad got to hear that Alex wasn't looking after himself. They took the unusual step of leaving Belfast for the best part of two years and taking a council house in Accrington to keep an eye on their son. His mum took cleaning jobs while his dad signed on full time at a sauce factory. Elizabeth was a lovely woman with a deep love for her family. His dad was a little chap with a pencil moustache. You'd never guess the two men were from the same family. Alex was the coiled spring, Dad was placid. I thought it was a great gesture to move house for their son's sake. Because he was a star in the making, they treated him with kid gloves. Alex lived on coaches and trains. He had no idea where the journey would take him. None of us did.

He beat me in a tournament in Accrington and his management team gave him a £200 bonus so that he could go back to Belfast for Christmas. Instead of doing that, he went to the Ace of Spades casino and blew the lot. That's the way he lived his life. He didn't take responsibility for himself. He was easily led.

Jim was the sober and sensible one, Dennis the understated comedian and Alex the circus act. He couldn't match Dennis's patter. One of Taylor's witticisms at an exhibition match in County Wexford infuriated him. It came a few months after Alex became world champion for the first time. He failed to show up at the venue so Dennis had to play against one of Alex's colleagues. He told the gathering: 'I know I'm playing the monkey, not the organ grinder. Alex should have been here tonight but unfortunately he was launching a ship in Belfast and forgot to let go of the bottle!'

He could never understand why Taylor was so popular with the fans. They had many confrontations. Taylor reported Higgins for misconduct during a tournament in Ipswich and later suggested that he'd deliberately played a foul shot to gain an advantage. Dennis said at the time: 'I know Alex doesn't like me that much but he can't say anything bad about me because I only say nice things about him.'

Alex did at least leave a congratulatory message on Dennis's answer machine after he'd beaten Steve Davis to land the world title, but magnanimity wasn't Higgins' strongest suit. As far as I can tell, it was the one and only time he said anything favourable about his compatriot. Jim recalls commentating for BBC TV in 1985 when Ireland won the World Cup Team Trophy after Alex snatched them back from the brink of defeat by beating Steve Davis. 'It was smashing to see Dennis and Alex, arms draped around each other, grinning like Cheshire cats and celebrating their joint success in a TV studio. Dennis said to David Vine: "What can you say about this fellow? He's absolutely magical!" '

What a contrast to the notorious World Cup event in Bournemouth five years later when Alex hit the roof about Dennis allegedly keeping the highest break prize instead of sharing it. He promised to have Dennis shot the next time he set foot in Northern Ireland. The inside story was that Alex wanted a float from the prize money to fund his gambling, and, as often happened in these situations, lost all sense of reason. There were still three matches against Canada to be played, and no guarantee that Dennis's break would remain the highest. Alex's threat was reported to the press by the tournament director, Ann Yates, not by Dennis. He'd have preferred to keep the whole thing quiet.

After a professional lifetime of tension and ill-feeling, Dennis wanted to keep his thoughts about Alex to himself. Measuring his words carefully, he did, however, tell me this.

Alex played some of his best snooker when he was drunk. If he overdosed, he lost it. I could have said a lot against him about the threat to have me shot, but I chose not to. For one thing, we had agreed to share the money and for another, my highest break was overtaken in the final anyway.

I did things to help Alex when he first came to Blackburn. I got him a flat and a television set when he was eighteen. He was already a pain.

For all his flamboyance, Alex wasn't in the same league as Steve Davis, Stephen Hendry or Ronnie O'Sullivan. I've played them all. Alex could humiliate you with wonder shots but I always knew the wheel would turn. You always had a chance of beating him. When Alex screwed back, the audience would respond because it was him. If someone else played the same shot, they took no notice.

Apart from the disagreement over the highest break prize, Alex turned another story completely on its head. He said I was after one of his sisters. What a joke! The truth is that *he* wanted to marry one of *my* sisters but she wanted nothing to do with him. Being turned down by Molly started the ill-feeling between Alex and me.

Here's how Alex described their relationship.

I first knew Dennis Taylor when he was fifteen and covered in spots. We were never close from the start. I was a star long before he was. When I won the all-Ireland title, Dennis was insignificant. In contrast, I travelled up and down Ireland for £20 a night getting through more work than pros like John Pulman. Dennis and I were chalk and cheese in temperament. I'm happy-go-lucky, Dennis is dour. I was amazed when he won the World Championship but I guess every dog has his day.

I wasn't keen on Dennis but I did like his family and once

> took a shine to his sister, Molly. She was very pretty. I was due to play an exhibition in their home village, Coalisland, and purposely stayed on to play in a little local tournament because I wanted to be near to Molly. We had tea and cucumber sandwiches in the parlour, with Dennis doing his best to protect his sister from me. It was a crush which only lasted as long as the tournament. I thought I was in love and promised her we'd get engaged, but what did *I* know about love?

As expected, Dennis stayed away from Alex's funeral.

The Three Musketeers toured the northern clubs doing exhibitions. Dennis and Jim laboured for between 10 shillings (50p) and £1 a night. By contrast, Banktop Working Men's Club raised Alex's fee from £3.10 shillings to £5 a night. Jim was easy with that: 'We accepted Alex's rates because we knew what a great crowd-puller he was. The snooker clubs sold out when he was around.'

The threesome had to abandon the Benarth club when bulldozers appeared on the horizon. They gravitated to the Elite in Accrington in 1970. One year later, Alex got his pro ticket and stunned the snooker world by promptly beating John Pulman, Rex Williams and John Spencer to become world champion at the first time of asking. Spencer, now a beaten finalist, acknowledged that while *he* might be the symbol of supreme professionalism, it was Alex who'd set the game alight. As Jim puts it: 'John was like a Rolls-Royce purring around the table. Alex was the opposite. The boy from Belfast was fast, aggressive and exciting, like a racing car screaming into the hairpins.'

Neither Dennis Taylor nor Jim Meadowcroft was earning enough to make a living from snooker. The rewards were still modest and they had to supplement their incomes elsewhere. Dennis worked for a television distributors, while Jim was a driving instructor. Alex managed without a day job because he was able to command bigger fees. It certainly didn't start off that way, as Jim recalls:

> We played round-robins for sixpence a time. At one of them, Alex knocked in ten centuries plus several eighties and nineties. No-one stood a chance against him. It was a sensational display. After the eighth century, Alex asked the club owner: 'Can I have a meat pie and cup of tea if I do it again?' The owner agreed and Alex banged in two more for good measure. A meat pie was meagre return for such a performance.
>
> I'd never seen so much talent. Still haven't. The reason Alex didn't win more trophies was because he loved playing to the gallery. He wanted to hear spectators roar rather than applaud. He deliberately took risks. Nobody has been able to fire up a crowd the way he could. Even at Benarth people would travel several miles just to see him play. There was no televised snooker in those days. There weren't many column inches in the newspapers either. Rumours of Alex's brilliance were spread by word of mouth.
>
> I remember a Blackpool fishmonger and part-time snooker coach called Frank Callan being horrified to see that Alex was charging £35 a night for exhibitions after winning the world title. Frank had a fish stall at Bacup market and often popped into the club for a chat. He coached Steve Davis and John Parrott in later years. I told him he shouldn't complain about £35 to watch snooker's world champion. Was there any other world champion from any other sport who'd perform for that kind of money? Of course not.

Jim and Dennis turned pro around the same time as Alex, but they resented paying 10 per cent of their earnings to the Billiards and Snooker Control Council. Eventually, the players formed a breakaway union, the World Professional Billiards and Snooker Association. Onwards they marched with little or no media interest in anyone but Alex.

Luckily, the club scene was vibrant. The number of bookings increased, enabling Dennis and Jim to give up their extra-curricular commitments. Snooker at last gave the Musketeers. There was near full employment in Lancashire and beer prices at working men's clubs were low enough to attract plenty of custom. Thanks to proceeds from the bar and a healthy income stream from fruit machines, clubs could afford to engage stand-up comics and live bands at the weekend. The likes of Higgins, Taylor and Meadowcroft kept the tills busy during the week.

The picture looked a lot rosier but the new snooker sensation wasn't firing on all cylinders. Jim got a disturbing glimpse of Alex's other persona. He imagined the world champion would be full of optimism about the future. He found exactly the opposite.

> I called at the small terraced house he rented in Accrington. Alex was slumped in an armchair like a little old man. He was pale, unshaven and bedraggled. He hardly lifted his head to greet me. At the age of twenty-two, the King of Snooker looked a broken man. You'd have said his career was over, not just beginning. I was frightened. I hadn't seen him like this. I asked him what was wrong. He just said: 'I've got no work.'
>
> He made it sound like a terminal illness. I came to realise that Alex needed work to justify his existence. It was his raison d'etre. He could only be happy if he was busy. Talking to him, it seemed that a lonely young chap from a different land had conquered the world, only to discover there was no pot of gold waiting for him. The world he'd conquered didn't seem to notice. I tried to reassure him and convince him he was a great player. Nothing I said sank in.

> That's when we first suspected that Alex had psychological problems. He was a manic depressive. They call it bipolar today. It was a serious condition which required treatment. He would never have accepted that. It wouldn't have surprised me if he'd been diagnosed as schizophrenic. It would have explained Alex's extreme highs and lows.

Jim witnessed an even deeper trough ten years later. This time it was Steve Davis who triggered Alex's depression. Davis won the World Championship in 1981, a year after Alex slaughtered him in the quarter-finals of the same event. Alex felt there was something unjust in Steve winnnig the title. He couldn't handle the thought that Steve was hogging the limelight. It was nine years since Alex had won the title and he was beginning to despair of repeating the feat. To make matters worse, Alex played Steve in a series of challenges organised by *The Sun* – and lost every one. His frustration turned inwards. His self-esteem was at ground level. A week later, and against his normal instincts, Alex booked himself into a nursing home suffering from physical and mental exhaustion.

Jim was concerned. A couple of weeks later he called Alex's new wife, Lynn, to see if there were any signs of improvement. There wasn't. Lynn needed support. She told Jim: 'He's in a terrible state. I don't know what to do with him. Would you mind coming over to cheer him up?'

Jim got there in the early afternoon. Alex had just crawled out of bed looking hungover. He'd obviously been drinking heavily the night before and was still in his dressing gown. Jim says: 'We sat and talked for ages. Alex was desperate for a boost – anything to lift his confidence. I told him he was a brilliant player going through a bad patch. It happens to all top players. He had to drag himself up off the floor and remind everyone how good he was. Snooker was his life and his family's future.'

Within six weeks of that conversation, Alex won his second world title. His first round victim was none other than Jim Meadowcroft, beaten 10-5. So much for the pep talk! Alex maintained that winning the title sparked envy among players and officials who didn't like the way he'd become bigger than the game. He was the last person they wanted as world champion. As though to irritate them further, Alex stole the headlines by irrigating the Crucible's foliage when he couldn't get to the toilet. Jim smiles when recalling the day Alex Higgins was bigger news than the Falklands War.

> Alex was practising late on one of the Crucible tables. You weren't allowed to do that. A television engineer was working nearby. He saw Alex peeing in a plant pot, and, as we know, all hell broke loose when he reported it to the WPBSA. I was having breakfast with Alex at the Grosvenor Hotel next morning. It was the day after we sank the *Belgrano* but *The Sun* and the *Mirror* had Alex peeing in a plant pot as the front page lead. The *Belgrano* was relegated to a few paragraphs at the bottom!
>
> The debate about Alex Higgins will go on and on. There's no doubt in my mind that he was the only true genius. I was very fond of Alex but I wouldn't have wanted to swap skins with him. There were so many sides to him, it was difficult to know which one you were dealing with. I don't think I've ever met anyone so driven. Snooker was the only way he could express himself. He was driven until he was out of control. In the end I felt sorry for my fellow Musketeer because the press slaughtered him like they did George Best. They made him into a monster. He wasn't that.

8

HE WAS MY DAD

Lauren turned towards the darkened window of the sitting room, her blonde hair partly lit by the sodium lights across the road: 'I still expect to see his face pressed up against the glass and hear a little tap.' Her brother Jordan chuckled from the sofa. He was less talkative. He was still recovering from a night out with the lads after watching Manchester United beat Blackburn Rovers 7-1.

'That's what my dad did,' said Lauren. 'Just appear out of nowhere and give you the fright of your life. You never knew when he was coming or where he'd disappear to afterwards.'

'Cool guy,' laughed Jordan. 'I remember him standing between those trees while I tried to score a goal past him. He thought he was dead good at football. He told us he used to play for Linfield Swifts. Perhaps he did. He wasn't a bad goalie, to be fair. That's until one of my free kicks bent his finger back. He took it real well.'

It was just another Sunday at the detached 1980s house in Heald Green, Cheshire, where Lauren and Jordan have lived with their mum, Lynn, since she walked out on her marriage. They'd become a tight trio. Lauren says her mum's her best friend: 'Mum gave me all the stability and all the love I could have wanted. Considering it got off to such a bad start with Dad, I've had a very good life.'

Both offspring sported versions of that fleshy Higgins nose, most familiar to the Great British public twitching down a snooker cue in one of those unforgiving close-ups. I recall one of our more outspoken television directors at ITV breathing hard into my earpiece as he tightened the close-up: 'He's an animal!'

There the similarity between brother and sister ends. Jordan's the wiry, ginger-haired clone, naturally good at sport but incapable of sitting still. By contrast, Lauren's statuesque, glamorous and confident. 'She should have been the boy,' says Mum. Her reactions are sharp; her mind constantly challenging; her strongly held views about everything from men to money refreshingly close to the surface. 'I'd like to get married and have kids one day, but I'm probably too difficult to live with.' Shades of Dad.

Lauren went virtually unnoticed for twenty-eight years after that involuntary carry-on part in the Crucible. It remains one of the most memorable sporting clips on television, ranking alongside Maradona's Hand of God, Shane Warne's first ball to Mike Gatting, Seb Coe kissing the running track at the Moscow Olympics and Cassius Clay's knockdown of Sony Liston. Quite a gallery.

She says: 'I've watched those images time and again since Dad died. I just wish I'd been a bit older when his success came. Then I could have been more help to him on the way down when people grew tired of his antics. I saw all his bad sides. I knew how to handle him. Being at the top meant it was so much harder to fall, especially for my dad who didn't have the safety net of a family underneath him. He never came to terms with his fading presence.'

Ms Higgins studied law and works in Human Resources for a legal expenses insurance company in Cheadle. When I met her, she was studying hard to qualify at the highest level of her chosen profession. I'd back her to make it. The determination to succeed, notably absent in her brother, was passed down by Alex. Her academic discipline wasn't. That's her own doing. Despite her lively demeanour and positive take on life, however, Lauren was troubled.

She kept thinking about a hundred and one things she should have done for Alex. More accurately, things she *feels* she should have done – returned his calls more often; made a point of going to see him in Belfast; and accepted his invitation to a dinner in Manchester. This is the one that distressed her most. It seemed relatively unimportant at the time. It doesn't any more.

> I had no idea it was a Save Alex Higgins evening. He didn't tell me they were raising money for his tooth implants. Sometimes he didn't tell you much. Dad just said there was a dinner for him and could I be there? He gave me a day's notice. I tried to re-arrange my work schedule but couldn't. He didn't understand people who had nine-to-five jobs. He thought they could drop whatever they were doing like he could. I told him it was impossible to get away. He ranted at me. His last words were: 'Fuck off then!' Although he left a voicemail apologising, we never spoke again. I have to live with that.
>
> He should have told me what it was for and given me more of a warning. I'm sure my boss would have given me compassionate leave. I felt terrible when I found out. I feel worse now that he's gone.

It should be a consolation to Lauren that guilt is a natural by-product of bereavement. Blaming oneself is a tunnel through which the bereaved often have to travel. She has good days and bad.

> I can go several hours without stressing before it hits me again. The other day at work I was standing by the water cooler panicking about what to drink. Then I burst into tears and had to come home. I still wake up some mornings thinking it's too much to cope with. I'm still in denial. Dad had such

> bounce-backability that I can't believe anything could have destroyed his spirit. As sick as he was, I was convinced he'd climb his mountain. He always has before.

The manner of Alex's death and his parting words affected Lauren so deeply that she couldn't face a repeat showing of the award-winning stage play, *Hurricane*, at Belfast's Royal Opera House six months later. I invited her to be my guest. 'Thank you,' she replied, 'but it's too soon. I'd want to get up and shout if there was something I didn't agree with. I wouldn't be able to stop myself.' Perhaps it was just as well then.

Lauren did get up, bravely, to deliver a moving poem at her father's funeral. She was the only mourner to pay a personal tribute. Jimmy White, having prepared a speech, was overcome with emotion and had to hand it to the Dean of Belfast, the Very Reverend Dr Houston McKelvey, to read. Millions of viewers watched live on Sky or later on ITN and BBC News as Lauren read out loud, her voice tremulous but under control. She was the first to admit, lest anyone accuse her of plagiarism, that she selected the poem from the internet rather than write her own: 'The Dean got it wrong. I felt embarrassed afterwards.' The poem went like this:

> You never said I'm leaving. You never said goodbye
> You were gone before I knew it and only God knew why.
> There are no words to tell just what I feel inside
> The shock, the hurt, the anger might gradually subside.
> A million times I need you. A million times I'll cry.
> If love alone could save you, you never would have died.
> In life I loved you dearly. In death I love you still.
> In my heart you'll hold a place no-one else could fill.
> It broke my heart to lose you but you didn't go alone

> For part of me went with you the day God took you home.
> Things will never be the same and though it hurts so bad,
> I'll smile whenever I hear your name
> And be proud you were my dad.

She added the line: 'I love you, Dad, from Jordan and me.' A rapt congregation applauded as Lauren stepped down from the lectern and sat next to her mother and brother. Her mouth movements reminded me of Alex, a father in absentia but a father infinitely proud of his daughter. His eyes always sparkled when he talked about her, which he often did. He told me how much he regretted having so few years under the same roof as Lauren. He was, of course, his own assassin, but it didn't stop the hurt.

As we shall hear, communication between Alex's offspring and Will Robinson, the man who organised the funeral, was sketchy and strained.

> I didn't know whether or not I was allowed to say anything in church. I couldn't get hold of the Dean. Will Robinson gave me a contact number but the office was already closed. I certainly didn't expect cameras in my face. The poem summed up everything I was feeling. When one of your parents goes, part of you goes too. You feel as vulnerable as a child. I know he wasn't the best dad in the world but I'd survived the ups and downs, been sworn at, neglected and insulted but possibly grew stronger as a result. I remembered how tearful I was when he forgot my eighteenth birthday. I kept hearing 'Fuck off then!' in his whispered voice.
>
> While someone's alive, you think there's always time to put things right. Now the opportunity's gone for good. If I had a wish, it would be to hear Dad say: 'I'm sorry, Lauren. I could

have been a better father. I could have provided for you, your mum and Jordan. I could have been your strength.'

I'd have been within my rights to say I wanted nothing to do with him, but Mum didn't bring us up to think like that. I didn't have the best dad but I have the best mum. And in the end, it was Dad who missed out. He may have hit the heights in his professional career and had hordes of followers, but he had nothing and no-one to come home to.

So there was only a flimsy platform upon which Lauren and Alex could build a meaningful relationship. Once Alex and Lynn were separated, quality time with his children was reduced to a minimum. In any case, Lauren was wary of him. She'd been introduced to his drunken outbursts and lashing tongue at an early age.

I was quite advanced for my years so I'd know from the tone of voice when something was about to kick off between Mum and Dad. I tried to diffuse it. I'm quite good in difficult situations. I pick up on people's emotions quickly. It can be a good thing or a bad thing. When my parents were divorced, Dad would phone if he was nearby and turn up a few minutes later. We were always on tenterhooks waiting for him. I had to be on guard in case of trouble. I suppose I got conditioned to it.

I remember lots of times when we did normal things like sit down to watch television. Sometimes he read me bedtime stories. Sometimes he made them up. He was good at that. He loved poetry. He used to get me to recite a poem called 'The Marrog' which he first heard me read at school. It's about an invisible Martian with seventeen hands who sits at the back of the classroom. Dad used to get me to act it out. I was over the top but Dad loved it, especially the last line which goes: 'And nobody, nobody knows.'

Dad was still asking me to perform it when I was seventeen. I told him I'd forgotten the words. I hadn't but it would have been embarrassing. I think Mum had him whipped him into shape for a short while. Apparently, he changed nappies and made the tea. He hoovered the house once! I remember him sitting in his dressing gown watching the racing on television. I remember how he used to play games with us on the floor. But he was very strict. I was told off for putting my hand in a glass of orange juice to pick out the ice. He said it was rude. You wouldn't think so but Dad was big on manners.

These were isolated incidents. More often, Alex would turn up unannounced, spend a couple of hours at the house and leave. What else is a divorced father to do? It can be a thankless role. You only have to cast your eyes around shopping centres on Saturday afternoons. They're sprinkled with divorced dads and their children munching chips after a trip to the cinema and wondering where to go next. As Lauren rightly points out, it was even harder for Alex because he seldom had a home of his own to take them to. Staying with Dad for the weekend was out of the question. So were half-terms and holidays.

When I was seven, he bought me a big teddy bear and a candle-making set for my birthday. He asked if I wanted to go to his place. That was very unusual. Holly Haise had a daughter more or less my age so I was intrigued to meet her. When I got to her apartment, we played in the bedroom and she said: 'That's your christening blanket on my bed.'

It really upset me. I didn't want to go there again.

There's a character in *He-Man* called Evil Lyn. Dad bought us the toy model each. I can laugh now but it wasn't a very nice thing to do. He was always asking me if Mum had a boyfriend. It made me uneasy.

Alex certainly took an interest in his children's progress at school, though it didn't always have the desired effect. He eyes lit up when Lauren chose snooker for her project.

He could have been a big help but he always thought he knew best. Nothing I'd say was right. However, he did get Jimmy White to send me a signed photograph and told me how snooker evolved from billiards, so that was useful. He was unbearable when I studied psychology at college. He claimed he knew all there was to know about psychology. I was trying to write an essay and he wouldn't shut up – telling me what I should read and that he knew someone who could get me important books to read, etc. I screamed at him: 'You *don't* know everything. You're driving me mad. Leave me alone!'

Then I stormed out and ran upstairs to my room. He came knocking on the door. I told him to go away: 'Everything in life isn't about you.'

When you're seventeen to eighteen you just want someone to listen to *you* rather than the sound of their voice. It took Dad a long time to get used to the idea that I was an adult and had my own mind. There was a definite improvement after that. Dad learned that if he wanted a conversation with me, it had to be a two-way thing. I played him at his own game. If he kicked off, I just put the phone down. Perhaps he mellowed after his cancer.

Not long before he died we talked on the phone about whether he might have lost some of his aggression. There were signs of it, but he had his eccentricities till the end and he could still fly off the handle at any moment – perhaps out of frustration because his body wouldn't do what he wanted it to.

When we were younger, Mum was usually the one on the touchline on Saturday mornings in freezing cold weather. She kept him informed of everything that was happening at school and how Jordan and I were getting on. I'll never forget the embarrassment when he came to see me in a school concert. He swept in wearing his long coat and stood at the back of the hall. When the concert was finished, he had a huge bouquet of flowers delivered to me backstage. Imagine that when you're seven years old! I didn't know how to react. It was only little me, not Elizabeth Taylor in *Cleopatra*!

To be truthful I was glad when Mum and Dad split up. The atmosphere was horrible. They just didn't get on. Dad's temper was scary for a child. I have a vivid memory of being locked in my bedroom with Mum clutching Jordan and me while Dad was throwing things through the window. It was nice and peaceful when he left. I'd have sacrificed my dad's success for a normal family life but I know he wouldn't. I look at my mum's parents who've been married for sixty years and wonder what it must be like.

Fortunately for Lauren, famous parents were two-a-penny at the King's School, a private school in Macclesfield where she began her secondary school education. Shouldering a notorious surname like Higgins wasn't the obstacle it might have been elsewhere. Lauren was sharing sweets with the progeny of actors, writers and television presenters. Other parents, such as Steve Bruce, played for Manchester United. Things were more difficult when she changed schools.

Dad was in decline and losing more games than he won. Students at my school got crueller as his behaviour became wilder. They'd

> laugh because he was such a rotten loser. Nothing was ever his fault. The worst example was that BBC interview in which he announced his retirement and told officials they could stick snooker where the sun doesn't shine. It was obvious Dad was drunk. He was slurring his words. I was praying under my breath: 'Please be quiet, Dad. Will someone switch him off or take him away?' I was terrified of going into school the next day. It didn't bother Jordan. He let things wash over him. He can switch off. I'm more sensitive. I've been brought up to defend members of my own family. Though I might not agree with the things my dad said or did, he *was* my dad at the end of the day.

Jordan nodded. He'd been listening quietly. I asked him if it had been an advantage or disadvantage having Alex as a father. He answered self-consciously and in short sentences: 'I didn't tell people. Some said I look like him. I know he was world champion but it didn't affect me. Since he died I've watched a lot of his games on YouTube. I watch them all the time. I'm proud of what he did. He was a genius. Sometimes I watch him and think he looks just like me. I walk fast like him. I'm easily bored. I don't like sitting in one place. I have to be doing something. I got bored at the Man U game and left before the end.'

That's a pretty low threshold. If he thought 7-1 was boring, how would he handle a goalless draw? Jordan's good at snooker but better at football. Left-footed strikers like him are priceless. He was on Manchester City's books for a time and played semi-pro for Stockport County on a YTS scheme.

'Dad used to come and watch. He'd run up and down the touch-line holding a massive mobile phone. Then he'd stop and shout at me to pull my socks up – literally. He hated untidy dressers. It did my head in. I was so embarrassed. I remember asking to come off at half time. He was a bossy dad. It felt as though he had spies everywhere. He was right, though. I should have been a pro. I didn't train hard enough. I spent too much time going out. Dad and me argued a lot. He wasn't happy that I didn't take football seriously. He wanted to get me a trial with Linfield in Belfast. I walked out on Stockport when it was coming up to contract time. I lacked ambition. Manchester City said I wasn't motivated enough.'

Lynn interrupted: 'Tell Tony why you weren't motivated.'

Jordan replied: 'Because I had everything I wanted here. Thanks to Mum, I didn't have to work. I wasn't on Jobseekers.'

Jordan was due to begin an engineering apprenticeship in January 2011 and promised to have a go at joining Altrincham Town in the Blue Square Premier. They could have used some inspiration. Altrincham were bottom of the table at time. The last I heard, he was doing intensive gym work and staying off the booze. A New Year's resolution or a serious attempt to get his life in order? We'll see.

Lauren smiled: 'I think Dad wanted Jordan to be a footballer because it would have been his own retirement plan. Jordan could have looked after him. It was like finding a wealthy husband for me. He tried to get me to go to Dubai to meet some seriously rich men. He said now I was twenty-nine it was time to get married. Over there, they were billionaires, not millionaires! I refused to go. He *knows* money isn't my motivation. I've worked for everything I've had. No silver spoons. That's what made it annoying when people assumed we had a nice easy lifestyle because we had a celebrity father. If only they knew.'

Alex was extremely protective of his daughter and, like many fathers, suspicious of her boyfriends. As someone who was fatally attracted to blondes himself, he knew the temptations and the pitfalls. It was a double-edged sword having an attractive daughter. I've seen him puff out his chest and say how beautiful she was. I've also heard him worry about who she was dating and what credentials he might have. Lauren was under intense scrutiny.

> He picked holes in my boyfriends and intimidated them. No-one was ever good enough. He'd say derogatory things without even getting to know them. When they came to the house he just blanked them. Then he'd storm out of the room in disgust. Then he'd ring me and say: 'You're not still going out with that prick, are you?'
>
> I've not had loads of boyfriends which is just as well because he didn't take to any of them. Perhaps he was jealous of the time I spent with them and not him. I can hear my mum on the phone to him now, fighting my corner: 'She's not an eight-year-old child, Alex. She's nineteen. She can go out with who she likes.'
>
> There *were* times when he was caring and generous in his way. He probably thought he was an okay dad in the circumstances. He always told me he loved me. People at the funeral said he thought the world of me. That was nice to hear. I'm not a touchy-feely person so I find public displays of affection difficult. I hardly ever kissed him but he would never leave without giving me a hug or a kiss on the cheek.
>
> I only asked him for money once in my life. It was in January 2010. I'd applied for a £300 loan towards buying a car but it was late coming through. Dad put the money straight into my account. I was lucky. It could easily have gone to the bookies. I promised to repay him when my bank loan came through but he wouldn't hear of it.
>
> It was a worrying time for me because I'd recently had a cyst removed. Complications set in. The wound had to be left open to drain. It was packed every day but it wasn't closing up properly. I couldn't walk or work. I kept it from my dad because

when a similar thing happened before, he wanted to speak to the surgeon, the anaesthetist and half the blooming hospital. He knew best. They weren't to do anything without his permission.

He couldn't understand why I was in bed each time he called. He thought I was avoiding him. Mum accidently let the cat out of the bag and told him I was unwell. He was furious that he hadn't been told. He knew a cure for my problem. He told me to put lemon on it. That would do the trick. Dad had a herbal remedy for every ailment. I think he got them from his mother. The roles were reversed a few weeks later. He rang me to say he was suffering with piles. I said: 'That's easy. Put lemon on it!'

He thought that was very funny. Sometimes he tried too hard to please and got things wrong. Like the time I asked for a treadmill for my birthday. I didn't think I'd get one but I tried my luck. Dad said he had a friend who dealt in treadmills. He told me to meet him at Masters Snooker Club in Stockport. I was apprehensive so I took some money for a taxi back in case he misbehaved. I also took a friend with me. We were both in school uniform. There were lots of blokes standing around. Dad pointed to a rowing machine in the corner of the room.

'I've got you this. They're really good.'

'I didn't want a rowing machine. I wanted a treadmill.'

'Get on and have a go.'

'I don't want to do it in my school skirt in front of all these men.'

'Get on. Nobody's looking at you.'

'No! I've had enough of this. I'm going. Don't even speak to me.'

I ordered a taxi and left with my friend. I know he meant well but the deal was more important to him than getting the present

I'd asked him for. There was another example of Dad getting it wrong after I was attacked by a gang of girls in the school playground. They gave me a black eye. Dad took one look at me and hit the roof. I told him not to worry. It was a case of mistaken identity. They were after a different blonde girl. He wouldn't let it rest. Before I could stop him, he'd rounded up all the likely suspects and made them stand in a line in the garden. He stood over them with his pen and paper like Hercule Poirot. Mum was shouting: 'Ignore him and go home the lot of you!'

They were frozen to the spot. Dad asked each of them for a statement and took notes. I told my friends he wasn't a policeman so they should run away. They were too scared. The investigation dragged on but no arrests were made. None of the girls he'd assembled were the ones who attacked me. That was typical Dad. I was furious.

I knew he was proud of me though. He once said I was his greatest achievement. He put me on a pedestal. I gave him something to brag about. Not long before Dad went back to live in Ireland, I agreed to meet him for a coffee. I was eighteen at the time. He joked that people would mistake me for his girlfriend. He sat with his Guinness and we were chatting away, catching up when a group of young girls started laughing at us. They obviously thought I was his bit of skirt. I lost it: 'If you've got something worthwhile to say, say it. This is my dad. What's your problem?'

Dad started laughing. He said *he* was meant to be the troublemaker, not me. Another time, my friend and I went to meet him in Manchester. He took us to Henry's which was a really wine bar. He gave me money to buy clothes, then treated us both to champagne cocktails. We thought we were the business. Dad was younger then and looked great. All the women admired him.

I felt a mixture of shame and admiration for my dad. I was ashamed of his outbursts and often felt uncomfortable when he was near me, but when I look at what he achieved from modest beginnings, I'm proud. He put in the time and the effort to succeed. That's impressive. He wanted to entertain the crowd more than win matches. In years to come, he'll be remembered more for his personality than his titles.

People who played snooker wouldn't be where they are today if it wasn't for Dad. It was a boring game that nobody watched till he came along. Then everybody watched – old ladies, housewives, young men and children. One old dear left him a violin in her will. There was another lady pensioner from Tunbridge Wells who drove all over England to watch him. They weren't only interested in the snooker. They wanted to see his entrance into the arena, check what he was wearing and watch how he behaved. Even when the other player was at the table, most of the attention was on Dad. I used to watch a certain amount of snooker but I was a lot younger and not really interested when Dad was winning matches. I'd love to be watching him winning the world championship now I'm this age.

When they banned him from the game and he had to re-qualify, he asked if we'd go to Stoke on Trent and support him. Mum took us both along. It was so different seeing a hundred tables in action and hearing all that noise. People played shoulder to shoulder. Dad was playing a woman to begin with. I'm not sure whether he was being gentlemanly or trying to gain the upper hand, but he got me to present her with a bunch of flowers before the match. She had no idea who I was. I've often wondered if they were Dad's tactics. He was good at tactics. He was a very shrewd man. He'd frighten opponents to death by going up to them before the game, shaking them by the hand and fixing them with a long, piercing stare.

It's no secret that Alex had concerns about his son. He told his sister: 'Jordan's going to be a problem. He won't get off his arse and he's in with the wrong crowd.'

He needn't have worried. Jordan has qualifications in Leisure and Tourism, not to mention an FA coaching badge. He has a pretty full life and a job with a building company. After his father died, Jordan made several trips to hear tales of Alex from the regulars at The Royal, and, of course, Alex's sisters. He told me: 'I love Ireland and I love the people. They're very friendly. I went three times in a couple of months. I stayed with my cousins Lyndsey and Shelley. I get on well with Dad's family. They're always pleased to see me.'

That reality doesn't sit comfortably with Lynn, though she doesn't stand in his way. There's very little love lost between the two sides of the family. It's been that way since Lynn and Alex were married. The sisters thought Lynn was an opportunist who never loved their brother. They're wrong on both counts. Lauren thinks the Higgins Trinity are vindictive.

This might sound like a Middle East peace initiative, but Jordan's the potential bridge. He and Ann Higgins maintain a dialogue. There are still things to be discussed, such as the whereabouts of Alex's belongings and the destination of his trophies. Ann was eager to see Jordan get a job and detects an all-too-familiar penchant for self-destruction. She phoned him after Christmas 2010 to let him know that McGrath's Cash Conversion shop in Belfast still had the trophy Alex won at the Benson and Hedges Masters. That epic one-legged final against Stephen Hendry was Alex's last big hurrah. It turned out that he pawned the trophy for £400, but redeemed it a few months later. He told McGrath's to hang onto it. He might need to pawn it again.

Contact between Alex and Jordan wasn't so frequent. They weren't especially close and Jordan's a more private person than Lauren. Nevertheless, Jordan visited his father in Belfast a couple of years before Alex died. Predictably, they went drinking, although father had no chance of keeping pace with son. Alex couldn't get him out of the place. In despair, he phoned Lauren, who was enjoying an evening with friends back home.

'I'm exhausted, Lauren. Jordan's doing my head in. I've been trying to get him to leave the bar but he won't move.'

'Ha, ha. It takes one to know one!'

> 'It's all very well you laughing. What do I do? Get the guys to carry him out?'
>
> 'If you do he'll kick off. Just pretend you're not feeling well and tell him you've got to get home.'
>
> It worked. Lynn had been privy to the conversation. She laughed: 'It was hilarious. Alex would normally be the one out till five, six or seven in the morning. Now he was getting a taste of his own medicine. What goes around comes around!'

Jordan shrugged his shoulders and laughed. He's been back to savour the delights of Alex's local, the Royal. It's a watering hole he first visited the day after they buried his dad. He can't call himself a regular yet, but it may come. He says:

> I've got to know Gary and Lawrence, the landlord. They look after me well. I hadn't been to Belfast much while Dad was alive. Perhaps I should have done. Perhaps I should have seen more of him. He wanted me to practise snooker with him before the Legends tour in Sheffield. He asked me to be his driver but I didn't fancy it. Dad was worried about me. He thought it was time I sorted out my life before I went off the rails. He was right. I admit I enjoy gambling as well – but not big time like Dad. I have £2 accumulators but never win much. Mum gives me the money. My grandparents spoil me too. I'm their favourite.

I don't think you could say Dad and I had a relationship, but then I never knew him as a father at home. I was too young. Mum asked him several times to take me for a game of snooker but he wasn't keen. He bought me a set of golf clubs instead. He said he didn't want me playing snooker in smoke-filled places. He'd say: 'Snooker's not a good life. It's lonely. Play outdoor sports. They're much healthier.'

I remember telling him I once made a 60 break. I was very proud. Instead of saying well done, Dad said: 'Can you do it all the time?'

'No.'

'It's no good then.'

Over the last five years, as Alex grew weaker and more dependent, Lauren and Alex enjoyed a more relaxed time – as relaxed as anyone could be with Alex. She thinks he almost forgot that she was his daughter and came out with inappropriate things at the most inopportune moments.

'I haven't had a woman for months.'

'That's too much information, Dad. I really don't want to know.'

'I'd love to have a woman. Not necessarily for sex. Just for friendship.'

'Enough already!'

Nevertheless, she was pleased he could confide in her if he was feeling down or had problems.

He suffered a lot from depression in the last year. I felt so sorry for him when he couldn't eat. He hated the Build-Up supplement Ann used to get for him but I told him lots of people have to do things they didn't like and to stop complaining. It was like a thunderbolt when we first heard that he had cancer. The hospital was worried because he wasn't taking any food. I went

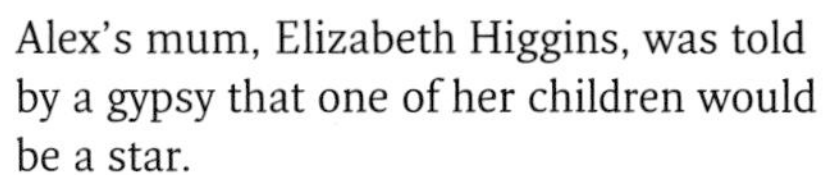

Alex's mum, Elizabeth Higgins, was told by a gypsy that one of her children would be a star.

A rare moment of shared joy with Alexander senior. Alex and his dad didn't have much in common.

20-year-old Alex in his natural habitat, the local club.

Always a dandy, Alex poses for his portrait as the new world champion.

Alex ignored the textbook and played shots on the move.

When Alex married Lynn Avison at the United Reform Church in Wilmslow, he met his match in every sense.

The essence of the man – frequently caught in personal turmoil.

Jimmy White was furious when his best mate died. He'd have strapped Alex in a chair and force-fed him if he could.

All smiles on the surface but Dennis Taylor and Alex, two Ulstermen, had a serious clash of personalities dating back to their youth.

Alex won a second world title at the Crucible in 1982, with a little help from cigarettes, but the smoke troubled Willie Thorne.

Jim Meadowcroft and Alex were two of the Three Musketeers who took the Lancashire club scene by storm. Dennis Taylor was the third member.

Lynn and Alex celebrate his sensational victory over Steve Davis in the 1983 UK Championship final, although the rift between husband and wife was growing.

Alex adored his children, Jordan (*left*) and Lauren, but the family life he wanted had no chance of materialising.

One of the great sporting images – Alex insisted on his baby daughter, Lauren, sharing the limelight when he won the 1982 world title.

Alex often said that Lauren was his greatest achievement. Her boyfriends were in for a hard time.

Alex's secret son, Christopher, met his father just once. Why he was ignored for so long remains a mystery.

Lynn and the couple's two children have become a tight unit since the marriage break-up. Lauren says her mum is her best friend.

Above left: Barry McGuigan (*left*) with his hero. He and Alex receive awards at an Irish sports stars ceremony in 1982.

Above right: The feeling was mutual. Alex was ringside in 1985 when Barry beat Eusebio Pedroza to win the world featherweight title.

Left: Never far away! Len Ganley (*centre*) refereed many of Alex's big matches and travelled the world with him.

into panic mode. It was the first time anyone in the family had had a life-threatening illness. It made me cry when I went to Belfast to visit him. His body had been through two operations and forty doses of radiotherapy which was a huge amount. He always put on a brave face. I pulled his leg: 'Right what have you been up to then? Annoying nurses up and down the ward?'

I hugged and kissed him – something I don't normally do. He looked so forlorn lying there. He told me how much he loved me. I said it back to him. Normally I found that difficult to do. I *did* love my dad. Although he'd done bad things, Mum didn't poison us against him. Eventually he beat cancer so it was a massive shock when he lost all that weight and aged. It was the ageing that upset me most. He was only sixty and looked eighty. People were horrified when they saw him and of course he was aware of that. Friends asked me why somebody didn't do something to save him. I told them we couldn't do much. He was his own man and did what he chose.

Not many people would have survived that amount of radiotherapy but Dad was incredible. He'd be knocked flat then bounce back up again. He was always on his feet, dancing like a gazelle, off to his next appointment. He was a permanent nomad. People think he was destitute but he did *have* money and he did *earn* money. It's just that he chose to gamble it away. He got £100,000 for his book but it had gone in three months.

I tried to stop him gambling so much. You could tell him in the morning that he should put a couple of grand aside for a rainy day. He'd say 'Yeah, yeah, yeah' but by afternoon he'd blown the lot. Jordan's been to the races with him and watched him bet astronomical sums of money. Unfortunately, Jordan's picked up the habit now. It's the last thing we need.

I suppose Dad's passion for the horses gave him real

enjoyment when there wasn't much else to get excited about. However, I'm not sure an addiction gives you enjoyment. He did what he loved doing and at the end it was his downfall. Most geniuses have flaws but it's not obligatory! David Beckham seems to manage all right. I think Dad's issues were no different from lots of other people's. They just dealt with them better. Dad was allowed to get away with unacceptable behaviour at the height of his fame and he thought it was okay to carry on.

It's horribly frustrating that he got over cancer, then died of something he could have avoided. When he decided to eat in order to have the implants, it was too late. It didn't matter that he was eating sponge cake with Charlie Hawley or cream teas with Cecil. The damage was done. When I heard that Charlie had to take him through the airport in a wheelchair, I was horrified. That's just not my dad.

What pisses me off is why the tooth implant wasn't done years ago. If you can't function as a human being, somebody somewhere should be able to help. We can't blame anyone else, though. We have to ask the question: did Dad care enough about himself? The answer has got to be no. He always had an excuse for not going to the doctors. All he seemed to care about was getting his bets on. It's such a shame.

Jordan: 'I saw Dad at our house about two months before he died. He stayed for a few hours. I was pleased to see him but cut up about his condition. He could hardly talk or walk. He never complained, though. And he didn't discuss his illness with us. He should have done. I tried to phone him several times when he went back to Belfast but he wouldn't answer. I suppose that's because he couldn't.'

The funeral drove a deeper rift between the two sides of the family. It was choreographed by arch choreographer Will Robinson, who described himself a friend and former agent of Alex. Lynn, Lauren, Jordan and Charlie Hawley pleaded ignorance of Will. Alex's son and daughter felt that obstacles were put in their way. The most tragic day of their lives was being organised with no opportunity for them to be involved. Lauren:

> The way Will and the sisters treated us really upset me. Jordan and I were his kids for God's sake. We felt we were kept in the dark and were not told anything about the funeral or the post-mortem until the last minute. They reckoned we didn't have much contact with Dad and didn't really care. Ann knows deep down what he felt about me. He'd have blown his top if he'd known how they kept it among themselves. Maybe they thought that we'd steal the glory. What glory?
>
> Five newspaper 'exclusives' appeared before the funeral. I think they were all arranged by Will Robinson. I've got text messages from Jean's daughter, Shelley, warning me to stop slagging Will off. But he deserved it. I didn't hear that he was planning the funeral until five days before it took place. He only sent me tit-bits of information. I had to phone and ask why ex-players were to be pallbearers but no-one had thought to ask Jordan. I left a message with Will that I wanted to speak at the funeral. I didn't hear back until two days before. I was beside myself with worry.
>
> Jordan eventually helped to carry the coffin but only the short distance from Jean's house to the road. That was bad. My brother felt that it was his dad and his duty. The team that carried the coffin from the hearse into the cathedral did it as a publicity stunt. Maybe that's why Will Robinson put himself in full view of the cameras. Let's be honest, he wasn't in the greatest physical shape for that job.

Ann did a lot for Dad and I'm grateful, but I got the impression that he didn't have much time for Jean and he was barely talking to Isobel. They fell out over a diamond ring. It's been a running sore for a long time.

Nevertheless, a complicated funeral of which Alex would surely have been proud *did* take place. If Will Robinson hadn't organised it, who would have? The World Professional Billiards and Snooker Association? I don't think so. Belfast City Council? You're joking. And if the media-savey agent had half an eye on television and newspaper exposure, so what? Wasn't Alex's entire career about media exposure? He often said he wanted a bigger, better funeral than George Best's. Lauren's answer had the benefit of hindsight.

I'd have organised the funeral. I have the ability to rise to the big occasion. More than that – I'd have paid for it out of my own money. And it wouldn't have cost £12,500. We'd have made it a more personal affair, with guests Dad would have wanted, not people grabbing a photo-opportunity.

I had suspicions about the Save Alex Higgins campaign when the money raised for his teeth was re-directed to pay for the funeral. I was told the campaign didn't have a charity number and was advised to report it to the police. They called back to say they'd spoken to Will and the reason it didn't have a number was because it was an *appeal*, not a charity. It's different legislation. That was clever. Will told them he could account for every penny and there was no more the police could do.

I tackled Will about the discrepancy between the fund for the implants and the cost of the funeral. Also about the way funeral arrangements were conducted. He smiled wearily.

> Any questions about my integrity are completely out of order. I didn't put a foot wrong. Yeah, the Siobhan story I gave to the newspaper may have touched a nerve. I'm sorry if it added to the sadness.
>
> I didn't make a penny out this. In fact the expedition to Spain and the funeral cost me money and work as well as a downgrade from my normal roster of artists. I work with multi-million pound international stars, not sick people at the end of their careers. That's the commercial answer. The human answer is that Alex was a friend of mine. I thought I owed it to him for what he did for me when I was a kid. I felt mortified for him when I first saw that picture in the *News of the World*.
>
> We raised £15,500 for his teeth and the funeral cost £12,000. The rest went on my trips to Spain, London and Belfast and huge telephone bills. Alex didn't pay for a thing. If someone asked me to organise a funeral again, my answer would be categorically no! I don't need the aggro. I don't need the accusations. But I have no regrets about what I did.

Lauren feels that he *should* have regrets, principally about his newspaper exclusive on the day of her father's funeral. She says: 'To have to read a degrading story about my dad being held upside down and shaken because, according to Will Robinson, he tried to kill himself, was devastating. A true friend wouldn't have done anything so tasteless.'

Some of the congregation, Lauren among them, were less than enchanted by the Dean's address. It was certainly thought-provoking, not to say very direct. He told a packed cathedral and millions of television viewers: 'Alex, at a very young age, encountered two of the greatest temptations possible – fame and fortune. He found it difficult to cope with both. He wasn't the first to find this difficult and he certainly will not be the last. Daily we see reminders in news about so-called celebrities who despite the best of provision of personal coaches and gurus are making a pig's mess of their lives.' He concluded: 'When things turned sour for "Higgy", he came home to the city in which he was born, to the place in which he was raised, to where he didn't have to say who he was. I believe that each of us needs to make a homecoming when we come to our senses and realise that we have fouled things up.'

Behind the scenes, Will had considerable problems getting the Dean to agree to the type of funeral he and the sisters wanted. (Lauren and Jordan weren't consulted.) Here's Will's version of events.

'He didn't want a fanfare in his cathedral. He wanted it text-book. Two hymns and he'd choose them. I thought it was wrong that he should dictate. Alex was a massive legend. Who was the Dean to put his foot down? He'd never even met Alex Higgins. He wouldn't have a procession. Told me it wasn't negotiable. I got around it by calling a meeting between the Belfast police and the undertaker. I wanted the police to plan it so that the Dean wouldn't have a leg to stand on. I presented the plan to Reverend McKelvey. If he still refused, he'd have been struggling to keep his job. He wanted an open casket in the chapel so people could file past. That would have been completely distasteful. As soon as the service was over, he was selling programmes with a photo of Alex scanned on the back. The sisters were fuming.'

Actually, the Dean emailed Lauren to ask if it was okay to sell programmes and give the money to cancer charities. Alex's sisters didn't like the idea. Lauren reminded them that she, not they, was his next of kin.

I made several attempts to speak to the Dean but he was unavailable for comment each time. Now to the question 'Who is Will Robinson?' According to Will, Lynn and Lauren must have a mental block because he met them both when Jordan was a nipper.

'I went to the house several times to help Alex see his kids. Sometimes the police had to move us on because Alex was breaking the order to keep away. Lynn should know who I am. Lauren may not remember.'

He added that Jimmy White asked him, not the Dean, to read his speech. Will backed off because he didn't want to get caught between the sisters and the children. 'I was in a terrible position so I passed it to the Dean.'

Lauren: 'Considering that I had to ask for a so-called documentary camera to be switched off at the burial ceremony, Will Robinson's remarks are ironic. He organised the filming. He didn't seem to care how we felt. There was a camera running during the funeral too. Will sometimes seemed as if he was more interesting in making money than paying his respects.'

Alex was buried with his mother and father. The atmosphere was tenser than it should have been. This is Lauren's description of the burial.

> Jordan and I were in a terrible state when we got to the grave. It's the one and only time I've seen my brother sobbing. The reality of putting Dad into a hole in the ground was overwhelming. There was an awful feeling of emptiness. We both tossed a rose onto the coffin.
>
> The three of us went to the Royal the day after the funeral. They did a lot to help Dad. I thanked Gary Audley and the landlord. They showed us the chair where Dad always sat. Jordan sat in it. I was on pins all day. I felt panicky. I'm sorry I didn't let the regulars take a picture of us but I just wanted to get to the airport and go home. I didn't want to be in Belfast any more.

There was an encouraging sequel to the furore about Alex's death and burial. It came from what, at the outset, appeared an unlikely source. Lauren and Jordan, not to mention their mother, had first been shocked to read that Alex had another son, Christopher Delahunty. The *Sunday People* first exposed it eight years earlier but a new 'revelation' appeared in the *Daily Mail* on the day of Alex's memorial dinner a month or so after the funeral.

To most people's surprise, Will Robinson announced at the dinner that Alex's son Christopher was among the assembled guests. So it was official. Alex's three sisters were there but Lauren and Jordan were not invited. Will thought it might be inflammatory to have both sides of the family at the event. Jordan, like his mother and sister, read the *Daily Mail* story: 'I knew nothing about Christopher until I read that. I didn't believe it. Dad always said the only kids he had were Lauren and me. But Mum told me the story could be true. She'd had an inkling of it.'

The excitement subsided until November when Jordan received a Facebook message from Chris: 'We have something in common.' He went to say that he was getting married and was having a stag do in a couple of days. Jordan said he'd like to go along and Chris said he'd be welcome. Jordan reported back: 'Chris is a nice guy. We got on well. Now I believe that he is my half-brother. We didn't discuss Dad much. It wasn't the time or the place for that. I'd go for a drink with him again. He'd like to meet Lauren but said he was nervous. I'm not sure why.'

Lauren sent flowers and champagne to Chris's home address, wishing him all the best for his wedding day. He and his wife-to-be were expecting a baby the following March. Said Lauren:

> At the beginning, I didn't know what to think. It was a shock. There was no reason for him to lie about this. I tried to imagine how I would feel in his shoes. It's not his fault that he's Alex's son. It must be hurtful to know that your father didn't publicly acknowledge you as his child. Jordan and Chris got on really

> well. It made me want to get to know him better myself. My dad might not have done what he should have done but there's no reason why we should compound the problem.

The story moved on quickly. Chris, Lauren and Jordan are regularly in touch with each other and visit each other's homes. I wonder what Alex would have made of it? Lauren: 'I'm proud to call Chris my brother. His mum did a great job of bringing him up without support from my dad. Here's another example of Dad missing out. He never got to know what a lovely son he had.'

9

HE WAS MINE TOO

The witness who knows least about Alex Higgins stood on the doorstep to greet me. He was in his carpet slippers and looking a tad weary after a twelve-hour shift at the wallpaper factory.

A row of neatly restored Victorian terrace houses standing together like soldiers on parade reminded me of the 1950s when factory workers went to work on a bike and milk was delivered by horse and cart. Women came out with shovels to gather manure for the roses. But this was Great Horwood in 2011. Cars were parked up and down both sides of the street, reducing the road to the width of a single vehicle. Most of the faces were English/Asian.

'You found it then,' called a smiling Christopher Delahunty as he stifled a yawn. 'Coffee's on!'

How bizarre that Christopher should spend the first twenty-six years of his life unaware that Alex Higgins was his father. Up to that point, 'Dad' was (and still is) Tom Delahunty, the stepfather who looked after him from the age of six. Now he was thirty-five.

Alex's sisters knew about their missing nephew. Alex's mother sent him birthday and Christmas presents each year. Most of Bowley knew that Christopher's mum, Joyce Fox, and Alex Higgins were an item. And they knew she was pregnant. It was hardly a state secret. The couple spent eighteen months together at Joyce's parents' house in this small Lancashire town. They went to the dance halls, drank at the pubs and sat in the back row of the local flea pit.

The only person in the dark was Chris. A thousand people,

including his parents, kept it to themselves. That changed one Sunday in 2002 when Chris got a call from his mum. She invited him over for lunch:

> I could tell there was something in the air. Mum and Tommy were cooking in the kitchen when Tommy said out of the blue: 'There's no easy way of putting this, Chris, but your real father is Alex Higgins.'
>
> I just said: 'Oh, really?' I'd heard of Alex Higgins but didn't put two and two together. Dad said: 'Yes, it's him,' and carried on cooking. Mum was in the corner crying. The subject of Alex still upsets her. I suppose I was a bit numb. Not being a snooker fan, it perhaps didn't mean as much to me as it might to someone who was.
>
> Obviously I'd wondered who my real father was for years. I asked Mum when I was eighteen but she didn't want to talk about. She said she'd tell me one day. Perhaps she didn't think I was responsible enough. I was a bit of a tearaway in my teens and early twenties. I'd be out from Thursday to Sunday drinking and doing club drugs. I left home at sixteen. I was banned from driving for hitting a stationary car then sentenced to six months community service for causing an affray. I had two affray charges. I'm not proud of them.

Like father, like son. I first met Chris at the memorial dinner for Alex a couple of weeks after his funeral. Chris missed the funeral – 'I wouldn't have known anyone' – but he went to the dinner because Alex's oldest sister, Isobel, invited him. They'd been communicating on Facebook – Chris in Great Horwood, Isobel in Queensland, Australia. I confess I couldn't detect any obvious family likeness. He didn't have the Higgins nose. He was taller and more strongly built.

Chris handed me a freshly brewed coffee and sat on the sofa to tell me the rest of the story. 'Mum said she met Alex at a nightclub in Blackburn. He'd already won the world championship but wasn't that famous. Their relationship wasn't documented because Mum never went after his money when they split. She's an easy-going person. She was probably naive. They didn't get married but I think they were planning to. Mum taught at a primary school and is retired now. Alex was with her till I was six months old, then he went away. Mum and I don't sit down and discuss it. She gets too tearful. I receive bits of information here and there. Alex was a big part of her life. It certainly wasn't a five-minute wonder.'

It baffles Lynn that Alex never once brought up the subject of Christopher. The only hint was when Alex's mother let slip that she was sending a Christmas present to a child near Blackburn. Alex passed it off as the son of friends he stayed with. Says Lynn: 'It seemed odd. I wish I'd asked a few more questions. There was absolutely no reason not to tell me. Why didn't *he* send presents? Why didn't he go to see the child? I wouldn't have minded. It must be horrible for Chris finding out the way he did and having a father who didn't care. There've been one or two trumped-up stories about illegitimate children but Alex always maintained he only had one son and one daughter.'

Lynn does, however, recall a mysterious incident when she stopped at a petrol station with Alex and Jordan in the car. Alex pointed to someone standing in the forecourt and said: 'There you are, Jordan, that's your brother.' Lynn thought he was joking because the man had reddish hair, like Jordan. Now she's not sure: 'It was a peculiar thing to say in the light of what we know now.'

Christopher incidentally has dark hair. There was never any doubt about him in Belfast. Alex's sister Jean even found a photograph of Alex holding his son on a snooker table. 'Mam showed me the photo many years ago. She said it was definitely Christopher sitting on the green baize. I remember one day Sandy saying he was going to England to see him. I told him we had the photograph but he hadn't seen it. I found it and gave it to him and I got it back when he died. It was in with the rest of his stuff. Sandy never mentioned Christopher before or after that. Mam sent Christmas presents every year. She said Joyce was a nice girl and they got on well. I think they met when Mammy and Daddy lived in Accrington to keep and eye on Sandy. It's strange that he wanted nothing to do with his son. Perhaps he kept it quiet to avoid paying maintenance. It's a mystery.'

Father and son eventually met in 2003. Chris had to organise it. A friend read that Alex was due to play an exhibition in Hull where Chris was living.

> I'd been trying to find my dad for more than a year. He was impossible to track down. I realised this might be my only chance. I left a message with the owner of the snooker hall and within ten minutes I got a call back from Alex's agent saying he agreed to meet me. I couldn't believe it was so quick and easy. I'd gone from not knowing he was anything to do with me to preparing to meet a national celebrity who happened to be my father. It was a strange feeling. In a way I was grateful he'd agreed, but in another I wondered what kind of mood he'd be in. Was it such a good idea? Although the meeting was ten days away, I was getting nervous.
>
> When the moment arrived, I got a lift to the Rising Sun Inn in Pontefract where Alex was staying. It was right opposite the racecourse. His agent met me in the bar and called me Mr Higgins. It was quite amusing. I was Fox to begin with, then Delahunty, but I've never been Higgins! I just walked up to my father and said: 'Hello, Alex, I'm Chris. Are you all right?' We went to a table in the corner and talked for two hours. He looked

frail but he told me he'd recovered from cancer. His voice was quite weak. I had to listen hard.

He confirmed that I was his son but there was no hugging. He just accepted it. He said he still loved my mum but didn't ask any questions about her. He remembered holding me in his arms when I was a baby. Then he told me he'd only been with twelve women in his life. I think there was some bullshit going on! He bought me lunch and a couple of beers. He only had soup. He asked what I did and how I was getting on but most of the time he complained about his ex-managers and how they'd ripped him off. He was quite angry. He seemed to think the world was against him.

We had a few games of pool in the bar. He showed me how to hold the cue properly. He let me beat him once. I hadn't seen much of him on television because I didn't watch snooker. I didn't see the final in 1982 but I've watched it since on YouTube. He said I should be golfer. I was the right build.

I wondered if there was any hint of an apology for disowning Christopher, or a rational explanation as to why he waited nearly twenty-eight years before breaking cover – and then only because Christopher took the initiative.

He didn't apologise in so many words but I could feel there was some regret. It was more of a case of what we could do to make up for lost time. He said I could be his bodyguard. Presumably that meant carrying his bags. Then he said he was playing in Thailand at Christmas and asked if I fancied joining him? He thought it would be a good bonding opportunity. I said it sounded a lot better than working on a building site on Humberside through the winter. He gave me his mobile number, then he went to his room to get ready for the exhibition.

While he was away I called my mum and told her the meeting was going okay. I promised to let her have the full story when I got back. Alex showed no interest in meeting her again. I got the impression they'd had a good relationship. That's why mum gets so upset. She didn't want it to finish, though knowing what I know now about Alex, nothing lasts very long. My stepdad was fine about me meeting him. He told Mum she should have got money from him. They're not money-orientated, though. Alex and Tommy met each other once playing snooker at St George's Hall, Blackburn. Alex didn't know who Tommy was.

After I'd called Mum, Alex said he was ready to leave. He looked dapper in his waistcoat, overcoat and trilby. We went to Hull in his chauffeur-driven car. He said hello to a few of my mates who came to the exhibition, then ignored me for the rest of the night. He played a few challenge matches for money, and did a few trick shots. It was a good show. Alex mingled with the crowd but didn't say a dickie bird to me. I couldn't understand that. Then he disappeared. I walked home. It wasn't far.

That was the last Christopher ever saw of his father. As far as we know, Alex made no attempt to keep in touch. Chris was left floating in midair: 'I definitely felt some affection for him despite his promises that meant zilch. When I was younger, I thought my father must be a tosser to walk off and leave us like that. But my anger had a few years to stew, so the ill feelings were gone. Occasionally when he was talking I thought I could see some of me in him. There's a possible likeness in some old photos I've dug out but nothing obvious that I can see.'

Although father and son never met again, they spoke on the telephone once more. It was the following December. Christopher called to wish Alex a merry Christmas, hoping that the trip to Thailand might still be on. Alex was at Heathrow waiting for his flight. He'd made no mention of Chris joining him and had clearly forgotten about his invitation. Disappointed but undeterred, Christopher tried to call him again the following Christmas.

'Someone else with an Irish accent picked up the phone. He'd never heard of Alex Higgins. Dad had changed his number without telling me. I never heard from him again. I'd given him my number but obviously he wasn't interested. He might have changed his number to avoid me. I felt hurt. Looking back now, I was glad I met him. It would have been shitty not to. At least he acknowledged to himself that I existed, even if to no-one else. I've no idea why he didn't tell Lynn, Lauren and Jordan. It's not as if my mum was an ogre. She didn't pursue him for maintenance. He didn't give her a penny. Thankfully she had a decent job so she managed.'

Through a freelance journalist friend of Christopher's, the story of Alex Higgins meeting his 'love child' hit the news stands. Chris signed what he thought was a lucrative deal with *The People*. Before it was due to appear, Tommy went around the streets to warn friends and neighbours what was coming. 'He needn't have bothered,' said Chris. 'They all knew. They'd known for years. It's peculiar that no-one marked my card before my stepdad did. I suppose it wasn't the sort of thing the older generation would pass on to their kids. In this day and age it'd be on Twitter!'

It finally broke in the *News of the World*. That's a mystery in itself because Chris thought he was talking to the chief northern editor of *The People*. He was promised a minimum of £10,000 for his story and allowed himself to be interviewed for three to four hours in a hotel room in Hull. 'I signed the contract but they shafted me. The reporter kept phoning to say it would be in the paper next Sunday, then the next Sunday and so on.' To his amazement, it surfaced in the *News of the World*. The contract he signed was drawn up by MGN (publishers of *The People*), 1 Canada Square,

Canary Wharf. It's dated 13.02.04. It agrees to pay Chris £15,000 for what it calls 'Splash and spread for interview concerning his relationship with Alex Higgins'. In fact, all he got for his troubles was the basic £750 disturbance fee. There was no apology or explanation. Chris didn't bother to challenge it. He thought there was no comeback. It might be worth his while to pursue it.

Seven years of silence were broken when Chris heard about his father's death while watching *News at Ten*:

> I felt empty and gutted. I took the day off work. I knew he'd been very ill. I'd seen bits in the papers about raising money for his tooth implants. He looked very different in the photographs from when I met him. He was like a living skeleton. I didn't know how to get hold of him and then it was too late. All those years I secretly hoped he might get back to me. It would have meant a lot if he'd followed up that first meeting. Now it was all over. There'd be no chance of seeing him again. Just crap.
>
> Meeting him once might not have achieved much but if I hadn't made the effort, I'd always be wondering. Now I think it's a shame his life faded out the way it did. He'd probably have had another twenty years if he'd looked after himself. Even though there was no proper relationship, I'm proud to tell people he was my dad. I'm proud that Tommy's my dad as well.
>
> I wasn't tempted to go to the funeral. It seemed inappropriate. I didn't know anyone and I wasn't invited. I watched it on the news. There were no tears but I did feel the finality of it all. Mum said it was an awful waste of a life. She said she still had fond memories.

Despite his exclusion from Alex's funeral, Christopher can at least console himself with the knowledge that his father's death triggered off a chain reaction which brought Chris and both sides of

Alex's family together. It was something they weren't able to achieve during his lifetime and probably wouldn't have happened otherwise.

Unlike her two sisters, Isobel is a Facebook user. Through this medium she invited Chris to Belfast to meet them all. His work prevented it, but Isobel persuaded him to join them for Alex's memorial dinner in Manchester. As Chris explained, it didn't go exactly according to plan.

> I'd just finished night shift and got up early to catch the Manchester train. Isobel said she'd phone to tell me where they were staying. I waited in Manchester until 6.30 on the evening of the dinner, but there was no phone call. I left my card at the Glamorous Chinese Restaurant where the dinner was taking place, then called my fiancée to say I was coming home. Around 7.45, I got a frantic call from Isobel. Where was I? I told her she'd missed me. I was home again. It would take two hours to repeat the journey. Luckily, my girlfriend, who was pregnant, offered to drive me back to Manchester and book in at the Travelodge. She stayed there while I went to the dinner.
>
> I walked in just as they were showing the BBC documentary about my father on the big screen. I stood at the bar on my own. I didn't know anyone. I asked the barman which table was Alex Higgins' sisters. He didn't have a clue. When the documentary was over, I took a chance and tapped a blonde woman on the shoulder: 'Excuse me, are you Isobel?' She threw her arms in the air: 'Oh, it's Christopher. I thought we'd lost you!' She'd seen a photograph of me in the *Belfast Telegraph* so she knew what I looked like.
>
> I was too nervous to eat anything. Will Robinson was master of ceremonies. He made an announcement and asked me to stand up. I couldn't. It was too daunting. Jimmy White came

> over for a short chat. He said I'd got the Higgins nose. Not sure he's right. To be honest, I didn't think he knew about me. I met Ann and Jean as well as Jean's daughters, Lyndsey and Shelley. They made me feel very welcome.
>
> The subject got around to Christmas presents. Isobel told me her mother – and my grandmother – sent me little things every year. I've no idea what happened to them. I checked with Mum but she said nothing ever came. We thought the presents must have been held back by Gran and Grandad because they didn't want me to know. They're dead now so unless the parcels are packed away in the loft somewhere, we'll never solve that mystery.

As we know, Lynn, Lauren and Jordan were excluded from the memorial dinner. They'd have missed the chance of meeting their long-lost brother if he hadn't contacted Jordan on Facebook. This is Chris's take on the stag do which brought the half-brothers together.

> Jordan and I got on like a house on fire. He's like me but a bit quieter. We talked about 'Dad' as if we'd known each other for years. Jordan said his Dad left him when he was three years old so neither of us, for different reasons, could say we knew Alex. We both felt sorry we hadn't seen more of him.
>
> Jordan told how he'd 'fucked up' at Manchester City. He'd tried his hand at being a roofer but lost the plot. From what I could gather, his mum and sister gave him enough to live on. There was definitely a common thread. We've both been reckless. I told Jordan he'd be an uncle soon. It was great of Lauren to send me flowers for the wedding day. It feels good to find a brother and sister apart from Laura, the one I already have from Mum and Tommy.

Before I left, Christopher pointed up the street and proudly announced that he and his new wife were leaving rented accommodation and buying their own house four doors away. With a baby on the way, and support from both sides of Alex's family, a new and fuller life was about to start. His eyes clouded over as another thought struck him. Shortly after hearing that Alex was his father, Christopher went touring with friends in the Republic of Ireland. Completely by chance, guests at the bed and breakfast where they stayed were watching a BBC documentary about Alex. Said Christopher: 'I caught a shot of him looking down-and-out in a betting shop. For no reason I can really explain, it made me cry. That was my dad on TV in a mess. My heart went out to him.'

10

HE WAS MY HERO

I was pleasantly surprised to see the Clones Cyclone, Barry McGuigan, at Alex's funeral. Belfast is a long way from Whitstable where the former World Featherweight Champion lives in rural splendour. His is the lifestyle that both of his fellow Irish superstars, Alex Higgins and George Best, would have enjoyed if they hadn't burned the candle so furiously. Apart from Ireland and sporting excellence, Alex and Barry had little in common.

Technically, they were from different nations. Alex was an Ulsterman and therefore British whereas Barry hailed from Clones on the Republican side of the border where the Euro reigns. It's one of those curious things that the two halves of Ireland compete against each other at football, yet they join forces for at rugby and cricket. With individual sports such as boxing and snooker, nationality is fudged.

From my travels in the north and the south while researching this book, it's apparent that Alex Higgins was as coveted in the Republic as he was in Northern Ireland – possibly more so. For his part, Alex loved the laissez-faire feel of the south. His most feral adventures were there. His one-man shows in Dublin, Waterford, Galway, Cork were always over-subscribed. Barry McGuigan's family were among his most ardent followers. He says: 'I went to Alex's funeral because he was a lovely man. He was my hero. I knew instinctively that I should be there for him. This was the end of his story. I wanted people to know how much I loved and admired the man. I accept that he had a bad temperament and serious flaws but he was a genius who brightened millions of lives. How many people can say that? It's a tremendous contribution for one human being to make. And at the bottom of it all, he was a good person.'

Alex, good? Well it's different. Many would be astonished at that view. Perhaps the goodness was submerged under an ocean of insecurity. Alex had programmed himself to be a lone ranger in a hostile world. He had to be selfish to survive. He had to prove himself every day. Most of the people he met were foes. He trusted few. You don't have to be *good* to be popular, but you do have to have to be witty, charming, exciting or original. When the mood took him, Alex was all of those.

Barry McGuigan emerged from a similar background to Higgins and George Best but followed a different path to iconic status. He's ideally placed to assess the slings and arrows of Irish fortune – to enlighten us why two of its three major sporting heroes destroyed themselves while the third survived sane, sober and intact.

> Although they had different passports from me, Alex, George and I were compatriots. I'd always been a Northern Ireland boxer. Another fighter, Paddy Doherty, and I were unique in representing both countries. Although I'm from the south, I boxed for Northern Ireland in the Commonwealth Games at Edmonton in 1978. That's because my father's family were from the north.
>
> My own little town, Clones, was originally meant to be in the north but after a big struggle, it ended up in the Republic. Ireland was a dangerous place in the 1980s. Although I won BBC Sports Personality of the Year, I turned down the MBE twice because I lived on the border. We called it Comanche country! I'd taken a British passport but my family was Irish. I

was conscious of the possible effects on them. They offered me the OBE as well but I turned it down.

Funnily enough, five of the six roads that lead out of Clones take you into the north! I had trouble all through my career trying to work out whether I was British or Irish. I've always been Irish but I've tried to eliminate that sectarian line across the border. It never meant anything to me. Alex was of a similar persuasion. I couldn't speak for George Best but it never struck me that he had religious or nationalistic leanings. He just wanted a good time! They both did.

I turned pro during a very dark period in Northern Ireland's history. The kerbstones were painted red, white and blue on one side, green and white on the other. King Billy versus the IRA. I thought, my God, I'm not going to contribute to that!

My dad always sang 'Danny Boy' before I boxed, but I wouldn't wear any colours that might segregate the audience. I wanted people to support me without feeling threatened. Sport was a great unifier. Alex and George appreciated that – especially Alex, who milked it for all it was worth. What you have to remember, though, is that Alex took himself out of Ireland before the Troubles. So did Dennis Taylor. They were tucked up in Blackburn. I was in the middle of the riots!

Alex once told me his greatest achievement would have been to turn the crowd support he commanded into some practical use for the sake of Northern Ireland, but confessed he didn't know how to go about it: 'Barry McGuigan proved it could be done. He achieved what politicians have failed to do since the dawn of time - bridge the Great Divide. The plight of the ordinary man in Belfast worries me. Things weren't so bad when I was a lad. What I see today makes me weep. We've got one of the nicest cities in the world. It's full of close-knit families and people with warm hearts. They care about each other, yet they tear each other apart. I was only a humble snooker player, so I wouldn't know how to stop the violence and the hatred. The safest thing for me to do was keep playing snooker. I didn't have the same driving commitment as Barry. I admired him for that.'

Barry continued:

> The advantage of snooker and boxing is that they're contained in a hall, not a stadium with 50,000 people. Unless you're up against a fellow Irishman, *all* the spectators are on your side. Alex never had to tippy-toe that neutral line like I did. There was no question of politics in his case. He played in the all-Irish championships because that's what snooker players did. I know he caused a huge stir when he threatened to shoot Dennis Taylor. That was just splenetic bad temper. I'm sure it wasn't nice for Dennis but we all know what Alex was like. He hurt many down the years but it was forgotten a couple of days later – at least by him!
>
> Unlike Alex, George Best was innocuous. There was no side to him. Verbally, Alex could be brutal but physically he was a weak individual. He ran away from most fights. Despite his aggressive attitude and his drunkenness, everybody loved him. It was amazing how he got away with it.
>
> My family were all Higgins fans. We'd been plagued with boring snooker players who showed no sign of human emotions, then in blew this powerful gust of wind and the game was suddenly transformed. Flair and speed replaced the snail. Laughter and tears replaced the stiff upper lip. I made a point of watching Alex live when I could. He transcended sport. Few people are capable of that.
>
> The effect in our household was electrifying. My grandfather, Johnny Rooney, and all my mother's brothers were big snooker

> and billiards players. Grandad was an exceptional player. He raved about Hurricane Higgins, the new sensation. Me too. We all knew he was bonkers but that enhanced his appeal.

I was eager to know how and why Barry avoided the alcohol trap which killed Best and damaged Higgins. When it comes to the twin pleasure/curse of boozing and betting, few indulge more enthusiastically than the Irish. I'm in awe of two nations whose menfolk begin drinking when the pub doors open at daybreak and stick at it, with minimal solid sustenance, until closing time - and after.

Some bars are stunning - notably the historic Crown Liquor Stores in Belfast, which is so ornate it feels like a cathedral and so charmingly partitioned it feels like a carriage on the Orient Express - and have a special ambience which makes them popular from Moscow to Melbourne. However, many others are dark, soulless, frequently men-only establishments where 'craic' is conspicuously absent and customers spend all day transferring their stares between industrial supplies of the black stuff and the next race on the telly. Alex's local, the Royal, is a bit like that - a functional alehouse with bland furniture and puffy-faced customers. It warms up on karaoke nights - if that's your bag.

It was noticeable that many of the people with whom Alex surrounded himself either had a drink problem or had suffered the side effects of alcohol - blood pressure, heart trouble, etc. They include his parents, several ex-snooker players and most of his Irish friends on both sides of the border. His sisters could be enthusiastic tipplers too.

So what is it about the Irish and booze? Is it a national disease or do we exaggerate it? The former snooker referee Len Ganley was an alcoholic. Still is. You don't get rid of it. Len has an interesting theory: 'Unlike Englishmen, the Irish never learned to be satisfied with a quick one after work. It's a foreign discipline. Irishmen go to the pub after work and *don't come out*. It's always been like that. It's something peculiar to the Celtic nature. Women are often the worst. Some of them can drink men three times under the table. In Ireland, if you give up the booze they call you a traitor. You're letting the side down!'

Barry McGuigan is teetotal - and not just because he was a professional sportsman. Boxers get bladdered too. He's teetotal because he was sickened at an early age by the corrosive effects of alcohol.

> They say the Irish have a low vitamin D count and therefore a genetic vulnerability to alcoholism and addictions in general. In the 1970s, Clones had a population of 2,600 but boasted twenty-four pubs. There was only one main street and a couple of side streets. The drink/driving laws reduced the impact, but there was a lot of misery. You could see it in almost every family.
>
> When I was a kid, Dad drank too much and Uncle Seamus was an alcoholic. So was my old trainer, Frank Mulligan. He was dried out fifty-two times! He wasn't the greatest trainer but he attached himself to me because, while he had a purpose, he had the motivation to keep off the booze. Frank and his drinking problems were the reason I left that stable.
>
> After my disappointment at the Olympics, I was getting ready to box against West Germany in an important amateur competition and Frank was back on the drink. I gave him two days to get off it, otherwise I was going to Belfast to work with Gerry Storey, the national coach. Nothing changed so I had an acrimonious split with the club. Drink destroys people and ruins lives and yet there's supposed to be something macho about it. Alex thought drinking was fun. It played a large part in wrecking his relationships and his family life.

When my dad stopped drinking, he couldn't sleep properly for six months. His tipple was the hard liquor – whiskey. I didn't see it because he never drank in front of me. Frank Mulligan was a whiskey man as well. He fell into hedges and got knocked down by cars. It was awful. His poor old mother used to put him to bed and take whiskey up to him. It was the only way of keeping him 'safe'. He used talk about the DTs and seeing rats running up walls.

I was an impressionable kid. I worked with my mother in the grocery shop when unemployment was rife in Clones. They handed out the dole on Fridays. On Saturdays, you'd see mums carrying children on their hips and crying. Their husbands had spent the money in the pub. They asked for goods on tick. Mum always obliged. I swore I'd never go down that road.

That made me a loner. Boxing was swimming with booze and boozers. It was almost a professional asset. I guess there was no great harm if they could control it but my fear was that I'd turn out like my dad – or worse. I'm a fairly compulsive individual so I figured the best thing was not to drink at all.

Alex wasn't so lucky. He grew up in a sport which encouraged smoking and drinking. It was part and parcel of life in a snooker hall. And when he got out of those places, he'd join other Irishmen sitting in dingy pubs all day. They drank but rarely ate. It was a dangerous way to live. I'll probably get slaughtered for saying this!

Some of that alcohol dependency was provoked by the Troubles. People lived in fear. Families huddled together and stayed indoors. The men huddled together in darkened pubs and clubs which were more like air raid shelters. No-one wanted to be noticed. You wouldn't dare go to the other side of town. In that atmosphere, drink was a solace. Alex missed most of that but the legacy lingers along every street in Belfast and Dublin. Drink is an essential part of our culture.

To find out more about that, I met a former inspector of the Royal Ulster Constabulary, Alan Beattie, at his old headquarters in Bangor. Alan told me that drink was officially recommended for police officers during the height of the shootings. In fact, it was a *prescribed medicine*.

> In the sixties we sometimes worked 22-hour shifts with no overtime. We'd sit in a small police station in Armagh, Newry or Londonderry waiting for the violence to erupt, sleeping on camp beds with an hour off for tea. We were encouraged to have a couple of vodkas to help us relax. When we were dealing with riots every night of the week and being shot at with Thompson sub-machine guns, we needed something.
>
> Squaddies from the army brought a drink culture with them. Even I started drinking because of the stress, and I'm from a Presbyterian family with no history of alcohol. I was downing vodka and beer. It got out of hand. Lots of policemen were alcoholics and that included George Best's sister Julie who worked for me briefly. I didn't know she was an alcoholic when she joined. Julie lasted a day and a half. She couldn't cope and had to take four years leave. George's mum was alcoholic too. Before that she was a very good athlete.

Illegal shebeens sprang up all across Northern Ireland. They were the breeding ground for extremists from both sides. It was one of Inspector Beattie's duties to police them. That meant closing them down and confiscating the drink. Eventually, Sir John Hermon, the RUC Chief Constable, ordered a crackdown on the three evils within the force: drink, dames and debt. Gambling was, and is, another art form in Ireland. It might, indirectly, have cost Alex Higgins his life. He squandered enormous amounts of money and time in the betting shop when he should have paid more attention to his life-threatening condition. Having once been flattered to have Alex in his camp, Barry McGuigan was appalled to see his hero disfigured.

Alex came to all my fights in Belfast. When you consider he was living in England at the time, it was quite a commitment. He saw me win the world title against Pedroza and he also saw my last fight when Jim McDonnell beat me. Alex came into the dressing room before the bout and gave me a big kiss. It was slightly disconcerting, but he was a massive fan. He contacted me all the time. He said he liked my style of boxing. I suppose it was a bit like his style of snooker. After that we met at award ceremonies from time to time but I became concerned because he started to look seriously unwell.

It was tragic to see him end up the way he did. The reason I started the Professional Boxers Association was to try to prevent sportsmen destroying themselves like that. I was sick of rags-riches-rags stories. Too many guys like Higgins went to hell and back.

Maybe I'm an idealist but I firmly believe that people who've given their lives to sport and become national heroes deserve to have a comfortable retirement. Surely the least we can do is to repay them for the entertainment they provided? It was obviously difficult with Alex Higgins. He was incorrigible. I wanted him to have a good life but there are some people you just can't help. If you gave him money, he'd blow it in the bookies.

Trying to analyse his temperament, you'd have to say that Alex created chaos where there wasn't any. Mike Tyson was similar. Friends and family say he would have liked a quiet life. Alex used to say it but I'm not sure it's true. I don't think he could have handled normality. People who've ridden the roller-coaster at the highest level find it difficult to put their feet on the ground. It's like a class 'A' drug. Only the most grounded, level-headed people can handle it. When fame and success aren't there any more, it can drive you insane. Sportsmen whose days were neatly compartmentalised while they were performing found those days shapeless once it was all over. The routine goes. People recognise them for a few years, then a new generation comes along and asks: 'Who's that, Daddy?'

I count myself extremely lucky to have had the benefit of a solid foundation. I have an incredible wife and family who help to keep me straight. I don't drink, I don't blow my money, I don't go looking for birds. I'm not a party animal. Put me in Alex's place and it wouldn't have been so easy. Without a family and being the compulsive personality I am, I could have exploded. I'm anally retentive about temptation. I was afraid of booze and gambling because they might take me off the rails, so I didn't go near. I like my kids around me. That's more important.

I regret that Alex faded away. You hope the last fifteen years of his life never come to *you*. When the curtain comes down, no matter how good you are, you must have alternatives. If not, you end up bitter and twisted. That can only lead to trouble. That's partly why Best, Gascoigne and Alex Higgins went wrong. Drink did the rest.

The irony is that people living in the streets of south Belfast didn't even know he was dead. It upsets me that he died on his own. He had two ex-wives and two lovely kids but nobody was around when he needed them. I feel gutted about that.

11

HE WAS MY PLAYMATE

From the train window, the countryside around Dublin in December had little to recommend it. Flat, muddy and, apart from intermittent residues of snow, monotonously grey. The train pulled up at Newbridge where Sheikh Maktoum of Dubai has his stud farm. However, that wasn't my destination. I was being met by someone describing himself as 'a one-armed taxi driver'. Could there *be* such a phenomenon? Was it allowed?

As I climbed into Tom McCarthy's four-wheel drive, I had my answer. Tom lost his arm at the shoulder in a motorbike accident when he was sixteen. He'd run a variety of businesses over the years, including snooker clubs and a lap-dancing club, before finally settling on taxi driving. I wasn't unduly fazed until Tom picked up his mobile as he drove. Apparently you can do that in Ireland.

Alex's sisters told me I *had* to meet Tom McCarthy. Alex thought highly of him. The fact that Tom was a driver and knew the Republic like the inside of his trouser pocket was an obvious attraction to Alex but a thirty-five-year friendship needed something more substantial. I should have guessed what brought them together. It was Tom's arm. Or lack of it.

When Alex agreed to open the Noggin Inn Snooker Hall at the height of his notoriety in 1980, part of the deal was a one-armed match against Tom. Alex strapped his left arm behind his back and the pair entertained a large gathering with the strangest show in town. Tom clipped a cut-down version of a snooker rest onto his prosthesis to give himself a stable bridge hand. He was capable of breaks up to 90. Ironically, he didn't *play* snooker when he had two arms.

Tom and Alex became instant friends. They signed an unwritten pact to turn Ireland into their playground. It so happened that Tom's Uncle Liam was a racehorse trainer and his cousin an amateur jockey. That was music to Alex's ears. He could see pound signs.

I should point out that the cousin in question, Dermot Browne, was eventually banned from racing for ten years after a doping scandal. Dermot was a 'needleman', the term for someone who injects horses with sedatives to slow them down. Alex was regularly on the phone to Dermot for tips. Having made his selections, he rang Tom at his snooker club in Waterford to get the bets on. It could be £500 here and £1,000 there - often with the warning: 'Hurry up, babe. This thing's off in ten minutes!' It didn't seem to occur to him to do the errand himself. They'd divvy up the winnings - if there were any.

Said Tom:

> We must have lost £250,000 over the years. Alex got good info from Dermot and other jockeys he befriended, but as soon as he had a winner, he blew it on the next race. If there wasn't a next race, he turned his attention to the dog track. It was a crazy way to live. Alex bust a gut to get to whatever meeting was on, be it in Dublin, Cork or Galway. Distance meant nothing because I did all the driving. He did the drinking and the fighting.
>
> When he was world champion, I brought him to Ireland for a week of exhibitions. He cleaned up £30,000 in five days. It all went on the horses. We had lots of disagreements about money. He didn't keep any aside for petrol or food. He didn't know what tax was. His view was that tomorrow could look after itself.

The here and now was all that mattered. I got sucked into it because it was exciting and I was easily led. Alex had an incredible way with him. It was difficult to say no. He told me how much he missed our adventures when his body couldn't take them any more. If I ever complained about money problems, he'd say: 'You think *you're* having a lean time? I haven't had a fuck in four years!'

Then he'd reminisce about Siobhan. He never stopped talking about her. He was a womaniser but it sometimes took second place to gambling and larking about. Like Shay Brennan when he went clubbing with George Best, I benefitted in the female stakes. We knew we wouldn't be left out. If Alex or George got the best looker, we'd get her pal. Alex was fussy about his women. They had to be stunners. He had a thing about blondes. He'd say: 'See that one by the door? She'll do.'

Then he'd move in with the chat-up lines. To be honest they weren't great. If he didn't make an immediate impression, he'd get bored and leave. Once he had his cancer, women weren't the priority any more. He'd done his shagging. It was the betting office, Vat 19 and a joint. He wasn't an alcoholic though. He'd binge drink but he could go without it.

Life's one big party in the south. The pace may have been too slow for Alex but he was feted here more than he ever was in the UK. He loved being a big fish in a small pool. He loved the hero worship. Alex was the reason I took up snooker. He was a magnet for me. Watching him gave me goose pimples.

Mind you, getting him to venues on time was a nightmare. One summer afternoon when we had a little time to kill before an exhibition match, we took my kids to the seaside at Tremore. Alex made a beeline for the dodgems. The chance to drive a car was irresistible! He crashed around in his baseball cap loving every minute. A crowd gathered to watch. Time was marching on but I couldn't drag him away. Eventually I did and we set off for the exhibition. Alex pushed the passenger seat back, put his stockinged feet on the dashboard and rolled a joint. Then he nodded off. It was par for the course. Later, he woke up and quickly sized up where we were:

'Look, Tom. There's a bar! We'll pop in for a drinky.'

'Alex, we're supposed to be on location in ten minutes.'

'They can fucking wait, babes. It's Alex Higgins.'

I'd stayed on the ring road to avoid temptation. It didn't work. He had a mental map of pubs and betting shops across the Republic:

'If you take the next left, there's a William Hill's half a mile up the road.'

'Your socks stink.'

'Okay, babes. I'll get some new ones from Louis.'

By Louis he meant Louis Copeland who supplied him with all his clothes. We'll hear from him later. Alex usually had the last word. He had a solution to most crises, which was just and proper since he created most of them. Tom brought two instances to mind. The first was an appointment with Cliff Thorburn in the Benson and Hedges Masters at Goffs, the most famous bloodstock sale-room in Ireland. The hub of their Goffs empire is an auction arena in County Kildare about thirty miles from Dublin. It has tiered terracing so it doubles marvellously as a bull ring for snooker. When Goffs is full, as it usually is for the closing stages of the B & H, the atmosphere's more electrifying than Wembley or the Crucible. Alex and Tom got into a spot of bother before the Thorburn match.

We'd been out on the piss, pulling birds and backing horses. It wasn't the ideal preparation. The tournament director Kevin

> Norton, was fuming. Alex and I went to the Cadean Hotel for a quick change of clothes but they tried to stop me getting in. Alex shouted: 'If Tommy doesn't get in, I'm not playing. Stick that up your arse, Mr Norton!'
>
> He was speechless. Alex got changed and I climbed into the courtesy car with him. We reached the venue with moments to spare. I could hardly stand up. Alex wasn't much better but at least he had a table to lean on. In no time he was 5-0 down to Thorburn. He carried on drinking through the match. He had more during the break and just when you thought he was dead and buried, he sauntered back into the hall to beat Thorburn 6-5! Only Alex could do that.

The second example takes us to a nightclub in Waterford. With a sozzled Alex and Tom among the undistinguished clientele, there was a fair chance it would degenerate into a free-for-all.

> We ended up brawling with a bunch of loudmouths over a woman Alex was chatting up. He just barged past her fellah and went for it. We were on the dance floor with the music blaring and these guys trying to knock Alex into the middle of next week. I dived in to help but in the scuffle, my false arm flew off. One of the women we were fighting over fainted and fell to the floor. She thought I'd been amputated in battle! Security men muscled in to revive her and escort us out of the nightclub. To everyone's astonishment, I carried my arm with me. They couldn't understand why I wasn't in pain. Alex's waistcoat was a bigger worry. It was the one he wore while winning the world title and it was badly torn. He turned to me as cool as you like: 'May I present you with what's left of this waistcoat, Tom? You can get it stitched. You won't need both armholes anyway!'

We all fell about. I did get the waistcoat stitched and wore it for a while before auctioning it for charity.

When Ireland tried to pay tribute to Alex's victory in the 1982 world final, it backfired horribly. Alex was celebrity-in-chief at the Texaco Sports Star Awards in Dublin's Burlington Hotel. Tom recounts the unsavoury details of that evening and the morning after.

We'd just sat down to dinner when Kathleen Watkins, the wife of RTE's chat show host, Gay Byrne, walked over to ask Alex for his autograph. Big mistake. He said: 'Can't you see I'm fucking eating?' She tried to apologise but he was abusive. Pestering him for autographs while he was doing something else always set him off. He couldn't go for a piss without being bothered. I told him he was out of order. He said: 'This is what my life's like, babes.'

Word spread through the dining room like wildfire. Everyone was looking. Nevertheless, he got his award. It was a carving of Alex holding his cue. Really nice. We stayed for ten minutes, then Alex decided to leave. Neither of us had our wives with us and everyone else was paired up. It looked like a boring night. He said: 'I'm not fucking staying. Let's go into town and get a few birds.'

We left his trophy at reception and went. We must have done half a dozen nightclubs dressed in our monkey suits. Our favourite was the Lower Deck in Portobello where all the great singers performed. Alex was mobbed everywhere he went. Women were lining up. We picked up two nineteen-year-olds and took them back to the Burlington. The night porter stopped us in the lift. He said no ladies were allowed. Texaco had booked the rooms only for Alex, me and friends. You can imagine Alex's reaction: 'What do you mean, you arsehole? These are my fucking friends!'

He went berserk. The porter said he wasn't putting up with that kind of abuse, whether Alex was world champion or not. He called security. The security guy told us we'd been ejected. We asked to be allowed into our rooms to collect our stuff. The security guard said he couldn't let us. The night porter would do it. We were furious because we knew he'd fling everything into the suitcases and was bound to miss stuff in the bathrooms. We sat there with the two girls waiting for the porter to come back. It was very embarrassing.

When he did, Alex turned on him again: 'Give me my fucking trophy and book us into the Gresham.'

The porter gave him the eighteen-inch trophy and said: 'You're not like your father. He was gentleman compared to you.'

Alex saw red and chucked the trophy at him. The bloke ducked and it crashed into the mirror behind him, shattering into fifty pieces. We grabbed the girls and ran out to hail a cab. When we got to the Gresham they said they were full. We tried two more hotels but it was the same story. The porter had us knocked everywhere. We ended up at the Skylon on the airport road. It was a seedy, run down place. All they had was a room with two single beds. We pushed the beds together and shagged the girls at the same time. We were all pissed out of our heads.

Tom and Alex had their pick of the best looking women in Ireland. They had their pick of everything. In different ways, he and Alex paid a heavy price for their hellraising. There were however, occasional acts of altruism. One of the most remarkable sequence of events, even by their standards, began at Galway Races in 1997. Tom recounts the story:

We had a week at the races, interspersed with snooker exhibitions in which we played each other one-handed. We were a big draw. Alex played with different hands behind his back. One of the venues was a pub called Sally Long's. It was sold out. A guy called John O'Hare who was in the audience asked us if there was any chance we could visit a handicapped day centre in Ballybane and say hello to some of Alex's supporters. I told Alex he ought to. I have a mentally handicapped brother so it was close to my heart. Alex said yes. I drove him there the next day.

It turned out to be a nine-hour bender. Alex played snooker with handicapped youngsters all day and into the evening. He was brilliant with them. Very few people have seen this side of his nature. There was no money involved. He did it purely as a favour. They topped us up with drinks. Everyone was getting merry, including the staff. Alex posed for a photograph with a group of youngsters. They were thrilled.

We said goodbye to the carers and went to get in my car. To our horror, it was empty. All the gear had gone. Alex said: 'Fucking hell, Tom – we do a good deed and we're robbed! Where's the justice?'

Alex had lost all his Louis Copeland suits, his briefcase, his money and his cues. We went back inside and called the police. Meanwhile Alex rolled himself a giant spliff. It was the size of Winston Churchill's cigar. The smell was awful. The Garda arrived. One was a rookie. Alex said: 'Let's get this sorted. We've been robbed. Two or three grand in cash, five top quality suits and all Tom's gear. That's what we get for doing a good turn.'

'Don't you be worrying, Alex. We'll sort it.'

While the officer was taking notes, Alex blinded with him toxic fumes. I dragged him over and whispered: 'We'll get nicked, Alex. Put it out!'

'Tom, fuck off!'

'Alex, I'm telling you.'

He knew he could only push me so far then I'd snap. I kept nudging him but he didn't care. Everyone was turning a paler shade of green as the bonfire burned in Alex's hand. The police didn't even notice. You could hardly see the rookie for the cloud hanging over him. A voice came from inside it: 'I remember sitting up till two o'clock in the morning watching you play.'

Alex nodded. He was virtually blowing smoke up the copper's nose. Poor guy couldn't see what he was writing. I was getting more and more worried. Alex said under his breath: 'It's okay, babes.'

They were so gobsmacked to find that Hurricane Higgins was the complainant, they completely disregarded the fact that he was in possession of illegal drugs. Alex was very clever though. He could read body language. He knew he was safe. Anyone else would have been locked up! The Gardee spent half an hour questioning us then said: 'Okay, Alex, we've got all the information we need. We'll do everything in our power to get your stuff back.'

Sean, who runs the handicapped centre, informed us in the middle of all this that there was a gypsy camp behind the building. Alex threw up his arms: 'Fucking hell, babe, that's where the gear is! We're going down there, Tom. You're coming with me.'

'Not in a million years. You can go on your own.'

Sean warned him against it. He said they were a rough lot. We could get into serious trouble. Alex brushes him aside: 'They've got the fucking gear. We're going in. If I have to go on my own, I'll go on my own!'

He got his way. We drove into the camp together. It was inhabited by pavees. Ireland doesn't recognise them as an ethnic group. They're classed as a social group. They reckon 60 per cent of the raw material in Irish steel comes from the scrap they gather. The site was a real mess – prams, pushchairs, bikes, engines, dogs, the lot. They know a stranger the moment he sets foot on their land. Alex got out of the car wearing his blue crombie overcoat and his Stetson.

'Hey, boss, I wanna see the head honcho.'

The pavee replied in shelta language. Something to the effect of: 'I don't know what you're talking about.' There was a lot of mumbling and jostling. A group of them gathered around us. I felt very uncomfortable. Alex gave them the low-down.

'You'd be doing Alex a big favour, boss, if you can get the gear back. We're skint. All we've got is what we stand up in.'

'Okay, Alex. Leave it to me. I'll put the word out.'

We get back into the car and I tell Alex it's a waste of time. The idea that travellers would help you find the stuff they probably stole in the first place was a joke. 'You've no chance of getting it back even if they have got it. By the way, look in the mirror.'

'Why? What's going on?'

'Don't look behind. Just in the mirror. There are three pavees behind us. They're ripping the engine out of a car – and they're all wearing Louis Copeland suits!'

I pissed myself laughing. Alex couldn't see the funny side.

Sean had booked us into a hotel in Galway. We had no money but the hotel agreed to look after us. Next morning, the local radio station announced: 'Hurricane Higgins robbed in Galway.' We're sitting in reception in the same clothes, unshaven and broke. Alex sighs: 'How bad does it get, Tom?'

Then this chap and his young son walked over to us and asked Alex if they could shake his hand. The father had been a fan all his life and was sad to hear the news. Was there anything he could do to help? Alex responded quickly: 'You haven't got ten grand, have you, boss?'

'Here's my card. I'll be in my office at 2.00 pm. Pop in and I'll see what I can do.'

He was a bank manager! He gave us £3,000. Alex had to sign and give his account number. The guy put it down as a short-term overdraught and gave us the cash. Alex returned the compliment:

'Boss, you're a real gent. Can I shake *your* hand?' He takes out a piece of chalk and says: 'Give that to your young son from Alex.'

Then, turning towards me: 'Tom, I think we're at the races.'

There's another twist in this amazing tale. Radio Galway announces that our gear's been found. It seems too good to be true. The Gardee tell us they'll bring it to our hotel. They arrive with two black sacks of waterlogged clothes. Alex opens the sack. There's no sign of his briefcase or cash, although it was hard to identify anything in all the mud. They'd taken all the valuables and tossed the rest into the river. It was hopeless. Our dreams were dashed. Alex thought for a minute:

'How far is Cork?'

'We're in Galway, Alex. We'd be on the road for a week! I've also got my wife blowing her top.'

'No, babe, just listen. We're going to see Oliver Reed.'

That's how Alex's mind works. There's always a plan B. After so many years on the road, he knows where there's a bolt hole if things get difficult. It's the same with his cannabis and coke. He always knew a collection point. He lived the way he played – always five or six moves ahead. He picked up the phone: 'I'm gonna stay with Oliver for a few days. Are you coming or what?'

'He's the last person I need to see right now!'

But I succumbed. I'd met Oliver once or twice. I drove Alex

to Castle McCarthy (no connection) where Oliver lived. There's one pub in the village – O'Brien's. He meets us there, gives us big hugs and says: 'This is the bloody life. Let's have a *real* drink.'

I could tell Oliver only wanted 'Hig the Pig' for entertainment. He treats Alex like a pet. He started teasing him. Before I knew, Alex was throwing shapes. I was sitting between them and it was obvious Oliver was looking for a fight. As usual, Alex was rising to the bait. I warned him to calm down. I said someone would get hurt and it wouldn't be me. I told him:

'I'm going home. I don't want to ruin your friendship with Oliver. He's a prick.'

'Okay, babes, you go home. I'll be fine with Ollie.'

I had my doubts. Oliver was a nutcase. He used to strip off in the garden and drink naked in the pissing rain. Sure enough, I got a phone call when I was driving home. It was Alex.

'I need your help, babe. This cunt's gone mad. He's trying to kill me.'

Oliver had pulled the branch off a tree and was chasing Alex around the garden, trying to beat him with it.

'I'm serious, babe. This is heavy shed. You need to get down here fast! I'm in the room.'

'What room?'

'The fucking bedroom! I've locked myself in.'

He rang me a back a few minutes later to say Oliver was jabbing kitchen knives into the bedroom door. Thankfully, his wife Josephine was there to calm things down, otherwise anything could have happened. Oliver wanted a session. Alex didn't. Those sessions are what killed Oliver in the end. He said afterwards that he had hardly any recollection of chasing Alex with lumps of tree. Alex made his escape the next day. He caught a train to Dublin and stayed there with a friend. Then he made his way to Louis Copeland's for a new load of clobber.

It was Tom McCarthy who broke the news to Alex in 1999 that Oliver had died after another session while filming in Malta. Alex burst into tears. Josephine had a job to escape him at the funeral. He was inconsolable and wouldn't leave her alone. She had to get Cecil Mason to rescue her. She told me she was too distressed to remember much about the day, but she does recall Alex's mobile going off during the service!

Tom thought Oliver Reed was bad news. Alex didn't need any encouragement to get wrecked. Tom had a close-up view of Alex's degenerate nature over three-and-a-half decades but he also saw some good points. He's keen to balance the picture.

> You'd see flashes of Alex's good nature here and there. If he really liked someone, he'd go out of his way to please them. He did with me – opening two snooker clubs I had in Waterford and stayed longer than the call of duty. Another beneficiary was dear old Paddy Comerford, a referee known and respected all over the world. He was eighty, the oldest ref in the game. Paddy had devoted his life to Irish snooker. He was a lovely little man. One night, he was refereeing a game at my club but seemed out-of-sorts. I asked him what was wrong. He said the World Amateur Championships were due to be held in Malta but snooker officials had told him he was too old to travel.
>
> It was a terrible insult. Those cretins on the Snooker Council of Ireland had never even *heard* of snooker when Paddy started reffing. He was longing to go Malta. This could be his last appearance. I told Alex the news. He was disgusted. As we know, he had no time for authority of any sort. We put in £400 each and bought Paddy's ticket to Malta. No-one knew it came from us. Paddy died shortly after the event. His family rang to thank us.

In 1996, two years after the first operation to remove cancerous growths from his mouth, Alex woke up with a sore throat and felt sick. He asked Tom to take him to hospital in Waterford. Now read on:

An arguments starts between Alex and two doctors the moment we walk into A&E. He refuses to wait his turn with fifty others so they put him in a cubicle. He's sitting there in his green baseball cap and white gown, explaining that he'd been treated for growths in a Belfast hospital but was still waiting for the biopsy results. They told him they had to get hold of his records before they could do anything to help him. You can imagine how that went down. He was seething! I went into the cubicle and told him to get a grip. They were trying to help him. He saw it differently: 'Tom, that guy's a prick.'

I said I wasn't getting involved. I'd wait outside. About twenty minutes later, I put my head around the curtain to see if he was okay. He was a changed man. His attitude had mellowed remarkably: 'Hi Tom. How's things? I'm doing fine.'

Did I say 'mellowed'? He's had a completely new lease of life. He's flying. Then I find out why. He's found a trolley full of medical equipment and wheeled it into his cubicle. He holds up a bottle of Novocaine – the stuff dentists use to numb your gums. It's cocaine in liquid form. Alex has sprayed his Rizla papers with Novocaine and is chewing his way through them! He offers me one.

'Here, babes, have one of these.'

'You can't do that, Alex!'

'No problem, babes. Put this bottle in your bag. It's good stuff.'

I make an excuse about needing the toilet. I'm thinking I'd better warn the doctors. Then I have second thoughts. What if they call the police? By now, Alex has lockjaw. He can't open his mouth. I have to tell someone. We go back to the cubicle but Alex has vanished. I go down the corridor looking for him. There's a woman mopping the floor. She's standing in a pool of water.

'Excuse me. Have you seen a guy in a baseball cap?'

'Yes, he's just run that way. He tried to jump over the wet floor sign but kicked my bucket flying!'

There was a pub in the road outside so I had a good idea where he might be. He knew the owner. Sure enough, there sat Alex in the corner wearing his white gown and green cap and reading his paper.

'Hi, Tom, how yer doing, babes?'

He had a pint of Guinness beside him and was studying the form as though nothing had happened. He didn't bother to go back to the hospital. His sore throat seemed to have got better.

We've heard about his penchant for alternative medicine. For someone who abused his body so relentlessly, it's interesting to note that he still had faith in some of his mother's nostrums and seemed to believe that Fisherman's Friends could repair his throat. Teabags were a new one, though. It surprised Tom. The pair were heading back to their hotel rooms after another hard day when Alex made an odd request.

'Tommy, I need some papers and teabags!'

'There'll be teabags in your room. What's the problem?'

'I just need some fucking teabags, babe.'

I go to the shop and get him a load of teabags. I leave them with him at the hotel and tell him I'll be back later. I'm praying he doesn't mess me about because the mayor's coming to the opening of a snooker club that evening. There's no reply when I knock on the door to collect him. I push the door open and there's no sign of Alex. I get a feeling in the pit of my stomach. Am I going to find a body in the bathroom? I do! Alex is motionless in a bath of brown water. I think he's dead. Then I see that he's covered in teabags. He's emptied some of them into the bath water and covered himself from head to toe with the rest.

'What the hell are you doing, Alex?'

'Just chilling out, babes. Teabags soothe the skin. You should try them.'

'Tell it to the mayor. He'll be here any minute!'

'No probs.'

Alex died on my son's birthday, July 24th. When I saw the photograph of Alex in Spain where he was supposed to have his implants, I knew he was a gonna. It was the only picture I ever saw of him with his head bowed. He'd thrown in the towel. I tried to speak to him when he came back to Belfast, but he couldn't get the words out.

I miss the guy a lot. He was Jekyll and Hyde but terrific company. Some people in Belfast probably regarded him as a pain. He'd turn on people without warning but always when he knew there were a few of us around to defend him. In the south he was always well protected. Alex made a lot of mistakes. He ruined his own life with drinking and gambling. I saw the lovely houses he once had. It was very sad that he ended up with nothing – not even a pad to call his own.

I remember him being asked on the day he was banned whether he could live without snooker. He replied: 'Can snooker live without me?'

That was the point. Without him, snooker began to die.

Two things struck me about the funeral. First, my estimation of Stephen Hendry went up because he took the trouble to be there. Second, my estimation of Barry Hearn went down. As chairman of the governing body, he had a *duty* to be there. I suppose it sums up Alex's relationship with the WPBSA. Neither of them had time for the other.

12

HE WAS MY 'FIANCÉ'

If Alex thought he'd found the Holy Grail in Siobhan Kidd, he was probably right. If Siobhan thought she could knock the bachelor out of him, she was wrong. If either of them imagined a tiger could change its stripes, they were delusional.

Passionate and romantic though it was at its height, the liaison between a sporting has-been who dragged himself through every hedge backwards and a pretty psychology graduate thirteen years his junior stretched most of our imaginations to breaking point. It was too good to be true. The way it ended suggests that Alex was incapable of a calm and lasting relationship. His partners couldn't work out which half of his split personality was the genuine article. Nor, I suspect, could he.

Alex managed to kill the love affair stone-dead. He had something to treasure but didn't know how to treasure it. Siobhan's sexuality possibly frightened him the way Cara's had all those years ago in Australia. He put it more succinctly: 'I had my chance and blew it.'

Siobhan (Shivvy) was a strong-willed twenty-four-year-old when she paired up with Alex. She had to be. Her determination to keep out of sight since calling off the romance in 1989 hasn't wavered. I tried to find her. She was variously reported to be working in the art world in Guernsey, Jersey or Australia. Each trail went cold. Even the funeral of the man whose marriage proposal she once accepted failed to tempt Siobhan out of hiding. She was invited but made no contact with Alex's sisters, which was a big disappointment to them. They'd welcomed her into the family with open arms. They'd been thrilled to hear about Alex's wedding plans. At the time, Siobhan described Alex as 'the gentlest man I ever met'. It makes you wonder what kind of company she'd been keeping! Alex was on the rebound from Lynn when he first dated Siobhan.

He'd noticed her at a Manchester nightclub where she worked as a hostess. His personal assistant at the time, Mark Howarth, detected a change in his behaviour. Alex would ask to be dropped of at certain points around the city, then mysteriously disappear with a 'see you later, babes.' Says Mark: 'I had no idea where he was going or whether I was supposed to pick him up again. I suspected there was a woman somewhere. He had a spring in his step.'

I saw Siobhan during the time I was interviewing Alex for his autobiography. First impressions were of a glamorous, classy lady. The next thought was: 'What's she doing with Alex?'

Around Christmas time, Siobhan moved into Delveron House, the smart Cheshire home Alex bought to save his marriage to Lynn. It was only six weeks after Lynn left. Lauren's and Jordan's toys littered the playroom while Alex was surrounded by dirty dishes and dirty washing. Most of it was piled up against the back door which no longer provided access. Siobhan did her best to inject some festive cheer by putting up a Christmas tree and hanging a few baubles on it. It was a sad time for Lynn and the kids. Jordan was aware of Christmas for the first time and wanted to know where his dad was.

Alex showed up at Lynn's new house on Christmas Day. He played train sets with Jordan. Lynn and Alex were civil to each other - quite an achievement considering it was only a matter of weeks since he threw a TV set through the window. Lynn thinks that's the moment when it dawned on Alex that he'd lost his family.

He did, however, have the consolation of a stunning new girlfriend. This is how he described her. 'She was a gem. She understood my situation. She had her own place in Didsbury but moved in with me. Apart from anything else, it was good to be with someone I could talk to. I have an active mind. Shivvy was very well educated. We'd talk for hours about books, history, films, whatever. She cooked for me, looked after me when things got difficult and came with me on the snooker circuit whenever she could. Our relationship was passionate. I wasn't used to a woman who woke up at seven in the morning wanting sex. She was one of those modern, energetic women who hold nothing back. I was an old man of thirty-seven. I wondered whether I could last the distance.'

He couldn't of course. They had just over two years together. As smitten as he was by this lovely young thing, Alex was still hoping to make it up with Lynn. He may even have been using Siobhan as a device, who knows? With respect to Lynn, it was the whole family package rather than his fraught relationship with her that he missed. Lynn says: 'Once the novelty of a new girlfriend wore off, he phoned two three times a day. Sometimes he'd arrive on the doorstep with a packet of bacon and say: "Will you cook this for me?" When he gave you that little-boy-lost look, you couldn't say no. It's odd that I enjoyed hearing from him after that terrible night when he was arrested, but I did. When I felt like forgiving him, I reminded myself of the awful things he did and knew I wouldn't go back.'

So Alex continued to live a double life. It troubled Siobhan who phoned Lynn to find out what game he was playing. Snooker with people? The pair had a meeting to clear the air. Lynn made it clear she had no intention of going back with him. Alex and Siobhan continued to live at Delveron House where Mark Howarth acted as estate manager. He mowed the lawns, tidied the house and even brought Alex his morning cup of tea with a copy of *The Sun*, the

Mirror and the *Racing Post*. For 'morning' read any time after 11.30 am. There was something else in the job specification.

'When the press got the scent, it was my job to sneak Siobhan out of her flat, drive her to Mottram St Andrew and sneak her into Delveron with a blanket over her head. Sounds ridiculous now but it was fun at the time. There was a lot of affection between Alex and Siobhan. It was different from his time with Lynn. Siobhan had her tantrums too but you had to push her hard before she'd blow up. Alex really thought he could get his life back together. He was happy when she was around. The three of us spent a lot of time together. I was the gooseberry while those two cuddled on the settee watching television. There was a very pleasant, relaxed feeling about the place. Mind you, Alex still expected her to bring his drink and fetch his cigarettes. He treated her like a servant. She didn't seem to mind - for now.'

Alex took Shivvy to Spain where he was commissioned for two-week series of exhibitions at a golf hotel in San Pedro. Staying at the same hotel were Michael Gaffney and his wife Breda from Dublin. Michael was an executive buyer at Dunnes, a department store with branches in Ireland, Spain and the UK. He didn't know Alex and he wasn't a snooker fan. They met in unusual circumstances.

> We were driving up the hill to the hotel at about 4.00 am. There was a car blocking the way. It was a battered old thing which kept revving, stopping, starting and rolling back. I couldn't get past it. I got out to help. There was a lovely young blonde at the wheel. She was panicking. She couldn't get control of the car. I told her to take the handbrake off. My sons and I held the vehicle steady as she put it in gear. A man got out of the car to help us push. I recognised Alex Higgins. He jumped back in as Siobhan

found traction and drove up the hill. They'd obviously had a good night out.

Breda and I went down to the pool the next day for our first dose of sunshine. I walked into the bar at midday and there was Alex Higgins again. He was snow white with skinny legs hanging out of a terrible pair of shorts which looked more like curtains. He called me over: 'Thanks for this morning, babes. Can I get you a beer?'

He called Siobhan over. She looked fantastic in her bikini. My wife joined us and we sat chatting over a few drinks. Siobhan asked if I played golf. When I told her I was keen golfer she said: 'There you are, Alex, you've got a partner.' It sounded as though she might be grateful for a break. We arranged a four-ball for the following morning. He was Protestant, I'm Catholic but it made no difference. We had a great game, then it was back to the pool with the girls. That evening, the four of us went for dinner.

The pattern repeated itself the next day – pool, golf, pool, dinner. I paid for the meal one night, Alex the next. He was great company and great fun on the golf course. He insisted on driving the buggy because it was his only chance of getting behind the wheel. He flew around the greens taking crazy chances. What a relief for the motorists of Britain and Ireland that Alex never took his test!

Frank Bruno was staying at the hotel. So was his manager, George Francis. They were preparing for a title fight. Bruno used to wander around the pool with his ghetto blaster deafening the sun worshippers. One day it was pleasantly quiet so I thought he must be away. Then I saw him buried in a magazine. I asked Alex what he thought Bruno was reading. He said: 'I can tell you. It's either the *Dandy* or the *Beano*!'

Siobhan said they were thinking of extending their stay. It was our first week, their second. Alex's exhibitions had finished so if they wanted to stay another week, he'd have to pay and get his flight ticket changed. They decided to stay. Siobhan drove him to Gibraltar airport to change their homeward flight. While they were gone we wondered how we'd cope with Alex for another week. He'd more or less hijacked the holiday. I was a bit concerned. Normally you meet someone on holiday a couple of times and move on. We had Alex every day and every night!

You could see he and Siobhan were very much in love but it was tempestuous. Sometimes they called us into their room and greeted us with a bottle of champagne. Siobhan was half-naked. It didn't seem to bother her and it certainly didn't bother me. I got on very well with her. One morning I looked out of our bedroom window and saw Alex by the pool at an unusually early hour. I thought he must be keen. When I looked more closely, he was gathering his clothes which were scattered everywhere. We discovered later that Siobhan had thrown them out after another blazing row. They had lots of them. The guy in the next room to them complained about the noise. Despite that, the second week went better than expected. Alex gave me his mobile number and we went home the best of friends.

A couple of days later I got a call from Doug Perry, his new agent. Siobhan knew Doug before Alex did. He played in a band and had an agency in Barnet. She persuaded Alex to switch from Howard Kruger and thought Doug would look after him better. I heard Alex and Kruger having some awful disagreements on the phone. Doug invited me to a five-a-side day Alex was having with Liverpool Football Club. Bruce Grobelaar, John Barnes and Ian Rush were there. Alex played in goal. He was useless.

He and Siobhan were living at her flat. I never went there but I saw a lot of her over the next year or so. Every time Alex was in

Ireland, I got a call. One of them was to say he didn't like his hotel in Dublin, so would we mind if he stayed with us and brought Siobhan with him? I have a five-bedroom house in Malahide which is *the* place to live in Dublin. Siobhan was in good form. That visit started a trend. There was a knock on the door on St Stephen's Day, which you call Boxing Day. There stood Alex and Siobhan. They just turned up. She had a present for us. It was a lovely Lowry print. She was working as an art restorer in Manchester. Alex said her job was 'touching up old masters!'

They stayed for two weeks! Fortunately, Malahide had lots of discreet pubs where Alex wouldn't be pestered by the usual hangers-on. He and Siobhan were out late most nights and stayed in bed most of the morning. Their sex life was pretty full. They seemed inseparable. It culminated one night in a hotel bar where the four of us were enjoying a quiet drink. Out of the blue, Alex asked Siobhan to marry him. She said: 'Get down on one knee.' He refused. She said: 'I won't marry you then!'

That was the end of it. I don't whether we'd just witnessed a proposal being rejected or whether they were pulling each other's legs. He told me afterwards he wished he'd done as he was told and got down on his knees.

Back in England, Mark Howarth saw serious cracks appearing in the relationship. Alex resented the fact that Siobhan kept her rented apartment and refused to move in with him lock, stock and barrel. He also got screwed up about her 'girlie' nights. According to Mark: 'They did his head in.' From Siobhan's point of view, the glamour of being in the spotlight faded as Alex's demands grew stronger and more ill-tempered. Things came to a head in dramatic fashion when Mark took Siobhan to buy a leather overcoat. He takes up the story.

* * *

She'd always wanted a leather coat and I knew a warehouse near Stockport that imported them. She chose a lovely full-length black one which was reduced from £200 to £40. She looked fabulous. Alex was fuming. He didn't like the idea that *I'd* bought it for her. He was insanely jealous. I was reprimanded for stepping out of line. There was a kind of cold war between us. It broke out into full-scale war when Alex came to play an exhibition in Warrington. The evening was going well until the disco started. Alex put his hand up a girl's skirt in front of her boyfriend and in front of Siobhan. The boyfriend went for him. Siobhan tried to separate them but Alex got her by the throat.

It calmed down for a while, then all hell broke loose. Alex grabbed hold of Siobhan and bit a chunk of leather out of the shoulder of her new coat. He had such a grip on her, we couldn't shake him off. Then he squared up to me and threatened to twat me. I said: 'Go on then. It's better you hit me rather than anyone else, then it won't get into the papers.' He promptly head-butted me and we ended up grappling on the pool table. I stopped the fight and said I was taking Siobhan and a couple of friends back to Delveron House where they were guests. I told Alex: 'It's up to you whether you come with us, but we've had enough. I don't work for you any more.'

'What do you mean, babes?'

'What I say. I don't mind if you get pissed. I don't care if you eff and blind and call me all the names under the sun, but the first time you lay a finger on me, we're finished!'

When we got to the house he tried to smooth it over. He invited me in. I told him no. I wasn't his fixer or his friend now. Siobhan refused to go into the house without me so I took her and the friends to my own home in Knutsford for the night. Alex was on the phone cursing and swearing all night and the next morning. He and Siobhan struggled on for another six months or so but my time with him was over. That was Christmas 1988.

Mark showed me a small jewellery box containing the piece of leather Alex bit out of Siobhan's coat, and five pink tablets. They were a sample of the betablockers he was taking at the time. It's a curious souvenir – probably worth more than he paid for the coat!

The end of the love affair caused consternation in Belfast where Ann, Jean and Alex's mother Elizabeth had all being hoping Siobhan was the one for him. Ann said: 'It was an awful shame. We all got on so well. She loved him and he loved her. She was the only one who got Sandy to live a normal life – for a while anyway. Sometimes real love is too intense.'

Jean, once thrilled to hear Siobhan accept her brother's proposal of marriage, was equally philosophical. She knew Alex too well to get her hopes up: 'They were serious about making a go of it. I think Siobhan grew tired of waiting. She wanted him to tie the knot. Maybe they spent too much time together. When you're with someone twenty-four hours a day you find out things about them and about yourself you didn't realise. Sandy was never going to be easy.'

Snooker referee Len Ganley was another disappointed onlooker as the relationship foundered. 'Siobhan was a class act. She reckoned Alex was gentle and caring. He could be, but only in short bursts. Having her on his arm was terrific for his morale. What a stunning trophy! Just being in her company was a dream. He was so lucky to find a woman who genuinely loved him. She went out of her way to make excuses for him when he embarrassed people. Alex hardly ever apologised to anyone for anything. She went with him to Hong Kong, Singapore and Dubai. It was a great relationship but he was always going to mess her up. I didn't know at the time but realise now that she was just another turn for Alex.'

Alex took the break-up badly. As was his custom, he tried to get Siobhan back. He was in denial about the awful confrontations they'd had - and about the tipping point. After Mark Howarth's six-year tenure, Will Robinson took up the challenge of minding The Hurricane. That would include trying to resuscitate him after a theatrical suicide attempt in front of Siobhan. We'll come to that after hearing Will's recollection of a torrid time.

> Things were going well for longer than you'd normally expect with Alex. Siobhan had an amazing way with him. He was in bed by 10.00 pm – not for sex, for sleep! That was brilliant because Alex wouldn't normally switch off until five or six o'clock in the morning. He didn't come home till it was light. Then he'd have young guys back to play snooker or cards for money. He was the hustler of all time till Siobhan stepped in. She'd collect him in her dinky sports car and off they'd go together. These rendezvous were hard to arrange because Siobhan had a full-time day job and Alex worked at night – the usual old problems.
>
> As far as I knew, the last straw was an argument they had in Delveron House. I think Alex pushed her into the kitchen door and one of her fingers went through a small pane of glass. She screamed at the sight of blood all over her hand. She ran to her car shouting: 'Look what you've done, Alex!' I don't think he was trying to hurt her. It was an accident. That was Alex's version anyway.

The story moves on a couple of days. Alex asks Will to pick up his betablockers from a twenty-four-hour chemist, while he goes to the pub. Siobhan's flat is just across the road. Here's what happened next.

* * *

Alex phoned to say he was now in Siobhan's flat so could I take the tablets there. Things were very tense. The three of us were sitting close together, struggling to make conversation. We watched Alex put both hands around a glass of lager and take a big gulp. Next, he emptied the betablockers into his throat and took another gulp of lager. The tablets were spilling out of his mouth and he was shovelling them back in. This took a matter of seconds. I was only twenty years old and I had a suicide attempt going on before my eyes. I wanted to dial 999 but Siobhan said: 'No, Will. No police and no media. We'll get him back to his flat.'

'We haven't got time. He'll die.'

'I'm telling you, Bubbles, it's the only way.'

I had a decision to make. Alex was losing consciousness. He needed to be in hospital. We've got him upside down. I'm holding his legs and Siobhan's slapping him on the back trying to get the tablets to come out. He starts being sick. Siobhan tells me to go. She'll call the ambulance and tell them Alex has suspected food poisoning. I went in the ambulance with him. He was mumbling: 'I love you, Bubbles. Don't leave me.'

We saved his life and kept the incident quiet. There's no way Siobhan would have him back after that but Alex wouldn't give up trying. A few weeks later, he got me to take him to Siobhan's flat again. She wouldn't let him in. Alex threw pebbles at her window. The neighbours were getting worried. Siobhan kept out of sight. We heard sirens and there was a flashing blue light coming down the road. I shouted: 'Alex, make a run for it back to the car.'

He dived into the bushes. We could see two officers coming towards us with torches. Alex decided to run for the car. He wasn't very fast. One of the policemen dived on top of him and they rolled over in the grass. We heard more sirens. Five police cars arrived with dogs. They took one look and said: 'Oh, it's Higgins.'

He ends up at Longsight Police Station. He doesn't want his solicitor. They call me in after an hour and he's sitting there chatting to the officers as cool as you like. 'Hi, Bubbles. You okay, babe?' He's telling them about upcoming exhibitions and putting dates in his diary.

They could have charged him with causing an affray but they held back. I think it was Siobhan who called the police. Alex was convinced she had another boyfriend in her flat. I don't know whether or not that's true, but I do know that Siobhan was bitterly upset that the relationship didn't work out. She really loved Alex. He became erratic when it was over. He was made bankrupt soon afterwards. By now he'd moved out of Delveron House and was living in a rented place in the hills. In icy conditions you couldn't get up the road. It was pitiful. Cancer was to follow.

Mark got to hear about the suicide attempt. He was grateful to be out of the firing line. He saw Siobhan six or seven years after the break-up when she was working in a Trafford art gallery. He said: 'She was sorry they hadn't stayed together but she knew in her heart of hearts that it wouldn't work. There was absolutely no way back. When Siobhan makes up her mind about something, that's it. All or nothing. Will tried to get hold of her to invite her to the funeral, but failed. She wouldn't have wanted anything to do with it. That chapter of her life was well and truly closed.'

Michael Gaffney had the job of taking the engagement ring back. No-one except Siobhan is sure whether or not she wore it or whether they were ever engaged. While on a business trip to Hong Kong, Michael returned the diamond ring to the Kowloon jeweller who'd sold it to Alex. He got a £2,000 refund.

13

HE WAS MY TRAVELLING COMPANION

This is Len Ganley's story. He had the frequently unenviable task of refereeing Alex many times at the height of his career. However, their relationship went much deeper than that. The two Ulstermen accompanied each other on the circuit for forty years. Their companionship began at the Jampot and endured until Alex's spectacular fall from grace and eventual demise. They travelled miles together, covered several continents, burned the candle at the sides as well as both ends and remained staunch buddies throughout – with the occasional blip, of course.

Len's had cancer for thirteen years. He's divorced and living alone on a daily intake of twenty-five drugs. They keep him going, but only just. He was and is a tough cookie. Some of that emanates from a near-tragic experience as a young father in Belfast. According to Len, his son Michael was kidnapped from the school playground and suspended by a rope from a tree close to the family house. Len was out of town working as chimney sweep. He cycled home to be confronted by the appalling news.

'If it hadn't been for a neighbour who cut him down with a kitchen knife, my son would have died. It was touch and go for a couple of days. I prayed at his bedside and vowed that if Michael survived, I'd give up the booze there and then.'

Michael did survive. He now works for the WPBSA. Perhaps not surprisingly, he wasn't keen to discuss the incident. Len believes it was a revenge attack for the time he spent in the British army:

'They tried to post me to Ulster. That was out of order. I refused to go and I quit the forces altogether. Belfast was a vicious place then. Alex was lucky. He was living and playing in England. The experience changed me forever.'

Rather than offer opinions, Len dispenses facts and issues statements, often with an air of menace, as if to say you'd better get this first time because I'm not repeating it! You can take the referee out of the game but not out of the man.

He and Alex were fortunate to emerge from their lifelong adventure in one piece. I hesitate to say unscathed. According to Len, they didn't have an argument in all that time - partly because you didn't argue with Len if you valued your health, but mainly because they clicked. The devout Catholic and the lukewarm Protestant. Laurel and Hardy. Don Quixote and Sancho Panza.

When he wasn't drinking, Alex was the nicest bloke you could ever wish to meet. He was amusing, clever and loyal. He often stayed at our house at the height of his fame. The kids loved him. He was a joy. I first met him at the YMCA. I was a player then and better than Higgins because he was six years younger. I gave him 75 start at snooker and 35 at billiards and beat him comfortably. I was as fast as Alex and slim in those days. Alex at thirteen had bags of ability but couldn't put breaks together. His game was all over the place. I didn't think of him then as a future champion. He wasn't even a contestant for the local league. He was a strange kid, quite introverted. He hardly ever came out of his shell. His face was covered in blackheads and he didn't wash properly. He just gave his face a rub. Altogether, he wasn't an attractive sight.

Unlike me, he didn't fit into family life either. I had twelve brothers and sisters. Meal times together were the focal point of the day. At the Higgins establishment they couldn't even *find* Alex for dinner let alone school. Yet look at the education he had. It was all in his brain. He was Billy the Kid, dodging the bullets, outsmarting the Apaches. He actually had a horse to go with it – for a while. But don't believe that bunkum about leaving home to become a jockey. Alex just wanted a punt with the stable lads. He didn't want to ride horses. He didn't want to do anything except find an easy way to make money!

The turning point came when he moved to England and met a better class of snooker player. Dessie Anderson and Jackie Rae were top professionals in the Blackburn/Accrington area. John Spencer was well established and so was Ray Reardon. Then along came Dennis Taylor and Jim Meadowcroft. Anybody who was anybody in snooker lived in Lancashire – with one notable exception. John Pulman was pulling up trees in Exeter, of all places. How unlikely was that? A fisherman/snooker player, and another introvert who could turn nasty. He could drink any man or woman under the table and usually did.

Alex only drank for fun then. The usual diet if you were Irish was a pint and a short followed by a pint and a short. Everyone who played the game drank. It was nothing to do with late hours. I defy anyone to stand at a table for that length of time *without* drinking. Only a few old stars drank and played at the same time. Alex mastered it. He once lost the first seven frames of a championship match to Eddie Charlton, got as drunk as a skunk that night, then breezed in the next day and potted every red off the table. Eddie had no answer. There wasn't an answer.

I went to see the world final in 1972. Selly Oak British Legion was packed with miners in cloth caps and men from the car factories. They were a lovely crowd but it was a horrible, dirty place. Britain was on a three-day week to save fuel so they played by candlelight. At the side of the table there was a big single candle with a glass globe over it. The globe kept slipping so the ref had to use a damp cloth to steady it or he'd have got his hands burned. All this while trying to referee the final! There was no overhead lighting and you could hardly make out the scoreboard.

No-one in their right mind would have played snooker in those conditions. Spectators had to sit on upturned beer crates because all the seats were taken. There must have been 300 in there. I went to give Alex some support. He looked up to me. He had no pals with him, although dozens of Irishmen from Birmingham came to cheer him on.

John Spencer was the favourite. He was one of the greats. He had to play the final with a different cue. He'd fallen asleep at the wheel of his Rover 90 a couple of weeks before the final and got his regular cue smashed to pieces. He'd already played Alex in Bolton so he knew what to expect. Nobody else knew much about Alex. Both finalists drank and smoked their heads off the whole match. Embassy were the sponsors so everybody was encouraged to smoke. When he beat Spencer, Alex got 6,000 cigarettes and a cheque for £450. He blew it the same night at a casino. Spencer went with him. He was a big gambler too.

When he was world champion, I signed Alex to do exhibition work for my children's charity. He came to live with us in Burton. We had a lot of fun. He got to know our six children and Michael thought the world of him. Alex was always good with youngsters. He'd give my wife a fiver to get them lollipops. They loved it when he climbed up three flights of stairs to play Scalextric in the loft. They raced each other for a penny. It had to be for money, didn't it? Alex was a kid himself.

He enjoyed eating in those days. If he was here now, he'd tell you about Rosaline's Ulster Fries. They consisted of soda bread, potato bread, three sausages, two eggs and four rashers of bacon. We'd all eat together. Unless you cleaned your plate, my missus was furious. Eating with a family made all the difference to Alex. There weren't many times in his life when he could do that.

Before he came onto the scene, I'd been hiring Graham Myles and Dennis Taylor for charity shows. When snooker fans saw the name Hurricane Higgins tickets flew out of the door. I sold more than 600 in one night! The money went towards wheelchairs and pushchairs for hospitals. We raised over £3 million in ten years. Alex put his heart and soul into it. When we presented wheelchairs to a group of badly handicapped kids, he cried over one boy who'd lost both legs and one of his arms in a road accident. We got the lad a computer with a pointer so he could use it with his head. Alex broke down completely. I'd never seen him so affected by anything. Even at the charity dinner that evening I couldn't console him.

I looked after him well. He was paid £750 a night for sixty successive nights. That's £45,000 for two months work! It was a lot of cash to cram into the tin box he carried. Even then, he could walk into an arena, see a crowd of 2,000, do a U-turn and demand more for his services. He'd say: 'You shouldn't treat me like this. Do you know who I am?' I'd tell him: 'Yes, you're the urchin from the Jampot who still thinks he's God's gift.' That usually shut him up.

When he finished all his stints, I drove him back to our house with his tin on his knee. He told me to stop at the casino. My heart sank the moment he said it. I knew the tin box would soon be a lot lighter. I'm not exaggerating, he did £45,000 in little over half an hour! Even I couldn't believe it. I've kept that tin box among my souvenirs. People think I'm mad but it represented an important time in my life – and his.

People have tried to calculate how much he must have

blown in his career. I'm telling you, Alex could have poured £20 million down the drain and never given it a second thought. Money was a gamble. Life was gamble. That's all it meant to him. He'd flag down taxis and say to the drivers: 'Do you know who I am?' Who gave a fuck? It was an excuse for a free ride. Taxi drivers never got paid. Nobody got paid. The world owed him a living. People were put on this earth to serve him.

Luckily for him, most were only too happy to oblige. He took full advantage. Wherever Alec hit town, he knew where to get free drinks. He survived on freebies. I don't know many people who'd do what Louis Copeland did. He'd send Alex ten suits, five topcoats, a couple of fedoras and a pair of spats for nothing. Everything Alex wore was a gift.

If things weren't free, he'd try everything he knew to avoid payment. A classic example was the time he stayed at the Strand Palace in London. One evening he told me to drop him off at hotel reception, then drive through the staff car park and wait for him at the bike sheds. I assumed he was going to pay his bill but didn't understand the bike sheds bit. I'm waiting in the car when I hear this bang, bang, bang on the tin roof of the shed. A suitcase comes bouncing on to the roof of my car. I wonder what the fuck he's doing. He jumps down off the shed shouting: 'Stick that in the boot!' Over comes another bag. 'Stick that one in too. I'll be down in a minute.'

Out of the corner of my eye I see him run along the hotel balcony, then leap off. He lands on the roof of my car screaming: 'Drive like fuck!' He's still clinging on while I pull away. Somehow he grabs the outside of the passenger door and clambers into the seat: 'Let's get out of here, babes.' He's running off without paying the bill and using me as the getaway car. I'm an accessory. What could I do – shop him?

The daft thing is that Alex didn't *need* daredevil escapes. He didn't need to do a runner. He was earning good money. The reason he didn't pay the bill is that he had no cash in his pocket. He wouldn't risk cashing a cheque because they'd deduct the bill from it. That was his attitude to life in a nutshell. Get away with as much as you can and laugh about it. It didn't matter that you might be damaging someone else's livelihood.

They'd have a seizure if he ever went back to the Half Moon curry house in Derby. I expect they've nailed everything down by now. One night at a roulette table, Alex lost the British Gold Cup trophy as well as his £6,000 winner's cheque. The next evening, he took a fancy to a bronze elephant in the Half Moon and walked off with it. I saw it in his hotel room. He said he'd put it in his house to replace the trophy. I was furious with him and took it back to the curry house myself. Alex's rationale was that he needed it more than they did. In any case, he said, it was a harmless bit of fun.

That same week, he stole two television sets from the Priory Hotel in Derby. Don't ask me how. He probably got his mates to do the dirty work. I've no idea what he did with the sets. Everything was a laugh to Alex until the police got involved. Then it wasn't so funny. For all that, I enjoyed spending time with him. We always had good conversations. There weren't many dull moments. He never learned to drive but I was happy to do it when I could. Then I had an idea. Why didn't I become his official driver? We were usually at the same venues. I didn't drink anymore. He did. It made sense. I discussed the idea with Alex's manager, Del Simmons. He agreed. I put it to Alex.

'Has it occurred to you that you don't need to travel everywhere by train and stay in hotels?'

'What the fuck are you on about now?'

'Let me be your chauffeur.'

'What?'

'I've got a motor home which would do the job perfectly. You could forget about draughty platforms, train timetables and taxis. You could live in it. No more hotels and rows with receptionists. All your clothes would be in one place and you'd have your own bed, shower and toilet. What more could you want?'

'Nice try, babes, but it won't work. I need my own space.'

Instead of formalising a proper financial arrangement that would have suited us both, I carried on driving him here and there when he needed a favour.

It was difficult for him to see the kids after he and Lynn split up. I went with him a few times when he was barred from the house. I don't blame her. Alex could be a frightening person. One visit I remember clearly was to deliver an envelope containing £300. Alex wanted Lynn to have it for Lauren and Jordan. She refused to open the door so I put it through the letterbox. I assume she kept it. In his own way, Alex *did* make efforts to look after his family when he had a load of cash, but I still had to stop him going to the bookies. It was as though he couldn't help himself. I'd say: 'This is important. Forget about doubling your money on the horses because you'll only lose it. You've got to pay it in for the kids.'

Len has experienced Alex's extremes of behaviour more than most. They alienated all but his most loyal friends. They terrified his wives and girlfriends; upset his sisters; embarrassed his children; offended strangers; had at least one tournament official on his back and kept the police busy. But what *explains* those sudden outbursts and swift plunges of mood? Why the violence? And why was it so easily forgotten – in his mind anyway? We shall never be able to prove this one way or another but two of his closest allies, Cecil Mason and Len Ganley, are convinced Alex suffered from schizophrenia. Jim Meadowcroft, agrees. Here's Len's opinion.

> His mental condition ticked most of the schizophrenia boxes as I understand the illness. On the one hand he was intelligent, literate and well-read. On the other he was crazed and dangerous. I've seen him talking to artists and judges on their owns terms. I've seen him charm an entire audience with his wit and repartee. Then the button would go. You never knew where or when. Heaven help you if you were in the line of fire!
>
> It's too easy to blame alcohol. He could be stone cold sober and still turn in a flash. It was genius bordering on insanity. He didn't apologise because he wasn't aware of the harm he'd done. Two unprovoked examples of cruelty stick in my mind. One involved a child, another a woman in a wheelchair. They were in direct contrast to his tearful reaction when he saw that young road accident victim. Alex could be two different people.
>
> The first incident was at St Peter's Snooker Club in Lurgan where Alex was doing an exhibition. A young lad picked up a programme and asked his dad if he could get Alex to sign it. His dad told him to wait by the toilet because Alex was in there. Then both of them made the mistake of approaching Alex at the urinal. They asked politely if he'd sign. Alex took the programme and said: 'Okay, sure. I can't do any better than this.' He peed all over it, then handed the sodden programme back to the boy saying: 'There you are son. Enjoy the evening.' His father wanted to chin Alex.
>
> The second occasion was at the Waterfront in Belfast where

Ken Doherty staged a magnificent testimonial to raise money for Alex. More than 2,000 people were there. I'm standing with Ken signing autographs and Alex is doing his best to avoid it. There was a big queue. For no reason at all, he walks over to a woman in a wheelchair who must have been in her late eighties and says: 'I don't sign autographs for paraplegics.' Then he marches off to the toilets. She burst into tears. As a consolation, I gave her a photograph of Alex winning the world championship which had been signed by him and Ken. It made her cry even more.

I saw him at the dinner table when a lovely looking girl came over and asked for an autograph as nicely as you possibly could. He told her: 'Fuck off. I'm eating my dinner!' She told him he was the most horrible man she'd ever met. That was Alex. Once he turned, there was nothing you could do. And they called him the People's Champion? No. He never was. To be the People's Champion you have to know the people. You have to be on their wavelength. The people who thought they knew Alex weren't real people. Most of them were drunks. They travelled the country so they could roll around legless and watch him play.

You have to be a family man to be a man of the people. Apart from a couple of occasions, none of his family came to see him. If you were looking for a People's Champion, Jimmy White was your man. He related to people big time. I've seen him in Bangkok surrounded by kids and signing autographs for hours. Alex would have fallen on his sword first. He didn't have the common touch.

People thought they knew Alex but what they believed was a myth. On the rare occasions when he was at peace, he could be a lovely man. And I mean *lovely.* He had a dry sense of humour and was very quick witted. There were times when he was really happy. There were times when he'd pick people out of the audience and get them a vodka and tonic – particularly a district nurse who followed him everywhere for thirty-odd years. She used to come straight from work, still in her uniform. This wasn't his usual behaviour though. Alex was the Alex Higgins Champion. The rest of the world could go screw itself for all he cared.

He didn't have an ounce of religion in him as far as I could see. His first and only time in the cathedral was inside a coffin. The only time I saw him with his mum's bible was at a testimonial evening at the Waterfront when dishing out free tickets to his mates from the Royal. He carried his bible in his trench coat in order to curry sympathy and get free drinks. He'd bring it out, and say a few words about his mother. It worked. People took pity and bought him a rum and coke.

We never fell out but I had to put him to sleep a couple of times, once when he was playing Ray Reardon in the Irish championships. Reardon was 19-2 up in the first to 21. Alex decided to go walkabout in Belfast during the break. That meant calling in at the Royal and a few other bars. I was in Ray's dressing room while watching him slick his hair back with water in the usual style and smartened up for the final countdown. Suddenly, Alex comes crashing in with a stupid announcement: 'Ray, you've been officially rebuked by some of my pals. If I don't win the first four frames tonight I'll . . .'

I didn't let him finish the sentence. I hit him on the jaw and hung him on the back of the door. The tournament director, Bob Kearney, came in. He pushed the door open, bashing the dazed Alex against the wall. He announced: 'Higgins has gone missing.'

I said: 'Don't worry, he'll be hanging around somewhere!'

Bob hurries off and the door swings back on its hinges. There's blood dripping from Alex's nose. Reardon's wondering what to do next. I tell him we'll get First Aid to clean Alex up. In comes this wee woman, takes off Alex's shirt, washes the blood off, then puts it on the blower to dry. Alex regains consciousness and looks at me.

'You fucking hit me you big, fat bastard!'

'I did too, and if you ever try to fix a match in my company, I'll do it again.'

'Lucky you cleaned me up. The boys are coming for you.'

'What boys, Alex?'

'The boys from the Royal.'

'Do you think they scare me? I was a bouncer at the Plaza and the Beehive when they checked in their pick handles before a dance!'

As it turned out, Ray *did* give him four frames to make it more of a spectacle for the fans. Though he was out of his head on booze and who knows what else, Alex still managed breaks of 116 and 90 plus. No brain no pain. Reardon finished it off 21-6.

I wouldn't say the WPBSA had it in for Alex as a body. Some members did but ex-players weren't among them. Reardon never decried Alex in his life. Nor did David Taylor or Rex Williams. He was their bread and butter. They were grateful. I wish I could say the same about Ray Edmonds and Doug Mountjoy. Ray couldn't keep his mouth shut while Alex and Doug fell out after Doug's daughter appeared on page three of *The Sun*. Alex wouldn't stop taunting him. Doug tried to hit back but Alex was too quick with the repartee.

Although she was from the same part of the UK, Ann Yates, the courtesy girl-turned-tournament director had little patience with Alex. He wouldn't let her forget that she started out as a courtesy girl. She in turn treated him with no respect.

We all knew the ban for head-butting Paul Hatherell signalled the beginning of the end for Alex. He knew it too. He deserved the ban but the WPBSA seemed intent on removing his livelihood. There was no way back from a five-month ban and loss of ranking points. Alex lost his credibility. To come crashing down from the one-time world number one to number forty-two was soul-destroying. People talked glibly about Alex losing a few thousand pounds. Who were they kidding? If you're in the top eight, you're pulling £120–150,000 a year in prize money. If you're in the top sixteen, you're looking at £60–70,000. The top thirty-two can expect to win £40–50,000, but the minute you're out of the top thirty-two, you're in cuckoo land. That's where Alex was dumped. All he could hope for was £8–10,000 a year.

Without question, the best match I ever refereed was Alex's 16-15 victory over Steve Davis to win the Coral UK Championships in 1983. Everyone remembers how he was 7-0 down and out of it. What people don't know is that Del Simmons was so furious, he tried to hit Alex during the break. That's completely out of character. He thought Alex wasn't trying. In those first seven frames, Alex didn't once ask me to clean the ball. He just grunted as though he wasn't interested. He was copying his opponent.

Who would blink first? Davis psyched Alex out by not getting the ball cleaned, however many kicks it got. In the second session, Alex changed tack. He asked me to clean the ball every time he came to the table. It signalled that he was on a different mission. It unhinged Davis. Now Alex was making phenomenal breaks – three in the 80s and five centuries. It was the best overall snooker he'd played that year.

Although Steve and Alex didn't have much time for each other, the biggest tension was between Alex and Dennis Taylor. It wasn't a Catholic/Protestant thing. Alex never cared about that. The rivalry and the jealousy on Taylor's part started when they played together as teenagers in the northwest. It continued when Alex won his first world title. Dennis didn't like that. He never won anything until 1985.

Dennis thought he was a better player than Alex. He'd cultivated an English accent while Alex was stuck with his broad south Belfast drawl. And Dennis was good at telling jokes. He made a fortune on the after-dinner circuit. Alex was hopeless at that kind of thing and resented it. Nor did Dennis like it when Alex was trying to get off with his sister. He warned him to keep away. Their uneasy relationship blew up at the world team event in Bournemouth when Alex threatened to have Dennis shot. I was there and Alex was completely out of order.

The row was about sharing the highest break in a match between Ireland and Canada. Alex kept the money for himself when *he* made the highest break three years before. The argument at Bournemouth was really about Alex wanting a cut of the £6,000 before the prize was even won! There were still three tournament matches to go. His team didn't win the break prize anyway.

The point was that Alex had blown everything on the horses and turned nasty when he needed money. Alex needing money can be an unpleasant animal. He loses all reason. It wasn't Dennis who reported it to the press.

Personally, I only get on with Dennis at arm's length. You might think he could charm the birds but he's spent his life caressing that persona. If he hadn't won the world title, he'd still have the persona.'

Although he was ill, Len made a point of going to Alex's funeral and to the memorial dinner in Manchester a few weeks later. He has strong opinions about the way Alex's life ended: 'I was always doubtful about the tooth implants. Why did Alex want teeth to eat all of a sudden? He hardly ever wanted to eat in the forty years I'd known him, teeth or no teeth. There was nothing to stop him taking protein tablets. There was no need to be under-nourished. He just didn't like spending money on something he might not need. That's the top and bottom of it. He thought he could stay alive but he wasn't sure for how long. No-one had the book to tell him.'

14

HE WAS MY HUSBAND

I was sad that he died so young but I have no feelings left for Alex. Neither love nor hate. They disappeared years ago. I was glad I made my peace with him. When they found him, I felt numb. Why did he die alone when his sisters only lived around the corner? That was the question on everyone's lips.

Alex was a large part of my life, whether I like it or not. We had nearly ten years and two children together. We travelled the world, met famous people and had nice things. Against that, he pulled tricks on me, hid money and neglected his family. He left his kids nothing. People would say: 'You and the kids must have done nicely out of the settlement.' I told them it was quite the opposite. I got nothing from the divorce. Everything I got was with the help of my parents, not Alex. I last saw him a few months before he died. I drove him to the airport. Funnily enough, it was the first time since I can remember that we didn't argue. It was really nice. We were like two normal people. He actually gave me a kiss on the cheek and I didn't back off.

It was always Alex who started the arguments, usually after a drink and often about trivial things. I don't think a lasting relationship with him would have been possible for anyone. That's a big statement, but he was a big problem. He could be very selfish – to the extent that nobody else mattered. There was a definite pattern to our relationship. Things would go smoothly for six months, then something in his head would explode. When we *did* get on, it was because I didn't drink. If both partners drink they can rub each other up the wrong way. I think that's what happened with Alex and Siobhan.

Everyone remembers the moment when Alex won the world championship and he called Lauren and me on stage. Some people said I didn't look happy. They were right. I was very *unhappy.* I didn't want to join him. For one thing it was *his* moment, not mine. But there was more to it. I had a sinking feeling. I knew this was the beginning of the end for us. I said to one of the player's wives: 'Here we go. This is where my problems really begin.'

And I was right. Now he was world champion again, he'd be in demand. That meant he'd be away a lot more and missing his home. He was devoted to his little girl but soon he wouldn't be seeing much of her – or me. I knew he'd be lonely and when he was lonely he drank. That could only spell disaster. So behind those pictures of Alex hugging us was a very different story. Just as he was becoming a real family man, the chance of a stable, loving home life was about to drift away. You could say the world title made him and ruined him.

Alex was very good at making up after a scene. He'd either be on his knees begging for forgiveness and promising to turn over a new leaf, or he'd be in floods of tears, desperate to hold things together. It worked every time with me. Jordan's just the same. You could forgive them anything.

I gave Alex several chances to make another go of our marriage but in my heart of hearts I knew it was doomed. Those who say I married him for money are talking nonsense. We were together for nearly ten years – much longer than Alex was with anyone else. That says something. And do you know what? He might have been violent with other women, but he never hit *me* and I never hit him. I felt like it a few times, but we didn't come to blows. The physical aggression in his relationships with Siobhan Kidd and Holly Haise was not part of our marriage.

It hurt to read the story Will Robinson put out on the day of the funeral, that Siobhan was 'the love of Alex's life'. What thoughtless timing. As far as I could tell, Siobhan felt vulnerable and uncertain with Alex. At her request, we met for a long chat when they'd been going out for a while. She told me life was difficult for her. She said Alex still loved me. He used to mention me quite a lot. She wanted to know if we'd ever get back together. I told her not in a million years and whatever she did, not to be soft with him. It didn't seem to me that she had him in shape.

I liked Siobhan. I told Alex he could bring her to my house. It wouldn't have bothered me. In fact I wanted him to be happy with her. He never brought her round though. Usually he just came on his own, or with his driver. There was no warning or checking to see if it was okay. He arrived in the middle of whatever we were doing and often caused another scene. We had to entertain the driver too. That's an example of Alex's selfishness.

He often phoned here in a crisis. We comforted him when he finished with Siobhan. He was feeling low and wanted to see the children. I took them to Bury, where he lived. I saw my gold cutlery in the house and asked for it back. I often wondered what had happened to all my possessions from Delveron House. He had the lot. He wouldn't let me have anything back. I also looked after him when Holly stabbed him. Lauren took the call to say he was badly injured and had been taken to Hope Hospital. She rushed off to see her dad but when she got there, Alex was gone. He'd checked himself out. The consultant was worried that he could lose a lot of blood and die. It was that serious. While we were wondering what to do next, he suddenly turned up at our house. No warning. I made up the sofa and he stayed the night. What else could I do? He said he was frightened because Holly's brothers were after him. Next morning he went on his way again.

Alex used to ring me in the middle of televised matches. You could see him on the phone in the background. He even rang me after the Paul Hatherell head-butt and said it was my fault because I wouldn't have him back. He asked us to support him after his first tournament ban. That was a major downturn in his life. He never recovered. I took the kids to watch him play in the qualifiers at Trentham Gardens. Alex was at the crossroads. His spirit had gone. I realised that if he didn't get his ranking points back, everything would change. He'd lose income. We wouldn't be able to pay the school fees. An awful lot hinged on those qualifiers. It was a shock to see hundreds of snooker players shoulder-to-shoulder in the big hall. Alex hated it. I could see why. Fancy the former world champion having to go through that! He was still trying to get me to go back with him. It wasn't going to happen but I think it helped him that we were there at least.

It's a fact that the two sides of the family don't get on – Lauren, Jordan and me on one side; Alex's sisters on the other. I didn't have much time for his mum either. She was a bitter, twisted alcoholic. Just like her son she underwent a personality change when she drank – and she was always drinking. We didn't like the way the sisters allowed Will Robinson to take charge of the funeral. Lauren and Jordan hardly got a look-in. they even had to battle for Jordan to be a pallbearer! Lauren would have handled things much better. She wanted to handle her dad's funeral but they took charge.

Things between the families weren't always that bad. Alex and I had Jean living with us for a while when she was pregnant. She didn't have two pennies to rub together. Her daughter was born here. Perhaps the Higgins women were jealous of me taking their brother and son away. That's silly if it's true. I'm a real family person. My mum and dad brought us up that way. I tried to include Alex's family as much as possible but they didn't like me. I think they were wary of me because I came from a middle-class background and didn't drink like they did. It really blew up when Lauren was born six and a half weeks premature. Alex's mum begged him to let her come and see her new granddaughter.

He wasn't keen because of his mum's drinking problem. I persuaded him that she had to be allowed to see our first child. She arrived at the house but kept disappearing in the afternoon. She said she was nipping out to the shops but you could smell the alcohol when she came back. Alex had made it a condition of her visit that she kept off the booze. One afternoon she came back legless. I made some remark and she launched herself at me, trying to kick me in the stomach where I had stitches from my Caesarian section. Luckily she missed but Alex jumped on her. She was like a wild animal – arms flailing everywhere. He couldn't hold her. Eventually, my dad and brother-in-law overpowered her. Alex tied her to the chair and the doctor gave her a valium injection. Alex was disgusted. He didn't bother with his mum for quite a while after that.

The way Alex and I came together was funny. It didn't look promising to begin with. Alex made the running. I'd heard from my sister Carol about this unusual guy at the nightclub. She said he was crazily dressed in an overcoat and bowtie and one of those Australian hats with corks dangling from it. He was obviously seeking attention.

Alex made a beeline for one of our friends. He persuaded her to be his cleaner. She wasn't even paid! She told us how chaotic his flat was – littered with clothing and money. I didn't like what

I heard. He'd click his fingers and expect her to come running. Foolishly, she did. Alex didn't give her a penny. He didn't even invite her out for a meal.

I met him about a year later, when I was twenty-two. My first marriage to a computer programmer broke up. I went back to live with my parents and spent a lot of time indoors until Carol invited me to George Best's club, Oscar's, for a rare night out. I had no interest in snooker. I thought it was an old man's game. When Alex walked into the wine bar, I was probably the only one who didn't recognise him. He wasn't used to that.

One of my friends cried: 'Look, Lynn, there's Alex Higgins!' I said: 'So what?' He was wearing a dinner suit and bowtie. I thought to myself who dresses like that in this day and age? He walked over to us like God's gift to women. I'd just come back from a holiday in Austria. He knew a lot about the country so I thought he must have been there. It turned out he'd only read about it.

When it came to my round, I asked my friend what she wanted, Alex dived with: 'Get me a large vodka and tonic.' I told him he could get his own drinks and left him standing there. He was shocked. He kept trying to chat me up but I wouldn't have it. Frankly, I didn't like the look of him. I had to congratulate him on his persistence, though. I told him I worked as a secretary at Manchester Airport. He wanted more details. I told him I worked for Serviceair and immediately wished I hadn't. He kept turning up at my office. My boss was a big snooker fan and allowed Alex to get through security. I couldn't get rid of him.

We were leaving the wine bar to go to a disco. Alex promptly ordered my friend to go and book a taxi and insisted on taking us. While she was away, he asked me out to dinner. I said no thank you. The cab didn't get far before Alex grunted something about wasting his time and jumped out at the traffic lights.

> What kind of bloke offers you a lift, then leaves you to pay the fare? We got out of the taxi and went for a drink. Alex followed us. He asked if I wanted to dance. I told him to go away.

Alex was intrigued. He was glad Lynn worked at the airport. He used it regularly so was bound to see her again. But he couldn't wait that long. He phoned the next day and repeated his dinner invitation. Again the answer was negative. Said Alex: 'Higgins doesn't give in that easily. She resisted for a while but eventually succumbed. They always do.'

Lynn's mother warned her, stay away. *She'd* heard of The Hurricane, even if her daughter hadn't. She'd read about him in the papers and it didn't make very good reading. If he wasn't drunk and disorderly, he was fighting or chasing women. Her advice had the opposite effect. Lynn: 'The more she went on, the more interested I became. It might be fun. I'd had a five-year relationship with a man I met in South Wales where we used to live. Then I met someone, fell madly in love and got married for a year. I was really too young to be tied down. I needed to breathe. Alex came along at just the right – or maybe wrong – time.'

The next twenty years would read like a bad soap. They included the pinnacle of Higgins' career, terrifying rows in front of the kids, arrests, break-ups, a suicide attempt and divorce. Even that wasn't the end of the story. Alex would continue to exert pressure and try to control his ex-wife's life. He'd spy on her, try to influence the kids and even attack an innocent man he thought was her new toyboy! But back to that first date.

> Alex literally whisked me off my feet. We went on a whistle stop tour of Manchester night life. He said he'd take me to the best Chinese restaurant in town. He knew everything there was to know about Chinese food from his visits to Hong Kong. Little

did he know that I was pretty well up on Chinese food. We had some good Chinese friends in town and had recently celebrated their New Year at a much better restaurant than Alex was taking me to but I played along with it.

I asked him to pick me up at eight o'clock but he said he didn't have a car and couldn't drive. Couldn't drive? Everybody drove. I thought he must be joking. He said he never had to make his own way anywhere and would send a taxi for me. I said I'd pick him up at Potters snooker club where he had to practise. I put on a lovely evening gown, expecting an elegant night out on the town. I was in for a shock. Alex was still playing when I got there. He wore a pair of jeans three inches too short and a jumper with a hole in the sleeve. He waved me to sit down and proceeded to show off. He chose the wrong person.

After half an hour of this, he said: 'Right, let's go.' I said: 'Go where? I'm not going anywhere with you looking like that. Goodbye!' I went to walk out but he caught me by the arm and apologised. He said there wasn't time to get home and, in any case, this was all he had apart from the dinner suits he wore for snooker. I had no choice. Off we went like the princess and pauper.

He made up for it, though, taking me to six clubs in an hour. I didn't drink much but he insisted on ordering me vodka in each club. I only drank a couple of them. Finally, we got to the restaurant. That was a real laugh. Alex tried to teach me how to pick up a grain of rice with chopsticks, but he couldn't manage it, however hard he tried. I pretended to be an avid learner until the food arrived. Then I showed him all I knew about chopsticks. He wasn't best pleased. I'd been warned by my friend that Alex thought his word was final. I resisted him every step of the way. It was like a duel.

Lynn had gauged it to perfection. Alex wasn't used to having someone contradict him. Girls allegedly fell at his feet. This one was a handful. Lynn wasn't sure whether there was any future in this liaison. If she'd known that Alex was a married man and had just returned from Sydney where things with his Australian bride were getting heated, she probably wouldn't have gone out with him in the first place.

Alex meanwhile was smitten: 'Lynn wasn't like any other girl I'd been out with. She was stubborn, cynical about the world of showbiz and difficult to impress. She disagreed with almost everything I said and had a wider knowledge than I was used to. I thought I was well up on pop music but Lynn's ex was a guitarist so I was scuppered there too. It's no exaggeration to say I fell head over heels in love on our first date. There's no bigger turn-on than a girl who's not interested. I could tell straight away that there was something between us. It was a mixture of attraction and repulsion which would cause loads of problems in the future. We talked a lot about our families. She told me her father was a keen snooker fan. That was useful information. If I worked on him, I might have a chance.'

Lynn's unsuspecting father Jim would witness more turmoil over the coming years than the average father-in-law could expect in two lifetimes. The young man he was about to provide with a temporary home would turn him off snooker for good. When you're summoned to rescue your daughter and grandchildren from a madman chucking television sets out of the window, and are then forced to make a mercy dash to Majorca where he downs a bottle of pills and leaves a suicide note, you wonder how your offspring ever got into this fateful union. As we shall hear, things were quite different in the early days. It's just that the early days didn't last long. What attracted Lynn to this bizarrely clad show-off then?

'He was so different from anyone I'd ever been out with – doctors, teachers and so on. All very respectable. My first evening with Alex finished at seven o'clock the following morning. I was worried what Mum and Dad would think. Nobody stayed out that late! I dropped Alex off at his flat. He'd earlier invited me in to see some photographs of his family. I thought oops, here we go. I had a bad experience with a dentist who invited me to see his art collection and finished with his hands around my neck in the bedroom, so I told Alex I'd wait in the car while he changed clothes. As it turned out, he was a perfect gentleman. I did go into his flat. He made me a coffee, showed me the photographs and I went home.'

Not being the sort of person to hang around, nor to miss an opening, Alex struck while he thought the iron was hot. The next day, he phoned Lynn's dad and said: 'Mr Avison, I love your daughter.' It was greeted with a stunned silence. Hurricane Higgins bowled over? He hadn't even met the guy. Seen him on TV, yes, but that was a bit different. Within a couple of months, Mr and Mrs Avison were putting him up! The flat Alex shared with Manchester United goalkeeper Alex Stepney was broken in to. It seemed the sensible thing to move in with the woman on whom he had grand designs. He stayed in the spare room for two years.

'It felt good to be part of a family again. I hadn't known it since I was fifteen. Lynn had gone out when I first turned up at her parents' house. Jim offered to take me to the nearest barbers for a shave and brush-up. I didn't want Lynn to see me untidy like on the first date. When I got back, I played snooker with Lynn's kid brother. I can be charming when I want to be.'

Lynn was shocked to see a snooker cue in the hallway when she got home from buying Alex some casual clothes to replace the moth-eaten sweater and undersized jeans. Surely Alex wasn't under the same roof already? Her mum nodded resignedly. They all sat down for tea together and the relationship was underway.

Lynn says: 'There was lots of affection between us. What I liked is that he never made a pass at me. I think that's why we stayed together. He knew I wasn't a pushover like all his other girlfriends.'

But the show had to go on. Although tournament snooker was growing slowly, the exhibition circuit was vibrant. Alex was booked most nights of the week - in more ways than one.

I had other girlfriends but nothing serious. Lynn was free to lead her own life while I was away, but I know she stayed faithful. She was that type of girl. We carried on like this for a year or so with me staying with her parents when I was back in Cheadle and Lynn coming to more and more events with me. It gave her a taste of what a professional snooker player's life is like. In my case, hectic. I had to make hay while the sun shone. She found the schedule as exhausting as I did. We had a row at one venue when Lynn and her cousin started laughing during the match. I could hear this childish giggling and looked around to find that the person disturbing my concentration and spoiling it for everyone else was my girl! She wasn't interested in the game of snooker, you see.

I put my cue down and marched over to her seat. I asked her if she was with me or against me. Lynn still wouldn't shut up so I sent for the doorman and said: 'Throw that woman out!' She told him she was quite capable of leaving on her own and left. I realised I'd been a bit harsh, dropped my cue to the floor and ran to fetch her back. She never did that again.

It was very useful having Lynn to drive me to exhibitions, though it almost cost us our lives one time. I was scheduled to appear in the Yorkshire Dales so we set off from London in fog and thick snow. The car blew up on the way so we had a long delay while we hired another. Now it was a race against time. We

> ended up high on a narrow road with a sheer drop on one side. I'm not the calmest passenger at the best of times. While Lynn twisted and turned through the snow, I was getting frantic. One false move and we were in the valley! She did brilliantly and we got there only half an hour late. They couldn't believe we'd made it in those conditions and handed each of us a large brandy to calm what was left of our nerves. Then they told us the road we'd come on was officially closed because it was unfit for traffic!

It's extraordinary that Alex never learned to drive. 'My father didn't teach me' was a lame excuse. He once tried to make up for it by buying a lawnmower to drive around the garden of Delveron House, the Cheshire mansion he bought to make another fresh start with Lynn. He got a pal to take him to an auction in Nantwich where lot 143 had caught his eye. He thought he'd be home and hosed only to find that by an extraordinary coincidence, the person bidding against him was Tony Knowles! The player who'd been partly responsible for introducing Alex to the northern snooker scene all those years ago outbid The Hurricane and drove off on the mower. 'Bastard!' shouted Alex as they fell about laughing.

He did actually ask Lynn to give him a driving lesson before they were married. She remembers it well: 'We put "L" plates on the new Renault Alex bought and set off through the centre of Didsbury. I didn't like the look of the traffic and told him it was too busy to risk a lesson. He insisted so we changed places. It was going all right until he turned into the main road. We were approaching a halt sign but Alex hadn't seen it. I shouted: "Stop!" By the time he slammed on the brakes it was too late. A van hit us on the driver's side. We pushed the car over to the side of the road and went into a Chinese restaurant which just happened to be nearby. They recognised him and brought him a brandy. The repair bill for the van came to more than £500. Alex never bothered to learn again.'

To be honest, it was probably just as well. Imagine this time bomb of nervous energy on the road in the dead of night with vodkas swilling around inside him! He'd have been banned within weeks. Britain's motorists were spared a potential horror. Alex settled for being one of life's passengers. Shoes off, feet on the dashboard, fag in hand. Lynn was one of the first of a team of volunteers to escort him around the country.

'Alex didn't care about distances. He bought me a Daimler and within a couple of hours of taking delivery, said: "Shall we go to Paris tonight?" He made it sound very romantic and invited our friends Geoff and Helen Lomas to travel with us. It was Paris via Hull where he had an exhibition to play first! We left Hull at midnight and caught the ferry from Dover at 6.00 am. Before I knew it, I was on the Champs Elysées in a car I wasn't used to. The others were asleep. I shouted to Alex that if he didn't wake up and give me some support, we'd all be killed. He mumbled 'You're okay' and went back to sleep. Eventually I found a lovely hotel in the centre of Paris. It was seven o'clock in the evening but Alex said he wanted another hour's sleep. I blew my top. I'd been on the road for twelve hours and *he* wanted another hour's sleep? It ruined the weekend. He tried to woo me with a red rose he bought from the hotel lobby. I told him where he could shove it. I stayed in my £150 room all night while they went out. Who was more stubborn - him or me?'

The more you hear, the less likely Lynn and Alex were to settle down to a contented family life. In fact she'd landed herself with the most impossible-to-live-with partner she could have found. Nothing could have prepared her for this. It's a tribute to her that they stayed together for the best part of a decade. None of his small coterie of close friends, Jimmy White included, could stomach him that close for that long. What made Lynn, an intelligent, level-headed young woman, think she could hold a tiger by the tail? She explained.

Alex wasn't like that to begin with. It embarrasses me now that people think I married a nutter. He wasn't. He was a hands-on husband. He helped me clean the house and did some cooking. If I asked him to pop down to the shop for a tin of tuna, he'd come back with five. He used to go shopping with me until it became unbearable in the supermarket with people asking for his autograph.

Alex was over the moon when Lauren was born. It was as if life for him was complete now he had a child of his own. Things felt right. He even changed her nappies. I honestly thought I'd chosen the right man. Alex without drink was the quietest, nicest person you could meet. I really mean that. Looking back over all those difficult years, I still feel that about him. Unfortunately, he had an intolerance to alcohol. It flicked a switch. He knew I wouldn't stay with him if he was drinking. I left him for six months to make that point. He didn't learn his lesson.

Eventually it dawned on him that bringing up babies was hard work. By the time Jordan came along, the novelty had worn off. You didn't find him changing nappies any more. For the time being, though, he was as good as gold. Sometimes I got frustrated when he sat around in his dressing gown doing crosswords. He'd sit quietly for hours, minding his own business. In many ways he was a loner. Though he wasn't allowed to drink at home, he'd occasionally slip vodka into his milk.

I know it's hard to imagine after all that came afterwards, but in the early days we were like any normal family. He tried to get home in the evenings. We had Christmas with my mum and dad and things were fine. We'd pop out for lunch together. We'd take Lauren to the park or the theatre or the circus. We bought her school uniform together. I'd have my parents round for tea. It was normal. In those days, Alex listened to me. He usually claimed he knew better but I'd hear him offering my opinions to other people as if they were his own. He often said how much he enjoyed being at home. He'd travel long distances at night just to be here.

Can you believe he actually ate food in those days? He loved simple, basic meals. His favourite was mince with carrots, potatoes, onions and tinned peas. It was a change from the junk food he had to grab between matches, or the late night Chinese meals he grew tired of.

The Alex of the last fifteen years before he died was someone I didn't recognise – and I don't just mean physically. You couldn't talk to him about ordinary things. He was in a different space somewhere. Part of me felt sorry for him but the other part remembers the nasty, spiteful things he did. You can't put those to the back of your mind.

His best qualities were his fatherly instincts, his sense of fun and his intelligence. If he'd had the schooling, Alex could have been a high-flyer. We had many laughs and he *was* romantic before we got married. He used to take me to this lovely French restaurant called Elysées. We'd have a candlelit supper and he'd often buy me one of the antique pieces of jewellery they kept in a glass case by the door. He liked things that glittered. They must have seen him coming. He couldn't walk out without buying something – not because I wanted it but because it gave him pleasure.

It *sounded* romantic when he phoned me from Trinidad to say he'd bought me a ticket to join him. He was playing exhibition games for ShellBP. He said I'd love it. The weather was marvellous and we'd be staying at a fabulous hotel once used by the Queen. When I got off the plane it was pouring with rain! July's the wet season in the Caribbean. Two blokes picked me up at the airport and we drove for hours in an open-topped cart. When we got to the hotel, there was newspaper stuffed in holes in the windows and the swimming pool was empty. It was just like Fawlty Towers. I asked them when the Queen stayed there. It was 1953, the Coronation year. I bet there was glass in the windows then!

We stayed three or four days but I wasn't happy. There was nothing to do. Alex played snooker at night and the highlight of the day was watching Spencer, the house cat, chasing lizards. Alex prodded a few out for him. I told him I was going home if we couldn't find a nicer place. We moved to the Hilton in Port of Spain, then Fig Tree Bay for an extra week.

The beach was full of muscle-bound West Indians doing exercises and showing off. Alex was puny by comparison. He was ten and a half stone wet through. He looked so funny with his skinny, white legs. He directed me away from the torsos. I suggested a swim in the sea. He said he couldn't swim. I was appalled. I'd never had a boyfriend who couldn't drive and couldn't swim. He refused to come into the water. Then he saw a length of rope on the beach. It gave him the idea to tie one end to the base of a palm tree and the other around his waist. Then he waded in. It was so embarrassing!

I persuaded him to take a trip in a glass-bottomed boat. We were in our swimwear admiring the coral but the chaps in the boat seemed more intent on admiring me. Two of them held me in the water to see the fish. Alex was fuming. I told them my boyfriend could do with a little help so they picked him up and carried him bodily across the water. He didn't see the funny side. And then he got sunburnt, so I told him to put sun cream on. He said: 'No, I'm fine. I know what I'm doing.' He ended up with sunstroke and had to spend three days in bed peeling and being sick. Did I say romantic?

The relationship was suffering because of the travelling we both had to do. I gave up my job at the airport because I was missing so much time. Most of the places I drove Alex to were

> working men's clubs. They were seedy and no place for a woman. I didn't like the lifestyle and I didn't like the hangers-on. It was all drink and groupies. Alex was increasingly moody. I told him I didn't want to go with him any more and went on holiday to the south of France with my parents. While I was there I bumped into an old friend.
>
> His mum and dad ran a business in Cannes. They wanted to give me a flat to stay on through the summer. It wasn't a proper relationship but it seemed a perfect way of breaking things off with Alex. I came home to sort a few things out before taking them up on their offer. Alex was terribly upset and begged me to change my mind. I realised I still loved him, despite his moodiness. He urged me to get a divorce. Then he went to see his solicitor to sort out his own divorce from Cara. While we were there he paid for mine as well. It was all over very quickly. We drifted into marriage. It seemed the natural step. I'd insisted on a long 'engagement' period because my first experience of marriage was too hurried. I wasn't going to make the same mistake again.

This was Alex's take on it: 'I had to toe the line for the first time in my life. Sooner or later I was going to have to make a decent woman of her. We got married with all the works – big white wedding, four bridesmaids and a page boy. I'd had years of gallivanting. What I needed was a base, a home, a wife and before long, hopefully, children. I've always loved kids. At the age of thirty-one, I decided it was time to have some of our own.'

In-laws became a problem. Lynn's mum, Betty, didn't like Alex at all. She tolerated him for Lynn's sake. Lynn sensed disapproval from the Irish branch when she accompanied Alex to a tournament in Dublin and met them for the first time. Alex had an easy win over Ray Reardon but then the problems began for Lynn.

I went to the ladies toilet. Alex's mum came in after me. They didn't know I was there. I overheard Elizabeth say: 'That fucking bitch is taking my son away!'

I couldn't believe my ears. I hadn't heard women talk like that before. I broke down in tears. Alex could see I was upset and gave his mother a severe telling off and said I'd done more for him than she'd ever realise. I think they turned against me because I was smart and good looking and didn't belong to their world. I suppose I had replaced them. Before I came along, they'd take him to tournaments and enjoy the limelight. They liked to be high profile in the audience. I was naive. I didn't know the front row seats were reserved for them. Now Alex asked me to take their place. I didn't want to. There was too much jealousy.

When he first took me to Belfast to meet his family, his mother wouldn't even talk to me. When we were introduced, she mumbled: 'So you're another one of his floozies, are you?'

I tried to mend fences by inviting them to England for Lauren's christening. We paid nearly a thousand pounds to bring his sister Isobel and her daughter Julie over from Australia for Christmas. I was never going to be accepted, whatever I did. Judging by their coldness at Alex's funeral, nothing had changed in thirty years.

My fears about problems in our marriage after Alex won the world title were justified. He went to London more often, visiting the night spots and mixing with a different crowd. He was riding high and full of himself. At times, I was desperate to walk out of the relationship but he'd say: 'You can't walk out on me. I'm the world champion.'

Like a fool, I stayed. I had to find out from friends what he was up to. He didn't bother to communicate with me. We loved

> separate lies after I discovered from another snooker player that Alex had been having an affair with a girl called Angie Gold. That was the absolute end for me. I began going to bed early and taking Lauren with me.

Alex: 'Left to my own devices, I was bound to wander from the straight and narrow. I'm not a monk! When love and intimacy disappear at home, what's a red-blooded male supposed to do? My wife had turned to stone. She always had Lauren in bed with her. That's where my late nights in front of the video recorder began. I was a stranger in my own house. My form suffered. Practice was by remote control. I couldn't concentrate. Lynn went to stay with her parents. I came home to an empty house with kids' toys strewn everywhere.'

Alex became a recluse, occasionally wandering down to the village pub at lunchtime but heading home and feeling sorry for himself after the first pint. Needless to say, his game was disintegrating. He was down to one meal a week. His staple diet was lager, tea and cigarettes - up to sixty a day. He telephoned Isobel in Queensland. The two kept in regular contact but this time Alex pleaded with her to intervene: 'Please will you tell Lynn I love her and want her back, but don't say I put you up to it.'

Lynn softened under a barrage of tears, apologies and promises. She agreed to give the marriage one last try. The couple went to Oliver Reed's villa in Majorca to find a way through their problems. They took Lauren with them. Jordan stayed with his grandparents. Within a few days, grandfather Jim was in Majorca himself, answering an SOS from Lynn. The attempted reconciliation backfired disastrously - and almost fatally.

Majorca was cool and windy. The mood was dark. Lauren was into everything, as toddlers are while Alex grew more and more fretful. Alex bought champagne to toast their togetherness but

Lynn accused him of being an alcoholic. His hopes and his world were slowly collapsing. Tension exploded when Alex suggested they join another couple on their boat. Lynn refused to leave her daughter with a babysitter.

'What came next was scary. He pulled out a knife and held it to his throat. I was terrified. I felt as though I was being held hostage. We'd gone on holiday at his request to see if we could sort out our differences, not to go on a boat trip and abandon Lauren. I could see straight away that he only wanted to be a family man when it suited him, which was every now and then. Five minutes in Majorca proved to me that it was the same crafty old Alex. There was a bottle of nerve tablets by the bed. He had them when we split up. He suddenly announced that he was sick and tired of everything and swallowed the tablets while drinking champagne.'

On his way out of the bedroom, Alex scribbled a suicide note: 'Now I've ended it all. I leave everything to Lynn Ann Higgins.'

Then he ran off, saying he was going to the bar down the road. If Lynn wanted to call a doctor, it was up to her. He didn't care. To add to this picture of misery, Lauren was being sick. Lynn continues the story.

> I panicked. I didn't see his note so I didn't know where he'd gone. I was driving the car with one hand and holding Lauren with the other. There weren't any seatbelts. We got to the harbour and I found Alex unconscious in the bar. I ordered an ambulance to take him to the main hospital in Palma. I checked into a hotel nearby and called my dad who came out on the next flight. The hospital was dirty. They put Alex on a life support machine. They asked me what he'd taken. I'd forgotten to take the bottle with me and tried to make then understand what tranquillisers were.

> It was touch-and-go whether he'd live. The doctors told me to prepare for the worst. I sat by his bedside, praying that he'd regain consciousness. How could I ever tell Lauren that her daddy committed suicide while we were on holiday? Alex was in hospital for forty-eight hours and Del Simmons had an air ambulance on standby. My father looked after Lauren. Alex pulled through but, according to the doctor, he'd come within ten minutes of dying. I went back to the villa to pack our things then got a call from the hospital saying he'd ripped the drip from his arm and run away! Somehow he'd got back to the villa when I was out, grabbed his passport and flown home without telling anyone.

Alex's version of his escape from Palma is straight out of *Mr Bean*: 'Running was beyond me but The Hurricane still managed to evade his pursuers. I had a head start on them, though I felt dizzy. I figured the last place they'd look would be in the hospital grounds so I doubled back and hid behind the shrubs. The nausea was bad. I lit up a cigarette. I only had a few pesetas on me so I had to get to the bank for money to buy my return ticket. I also had to get my passport from the villa without being seen.'

Lynn felt sorry for him. How could she leave him in that state? She promised to consider going back with him if he'd get professional help. Alex checked into Cheadle Royal, a mental hospital. Needless to report, therapy sessions failed to float his boat and he checked out after two days: 'On Day Two, I walked into the room and they were doing anagrams. I took one look and told the psychiatrist it was a joke. I was leaving. Ta-ta! I didn't pay the bill because one of the hospital staff tipped off the papers that I was having treatment. They apologised but I told them where to stick their £400!'

It's impossible to verify, but his family think this was the first time the name Alex and the word schizophrenia appeared on the same card. He wasn't there long enough for an official diagnosis, but doctors seemed to think his behaviour pattern was abnormal and clinically rooted. Despite his refusal to be treated, Lynn decided to go back to her husband. Things held together long enough for Alex to beat Steve Davis in the final of the Coral UK Championships in 1983. Considering he was in a self-induced coma only a month earlier, it was an incredible effort. That was the nature of Alex Higgins – from the abyss of despair to the summit of happiness in the blink of an eye. Only his manager, his wife and her parents knew anything about the crisis in Majorca.

Lynn had moved back with him shortly after returning from holiday. She was frightened he might try to take his life otherwise. The effect was immediate. She cooked some of his favourite mince and casseroles, he started eating again and his weight improved. So did his urge to practise. Eight hours a day at the Masters Club in Stockport was the sentence he imposed on himself. It was severe. Alex needed an audience to perform his best, but he stuck at the practice routine. He got his audience at Preston Guildhall in that memorable final.

He couldn't have had a worse start. The focus which took him to the final seemed to desert him once he was there. At the end of the first session, the scoreboard read: Davis 7 Higgins 0. Lynn was organising her daughter's birthday party at the time.

> While I was pushing the trolley around Sainsbury's, I overheard someone saying Alex was 7–0 down. I thought: 'Oh God, what do I say when he phones me?' I couldn't get home fast enough. I told him not to worry. Just relax and play his normal game. His reply astonished me: 'What are you talking about? I'm going to win!' I'd never heard him so confident. The press were knocking

> the door down to get pictures of Lauren's party. They wanted the image of my daughter enjoying herself while her dad suffered. I knew their tricks by now. All I could think of was getting the party games over as fast as possible so I could get to Preston.

Lynn needn't have worried. Plenty of well-wishers visited Alex's dressing room, but the crucial visit was from Del Simmons and Rex Williams. After the suicide attempt, Del was more apprehensive than ever about the potential damage to Alex of a shattering defeat. So was Rex. He handed Alex a half pint glass containing five vodkas with a topping of Coca Cola and urged him to have a sip before the second session. Alex said he didn't need vodka because he was already on Mackeson for its sugar content. Rex and Del insisted. Alex obeyed and took the 'medicine' in with him. He beat Davis 16–15. From that day on, he referred to his helpers as Doctor Rex and Doctor Del. Lynn watched the triumphant finale.

'I was so thrilled and so proud of him. The image of him lying so pathetic in that Spanish hospital bed flashed across my mind and my heart went out to him. At the trophy presentation, people were urging me to go onto the floor with him like last time but Alex shook his head. It didn't make any difference. I was virtually pushed into his arms. I felt certain the victory was down to Lauren, Jordan and me. Alex was secure again after our nightmare in Majorca. He was as happy as I've ever seen him – and that includes the world championship.'

As was his wont, Alex soon plumbed the depths of despair again. This time there would be no turning back. No happy ending. Maybe there were too many demons in his head for that ever to be the case.

Lynn says: 'I still don't know what to make of Alex. He was several people rolled into one. Sensitive and caring at times but vicious at others. He could be generous with money, then snatch it back off me when we fell out. When I left him for the second time, he confiscated a diamond watch he bought for me in Australia. He could have made life better for all of us by coming home from tournaments and exhibitions like other players did. It wasn't true that he was always on the road and working. In the latter years he had a lot of time between events. The fact that he chose to play golf instead of bringing up his kids is his fault, not snooker's. I tried to reason with him but he wouldn't see it. He knew best. If he'd come home, gone to bed and had a decent night's sleep he could have enjoyed breakfast with the kids and taken them to school.'

Alex couldn't accept that line of thinking. It was the familiar story of a professional man believing his partner didn't understand the pressures of work, and of a neglected wife believing that 'pressure of work' was an excuse to be unfaithful. They both had a point. Finding the middle ground was an impossible task for Mr and Mrs Higgins. This was Alex's reasoning: 'Lynn didn't understand that you can't just switch off after a match. It's all about adrenalin. I'm on a sort of high, more so than most players because of the way I'm made and the way I play. I couldn't just go to bed with a mug of chocolate like Lynn seemed to think.'

Superficially, the couple were back together, Jordan was growing up and Lauren was a bright, lively little girl. Because his daughter hadn't known any different, Alex's non-appearances at family events didn't unduly trouble her. However, the raging arguments did. Before long, she'd witness the mother and father of marital disputes. It's a memory that still troubles her today. In the meantime, her parents ticked over, nothing more. Lynn's decision to pardon Alex after Majorca made little lasting impact. He soon reverted to his selfish old ways.

We led separate lives. Me and the children on one side, Alex and his cronies on the other. The doting father I saw when Lauren

> was born quickly disappeared. Jordan never got the same attention. I gave Alex plenty of latitude while I brought up the kids. What I couldn't take was his awful temper. It was useless trying to discuss anything with him. He'd fly off the handle at the slightest excuse, then think he could make it up the following day.
>
> He bought me a Mercedes after one blazing row. As if that could solve anything! He frightened me after that win against Davis. He was full of pent-up aggression. He accused me of spending all his money. He told people he'd be well off it wasn't for me. Yet he's the one who spent £8,000 on a diamond. I told him the ring was too pretentious. He should take it back. Is that the behaviour of a greedy wife?

Alex went way beyond £8,000 in his latest attempt to break this descending spiral. He'd spotted a £235,000 house and grounds in the stockbroker village of Mottram St Andrew. Lynn was persuaded to take a drive past the house. Alex asked her to pull into the driveway. The house was empty so they looked in the windows. Alex's eye was immediately taken by the oak-panelled snooker room: 'I astonished Lynn by asking her if she wanted to live in Delveron House. I turned on the charm and before she knew it, we were making a fresh start.'

Lynn liked the house and hoped they could work it out. When they split up for good, Alex accused her of forcing him to buy it! He was very good at twisting the evidence. For a time, though, things looked more promising. Alex promised to cut down his commitments and stop drinking. Fat chance!

> He imagined I had all I wanted in this magnificent house with a two-acre garden. It was awful. The house was so isolated the kids didn't see their friends. People thought I had it made. Alex

> said I didn't know I was born. That was rich coming from him. How could he claim snooker was a hard life? What about men who spent their lives underground? It was Alex who didn't know he was born.

The storm was gathering. The blow-up came one day when Lynn caught her husband messing about with the Spanish au pair, Daniella. She heard Daniella leave the house. Alex went upstairs to say he was popping down to the pub for a quick one. Lynn accused him of going to meet the au pair. Alex flew into a rage and stormed out. Alex always maintained his innocence but here's how Lynn saw it.

> I heard Alex come back with Daniella. He said: 'Make me a coffee, Daniella', then whispered: 'Come into the snooker room, I've got something to show you.' She said: 'Are you sure your wife can't hear us?'
>
> I sneaked through to the dining room to listen. The au pair said she thought someone was at the door. Alex came running through to find me and blew his top. He said he was showing Daniella his cue. I said: 'Since when have you shown au pairs your snooker cue?' He went berserk. I ran upstairs, grabbed Lauren and locked both of us in her bedroom. We cowered in the bed while he smashed the windows in the door with his golf club. Lauren was screaming and clinging onto me. I heard Alex throw the television set through a bedroom window out in to the garden. He was wrecking the place. I called the police and my dad. I was worried sick that Dad would get there first and walk into Alex's fury.

Luckily, the police beat Jim Avison to it. Five officers dived on Alex and took him to Macclesfield police station where he was questioned, then locked up for two hours. They charged him with breach of the peace. In the early hours, he was driven back to an empty house. Lynn and the children had gone, this time for good. The divorce staggered on for five years and cost Lynn £70,000. True to his name, The Hurricane soon had his new girlfriend, Siobhan, moving in.

Out of their joint account, Lynn bought the house she now occupies in Heald Green near Stockport. She got it with a £14,000 deposit and eventually took out court orders to prevent Alex coming with fifty yards of her. Access to the children was a constant sore. Alex turned up regardless, quizzed the children about boyfriends their mother might have, threatened to withhold school fees if he wasn't allowed to see them and spied on his ex-wife from across the road. On one famous occasion, he forced his way into the house and attacked a young visitor. Lynn:

> I'd asked this chap from over the road to programme Lauren's new computer because we couldn't get it to work properly. Alex found out about it somehow. That's what he was like. You could change your mobile number and he'd have the new one in minutes. I don't know how he did it. He burst into the house and accused me of having a toyboy. He went for the poor chap, then grabbed a saucepan out of the kitchen and smashed the windscreen of his car parked outside. It was a ridiculous performance. He even accused me of being high on drugs. I've never taken drugs in my life. The guy who'd come to mend the computer dived into the cupboard under the stairs to avoid trouble because Lauren was hysterical. She pleaded with him to hide. Next thing I know, the *News of the World* ran a story about 'Toyboy found in cupboard'. I've never been so embarrassed. I daren't leave the house for what the neighbours might be thinking and saying. I sued the *News of the World* for £100,000.

Alex was permanently on my case, even when he was having a high old time with Siobhan. I couldn't make friends with anyone and feel comfortable. One evening I was at a restaurant in Rusholme, not far from where he and Siobhan lived. My mum and sister had organised a curry evening. Suddenly Alex walked past the window and saw me inside. He came in and asked what the hell I was doing. I said: 'Eating, what do you think I'm doing?'

'You shouldn't be out. Get home and look after the kids!'

He made a terrific scene. He even ordered the staff to throw me out. In the end, they threw *him* out. He was still ranting and raving. That was the evening Siobhan locked him in the flat and he jumped out and broke his ankle.

He had this kind of power over people. Or he thought he had. I haven't remarried because I wanted to give the children the family life they didn't have with their father. I didn't want to bring another man into the equation. I didn't want someone else telling my kids what to do. In any case, it would only create more problems with Alex. I had panic attacks because of the way he had me watched. Men don't interest me any more. Don't get me wrong, I'm not interested in women either. Lauren and Jordan are my world.

Lauren and Alex's sisters have tried to retrieve all his lost belongings. As befits someone who never had a permanent home, there are bits of furniture, clothing, trophies, medals and personal belongings all over the place. One of his old betting slips fetched £2,000 at auction so who can gauge the commercial, let alone the sentimental, value of his paraphernalia? Lynn thinks Alex put two Lowry paintings from Delveron House into storage when they split up. Is one of them the painting Siobhan gifted to Michael Gaffney, their mutual friend in Dublin? They suspect that Alex failed to keep up the payments for furniture he kept in storage. Finding the stuff now might require the services of Hercule Poirot!

One item, however, is in Lynn's loft. It's the famous blue case he dragged upstairs during one of his flying visits. Alex begged them to keep an eye on it because it 'contains a lot of important things'. Lynn peeped under the lid from time to time but couldn't bring herself to go through the case until six months after he died: 'It's full of bills, receipts and other documents. There are loads of newspaper cuttings too, especially about women. There's one about a well-known woman astrologer. She and Alex were supposed to be 'just good friends'. From what I've read of the love letters she sent him, they were a bit more than that!'

Perhaps there's a sequel to this book – *The Secrets of the Blue Case*.

15

HE WAS MY CLIENT

Charlie, the Timeshare King

It was a hectic day in Charlie Hawley's office. Everybody wanted to escape the wet English spring for a dose of vitamin D. Charlie answered the phone for the umpteenth time that afternoon.

'Hello, Gold Club Holiday Apartments.'

'Hello, I'm the manager of Alex Higgins.'

'And I'm Jack the Ripper. What can I do for you?'

Charlie winked at his secretary. A hoax call was just what he didn't need.

'Alex has heard about your apartments and would like to book one.'

Charlie paused. Maybe the caller was serious after all. He said his name was Doug Perry. It didn't ring any bells. Charlie decided to play along with it.

'Tell him to call in. We're open all day.'

'Okay, thanks.'

Charlie thought that was the last he'd hear of it. But the phone rang again a few minutes later.

'Hello, babes. Alex Higgins here. Are you Charlie? I've just arrived in Alderley Edge. Be with you in half an hour.'

Indeed it *was* Alex Higgins and this was the start of an on-off friendship and professional relationship lasted twenty years. I say on-off because that was the only relationship you could have with Alex. Half the time he'd be great company and a passport to smart places, for the rest of the time he'd either disgust you with his attitude or drive you to distraction with his selfish demands.

Alex's opportunism wasn't confined to the snooker table. He liked people who might be of use to him – and he used them mercilessly. Charlie wasn't to know it but he too would fall into that trap. He couldn't have imagined that, a mere twelve months later, a distraught Alex would grip him by the hand and say: 'Please help me, Chas. I think I'm going mad. I haven't got many friends and I upset people. What's the matter with me?'

But in the spring of 1988, Charlie Hawley, timeshare operator and ex-Grenadier guard, was flattered to get a visit from The Hurricane. He showed up five hours late with a gorgeous blonde on his arm. It was Siobhan Kidd. Says Charlie:

> You could tell he was besotted with her. The first thing he did was ask me to drive the pair of them to Rawtenstall. It took ages. When we got there, Alex said he was sorry but he had no money. Would I accept a microwave oven instead? He presented me with the biggest oven you've ever seen. I told him I didn't need a microwave and not to worry about payment.
>
> We spent a couple of hours laughing and joking in the small terraced cottage he shared with Siobhan. Next day they were on their way to my timeshare apartments in Puerto Cabopino. That's where they filmed *El Dorado*.
>
> I admit I was star-struck by Alex. Although snooker wasn't my sport, I knew all about him. Didn't everybody? He was the only reason I'd ever watch the most boring game on the planet. Who wants to see two old men knocking balls about for three hours?

Alex was having a difficult time with his agent, Doug Perry. He always had difficult times with agents, whether it was Dennis

Broderick, Del Simmons, Howard Kruger or – wait for it – Charlie Hawley. Extraordinary though it sounds, Chas, the chap he met out of the blue, would become Alex's marketing manager. He laughs when he tells me, not quite believing he took on the most unmanageable sportsman who'd ever lived. And by this time, he was having trouble just living.

'He wanted me to get rid of Doug Perry. He was a nice, genuine guy. Who was I to get rid of anyone? Because Doug was in London, though, I ended up running a lot of Alex's errands – taking him to and from appointments, collecting his washing, that sort of thing.'

Eventually, Alex dispensed with Perry and persuaded Charlie to be his minder. They signed a contract to that effect. That was Charlie's first mistake. There are thankless tasks and hopeless ones. This was in the second category. Alex was bankrupt, so what was the value of a contract? He'd also been abandoned by the woman he wanted to marry and was about to be banned from snooker for twelve months after hitting Colin Randle, a press officer at the World Championships – and threatening to have Dennis Taylor shot by paramilitaries. The self-destruct mechanism was in its advanced stage. However, Alex behaved impeccably on his first trip to Cabopino.

'I gave him apartment J61 which is a big three-bed place. I went with him. He stayed for three to four weeks the first time. He kept himself to himself. He got up in the morning and read his papers. He was brilliant. I liked him because he seemed calm. There were no flare-ups at that stage. He could see I had a bit of umph and might be able to help him. If he could get to know someone who didn't grab, grab, grab, it was valuable to him. People are still grabbing now he's dead.'

One of Charlie's first ventures was a sell-through video called *I'm No Angel* which both parties believed would go some way towards re-establishing Alex's reputation. He'd make £5,000 out of the deal, though Charlie had to be careful because of Alex's bankruptcy order. A local company, Swan Films of Wilmslow, did a good job in trying circumstances. Alex was always difficult to produce and his relationship with Siobhan was rocking badly. Says Charlie: 'He wanted the best of both worlds – to keep hold of her but to be out drinking with the boys whenever he felt like it. Siobhan just had to accept it. He'd roll back in a shocking state. No relationship can progress like that. He was the same with Lynn. It was obvious to me that those two loved each other, but Alex couldn't switch off after tournaments and exhibitions. He'd tell you how he used to come home from playing snooker to play with the kids. That was nonsense. He was in the bar till 2.00 am.'

Charlie pressed on with the filming as Alex drifted out of his love affair with Siobhan and took up with Holly Haise, a single mother who lived in Didsbury. 'Holly was very pleasant but this was yet another volatile relationship. She had a little girl. I'd either drop Alex off at her house or pick him up from there. She came to Belfast and Dublin with us when we were making the video. I only knew her for a year. She and Alex had some fun but they never seemed very close to me. I remember he took her to the States. They hired a helicopter in New York. Alex tried to get the pilot to land so they could pick up a McDonalds! He stayed at Holly's sometimes. He kept some of his clothes there but it was a strange affair. I had to calm things down when they were chucking plates at each other. I'm not surprised she ended up stabbing him.'

While making *I'm No Angel*, Charlie met Alex's great drinking pal, Oliver Reed. They'd struck up an instant friendship at a party thrown by Keith Moon, the Who drummer. Although Oliver was a good friend who kept in touch with Alex during his cancer treatments, he treated him like a plaything and Alex always came off worse in their drunken horseplay. He paid dearly for visits to

Oliver's luxury pads in Ireland and Guernsey. They almost cost him his life.

Charlie recalls his first meeting with Oliver: 'We'd been celebrating Alex's mum and dad's wedding anniversary and were due in Dublin the next day for an appearance on the *Gay Byrne Show*. It was a late night show, so I decided to give it a miss and catch up on some sleep. A figure suddenly appears at the bedroom door, blocking out the light. It's Oliver. He bellows: 'Charlie Hurley, ex-Grenadier guard, we're off to the show. Are you coming?' I declined and climbed into bed, hoping I didn't get the treatment. It was a short respite because the next day was Oliver's birthday. He insisted I change my flight back to Manchester and join him and Alex to celebrate. I spent a couple of hours drinking champagne with them in a Dublin restaurant, then made my apologies and left. Oliver gave me such a bear hug I could hardly breathe and Alex gave me a bottle of brandy from Oliver's collection. I asked the taxi driver if he'd pick Alex and Oliver up from the restaurant in about fifteen minutes time. He said: 'Those two? Not fucking likely!'

Apart from the occasional trip to Cabopino, Charlie lost contact with his client until 2008, two years before he died. Then he received an urgent call from Jimmy White's manager to say that Alex was supposed to be appearing at an exhibition in Bolton but was so ill they feared for his life.

> I said I'd be right over. I'd never seen anyone so undernourished in my life. If anyone really cared about him, they should have put him in a rest home, put him on a drip and got some flesh back on his bones. He looked like a 'messing rep', which is an old army term. He said: 'I've left you something in my will, babes.'
>
> 'Don't talk like that, Alex.'
>
> 'I want to go to Cabopino and end it all.'

> 'No way! I'm not clearing up your mess. You're a fighter. Get on with it.'
>
> Alex laughed but the situation wasn't funny. He was very low. He was due in Belfast soon to have his gums checked. That thought didn't appeal to him much. The evening was a charade. People still wanted to play a frame with Alex but he wasn't fit to be there at all. Watching him trying to knock snooker balls around was excruciating. He kept giving me a hug and holding out his hands to show how steady they were. Every time the balls clicked he jumped like a frightened rabbit. He sat there signing photographs of himself twenty years ago. I was embarrassed for him. And I wasn't the only one.

Charlie would have a large part to play in the tragic episode of Alex and his tooth implants.

Louis, the Master Tailor

Every smart dresser in Ireland knows Louis Copeland. His gentleman's outfitters in Capel Street, Dublin, is legendary. It was started by Louis senior in 1953. Pictures of his customers adorn the walls. They include Pearce Brosnan, Kevin Spacey, Tom Jones and President Clinton. Louis owes part of his reputation to Alex Higgins, but Alex Higgins owes his entire wardrobe to Louis. Whatever Alex wanted Alex got - free of charge and whenever it suited him. This is Louis's story.

> Our friendship developed after he picked up a couple of suits from me when after winning the world title in 1982. Every time Alex came to Dublin I gave him clothes, mostly suits and waistcoats. He loved colourful waistcoats. I had his fedoras and overcoats made too. He liked to be different. In return for free clothes, he wore my initials LC on television but it had to be

discreet. Alex was a snappy dresser. He knew a lot about clothes and even more about self-promotion. I benefitted from that. He was a difficult size, though. His normal chest was 38 inches and waist 32. Towards the end it became a 34 and 26. One day he decided he wanted spats. He'd been watching *The St Valentine's Day Massacre* on television.

I got a pair made for him and he danced around Dublin like Don Corleone. The BBC did a down-the-line interview with Alex from the RTE studio when Harry Carpenter asked him what he was doing in Dublin. Alex put his feet up on the desk and said: 'What do you think of these, babes? Courtesy of Louis Copeland, bespoke tailor extraordinaire.'

It was a great advert for me, though I didn't think spats would catch on.

You always knew when Alex was nearby. Drivers stopped in the middle of the road and honked their horns and people followed him through the streets like the Pied Piper. I was in awe of him too. He sent shivers down my spine when he walked into the shop. He even got me interested in snooker. He got *everyone* interested, including people who didn't understand the game. We expected fireworks and we usually got them.

When Ken Doherty was starting out as a teenager, I brought him to Blooms Hotel to meet his hero. Ken was captivated by Alex. They became good friends and Ken helped Alex a lot as time went on. No matter what people did for him, though, he was always going to screw up.

For a couple of years, Alex was the highest-profile sports personality in Britain. I was reminded of that at the Queen's garden party for all the top sportsmen and women in the country. Frank Bruno was there along with Ian Botham, George Best and a host of others. Alex invited me because he'd split from Lynn and Lauren wasn't old enough to take. It was an astonishing scene at Buckingham Palace. Two people commanded all the attention – Bruno and Alex. No-one seemed interested in the Queen. The Palace guards in their busbies sneaked up to Alex for his autograph. They even asked if he'd put on an exhibition for them on a snooker table in the Palace. Alex would have done it but protocol wouldn't allow. I bet the Queen would have loved it!

I saw Alex through some of his most traumatic times. The separation from Lynn was a big blow. I didn't meet her but I was often on the phone trying to patch things up between them, especially at Christmas time when Alex was at his lowest. I felt for Lynn because he was the most awkward bloke I ever met. I called him the Devil's Advocate. If you wanted him to turn left, you asked him to turn right.

He was ever so charming and ever so obnoxious – often with people who'd done nothing to deserve it and couldn't fight back. Not with me, fortunately. He knew which side his bread was buttered. I looked after him and I was always giving him things. If it wasn't clothes, it was money for gambling. Alex was always on the touch. He'd say 'Give me £300, Louis' in the same manner that others might say 'Have you got a light?' I'd give him £50. In his latter years, he didn't care who he asked for money. It didn't occur to him that we might want it back some day.

Alex was always pulling strokes. He really believed he could sue the tobacco companies for giving him cancer. Complete strangers were expected to drive him to Belfast at the drop of a hat. That's a round trip of 170 miles and they usually obliged. Why did we all do it? Because he was Alex Higgins, superstar. He wove a kind of spell and, for all his faults, I liked him. You couldn't help liking him. I suppose you'd best describe our relationship as love/hate.

Many thought it strange that Louis missed Alex's funeral but he sent a fedora to put on the coffin. Perhaps he was caught, like other acquaintances, in the admiration/revulsion dilemma. Perhaps Louis couldn't quite bring himself to pay such extravagant homage to a Devil's Advocate. Alex's boyhood ally, Cecil Mason, told me that after several years of pandering to Alex's every whim, Louis began to find 'prior engagements' when he knew Alex was coming to Dublin. He told the staff to put a few things on the rack for Alex but to keep other suits hidden around the back. Who would blame Louis? He last saw his client three months before Alex died.

> He'd been playing an exhibition with Ken Doherty in Killarney. As usual, he jumped off the train in Dublin and breezed into the shop. His voice was so weak that I couldn't understand most of what he was saying. I gave him six months to live ten years ago. He proved me wrong. This time I knew it was the end.
>
> The closest I saw Alex to happiness was when he was with Siobhan. They were very tactile with each other. I went out with them socially and you could see they were in love. Siobhan was a lovely, intelligent woman who seemed above the likes of Alex. I don't know what she saw in him. She spent her time covering up for him, whether he was kicking off in a restaurant or arguing in the betting shop.

Alex's sister Jean passed me two handwritten letters she found among his documents. They're undated and largely unpunctuated. One of them is addressed to Louis Copeland Junior, master tailor. It's a rambling note but it thanks Louis, his father and 'the magnificent staff'. It continues: 'From Mary in the office also people who took the odd hem up or made a pair of pants or suit of clothes feel and look so much better on each individual customer. If I have forgotten anyone I'm sorry. Thanks Louis for all the service one last thing Adrian Copeland is doing all right around Grafton Street. Louis senior can rest in peace he has two charming and industrious sons. He would be proud of them.'

Alex signs off with: 'My sincere best wishes, yours Alexander Gordon Higgins or Hurricane for short.' Beneath a smiling cartoon, Alex adds a short message to the Royal Bar in Belfast: 'Up your ass with a Scottish thistle. With best wishes, the man who sat in the corner listening. Cheers boys and girls.'

It's probably a goodbye letter written when Alex was in bed. Close friends say he didn't have the patience to write letters when he was active. The second one is entitled 'Gerry's Bar - den of eniquity penned by Paul Ryan. A new found place.' It's hard to follow:

'In the heart of theatreland I accidently fell on Gerry Bar. It was cellar bar full of surprises. I looked on the walls . . . and what did I see. A set of film stars past and present which my mother adored. I was fortunate to meet some of my late mother's screen idols in Gerry's Bar Bean Street. I was also fortunate to meet the proprietor Michael Dillon . . . Even in the twilight of my career, Michael always made me feel at home. It was only in the last six years that I was introduced to Gerry's Bar by a great actor called Jeremy Brett, aka Sherlock Holmes . . .'

Alex signs it, 'George'. The footnote says: 'All the individual who pass through Gerry door you must have talent or grace.'

To Louis Copeland Junior Master Tailor
He like his Father dresses me just like his. Grandfather
Master Bespoke Tailor. From Capel St. Dublin. Also many thanks
to Louis and Louis both Past + Present to the magnificent staff
the Copeland family have h[illegible] working for the Capel St. firm
from Mary in the office also the People who took the old
hem up or made a pair of pants, or a suit of clothes
feel and look so much better on each individual
customer. If I have forgotten anyone I'm sorry I've worn
Louis Senior's and Louis Junior clothes and as long as I live
these People at Copelands, Capel Street. Really care about
the customers, thanks Louis. for all the service
one last thing Adrian Copeland is doing all right around
Grafton Street. Louis Senior can rest in peace he has to
charming and industrious sons. He would be proud of

To Copeland's.
My sincere Best wishes
Yours Alexander Gordon Higgins

or Hurricane for short?

To The Royal Air
Sandy Row.
up your ass with a Scottish thistle
with Best wishes
The man who sit in the corner,
listening,
Charlie's Boys + Girls

Hugh Hourican, the Dublin Landlord

The surname's a coincidence. The fact that Hugh's bar is 150 yards from Louis Copeland's shop isn't. Alex spent sixteen years visiting the Boar's Head whenever he was in Dublin. It's a good example of the unique Irish drinking culture. Where else in the world would you find a bar serving Guinness at 7.30 in the morning? Guinness in its home town is supreme. They say it's because of the water. They insist it's a cut above the equivalent pint in Belfast. At any rate, Alex was a keen student of the national beverage, along with ambulance drivers, nurses, policemen and casino staff who'd come off the night shift straight into the Boar's Head. Originally Dublin boasted twenty-seven pubs with early licences. Customers came from the docks and the wholesale markets. Drink/driving and the smoking ban killed that tradition, but Hugh still finds enough takers for his pint-and-toasted-sandwich breakfasts. Alex rarely saw that time of day, but he had his routine and, as Hugh recounts, it didn't vary.

> He ran in the door with his duffle bag, his cue in its case and a red ribbon tied around it. He ran everywhere. To this day I don't know why the red ribbon. He put his things behind the counter, then ordered a Guinness and a bowl of soup. He sat at his special seat by the window because he liked to watch the world go by. Also, he was hidden behind the door and the pillar so no-one coming into the bar could see him. He had his television set alongside him and his dockets and newspapers on the shelf. This went on for sixteen years, from the time he was fit and well until six weeks before he died.
>
> He stayed for two to four hours and had maybe twenty bets. The bookmaker's two doors away so he had an easy run to place them. He only carried sterling so there was always an argument in the betting shop about the exchange rate when he collected

his winnings. He never had Euros. He couldn't be bothered to change his money so. I eventually agreed to do it.

Alex charged in one day after he'd been diagnosed with throat cancer. The pub was decked out for the World Cup '98 and full of people watching the England game on the big screen. Alex made a beeline for me and said he needed £100. He never asked me for money. We have an unwritten rule in the Boar's Head: If you lend a customer money, you'll never see him again.

I said: 'Jesus, Alex, you know I don't lend money.'

'If this wins, babes, £4,000 is yours. And I'll give you interest.'

He followed me upstairs and downstairs in his long mac and hat. People were watching him not the football. I told him I wasn't giving him the money because I didn't want to lose him as a friend and customer. He said: 'Okay then' and sat at the top of the stairs to watch the game. I felt bad about turning him down.

The next day he surprised me by coming in again. He had a pal with him. They ordered two coffees. I was waiting for him to explode at me. His pal went to pay for the coffee but Alex says he'll pay. He pulls out £4,000, gives me a wink and laughs. Then he tosses the bookies' dockets into the window. He'd obviously got hold of £100 somewhere. It was one of the few times I saw him win.

He was usually okay for money though. One Saturday, before going to a tournament in Killarney, he calculated he'd earn E200 from challenge matches and about E1,000 in prize money. All in all, that should keep him going till Thursday. When Thursday came, Alex ran in to say he hadn't made a penny. He was beaten the first night of the tournament so he failed to qualify for the prize money – and although he won £1,500 from challenge matches, he lent half of it to Jimmy White who was broke. Conclusion?

'I'm a magician. I turned Thursday into Monday!'

His appearance was terrible. I never asked how he was because he'd probably tell me to mind my own business. His personality didn't change when he was sick. There was still a sense of optimism. He talked a lot about his son and daughter. He was very close to Lauren but concerned about Jordan. I remember him saying: 'My son's a bit fucked-up. I don't know where he got that from!'

There seemed to be a ban on Alex seeing them but he told me he used to meet them on the quiet. I was sorry they'd become so distanced.

About a year ago he presented us with a signed picture of himself and Jimmy White. I didn't ask for it. He just turned up one day and said he'd brought us a present. It takes on extra importance now he's not here any more. It's on the wall in the bar. My regulars still talk about Alex. I lost count of how many phoned after he died. He never put a foot wrong here. He was the perfect gentleman and fun to be with. We miss him terribly.

16

HE WAS MY INSPIRATION

Willy Thorne

Alex Higgins and Willy Thorne had two things in common: a love of fast play and a ruinous passion for gambling. Willy blew £2 million and his marriage. Alex blew twice that amount and any hope of a proper relationship with his kids. He left them nothing. He had nothing to leave. In another century he'd have been given a pauper's grave and all because of gambling.

Willy recovered from bankruptcy and remarried. He was sitting in the comfort of his executive home in Leicestershire watching Channel 4 racing when I called. I raised an eyebrow. He countered quickly:

'I'm in control of my gambling now.'

I wanted to understand from a self-confessed addict what it is that draws intelligent people into crazy downward spirals. It might explain the mentality of a starving man who preferred to invest his salvation fund in the 2.30 at Kempton rather than in an operation which might prolong his life.

Although they could never be classed as close friends, Alex and Willy spent a good deal of time together in the UK and on overseas tours. They knew each other and each other's game well. Willy beat Alex as often as he lost to him. Familiarity didn't breed much fondness and they had many confrontations. Nevertheless, Willy had no hesitation in cancelling a television commentry engagement to be at Alex's funeral. He said:

I wanted to show my respects. As much as I disliked him, I honestly feel I wouldn't have enjoyed such a good standard of living but for Alex. We owe him a debt of gratitude. He brought money into the game. He lined our pockets. He attracted a new, younger audience. The old fogies were outnumbered. A generation of young players appeared from nowhere and snooker was suddenly exciting, edgy and lucrative – all because of Alex.

He inspired me when I first saw him play. I immediately said to myself: 'That's the way I want to play.' I was quick and could build breaks better than most, but I couldn't match Alex's invention. His safety play baffled most people. He was the best-ever shot maker, even if his aggregate of century breaks in tournament play was well down on Stephen Hendry, Steve Davis, John Parrott and me. His 69 against Jimmy White was rightly heralded as the best break ever seen. Alex's cue ball control was all over the place but he kept knocking the balls in. He developed shots most of us never knew. He'd play reverse side and send balls spinning all around the table. Alex turned a century break into an art form.

He was the ultimate showman. You know you're in the presence of genius when even fellow pros are lost in admiration. I loved playing him in exhibitions. I won a few but Alex played shots no-one else would dream of. Whereas I'd pot the reds and the colours in clockwork fashion to close a frame, Alex went in and out of baulk, flirting with hazard and loving the risk.

He beat me 13–10 on the way to winning the world title in '82. It hurt because I was playing my best snooker at the time. We had an argument of course. He called me a cheat and said I'd stab my grandmother for two bob. We sat alongside each other with an ashtray on the table between us. When Alex was in play, I stubbed out his cigarettes because the smoke was bothering me. He was angry: 'You cunt. You've put my fag out!' Then he'd light another, oblivious to my or anyone else's needs. Alex would have won more trophies if he'd scored more heavily when he was in control. It made him vulnerable to an in-form opponent. If his opponent wasn't playing well, Alex would always win. By not building enough frame-winning breaks, though, he left himself open to defeat by players who shouldn't have been able to hold a candle to him.

Talking of candles, I went to Birmingham to see him win his first world title. I practised with him before the match and in the intervals. He was twenty-three, I was eighteen. It was a weird atmosphere during the three-day week. We played by battery light in a dingy back room.

Alex was a wild man. He made his own rules. Nobody knew how to handle him. He was managed by a guy called Simon Weaver who asked if I'd like to drive Alex around and be his regular practice partner. I'd only just passed my test and wasn't sure I fancied being in his company all the time. I told Simon it wasn't for me.

I was a junior champion and played Alex in several early events. One I particularly remember was in my home town, Leicester. I usually had a bet when I played him. This time I was glad I hadn't. He beat me 10–2, including a 146 break which incorporated 16 reds. He had a chance of the world record. No-one had ever done it. Alex could easily have scored 148 or 149. For some reason he didn't bother. That summed him up. The journey was more important than the arrival. In those days, he travelled with cue and a plastic bag containing his dress suit and shirt. He often stayed at the Falcon Inn in Braunstone, a rough place on a council estate just outside the city. He'd come knocking on our door with a bag of washing. Mum would take him in and iron his clothes.

Over the years I probably went out with him socially a couple of dozen times when it might have been 300. That's because he was so changeable and so dangerous to be with. He also drank and I didn't. I was of limited use to him. Each time you went to a restaurant or nightclub he'd embarrass you in some way. If it wasn't an argument with the waiter, he'd be chatting up a bird and her boyfriend would appear. Time and again you ended up being the peacemaker.

We nearly had the mother and father of all fights at 35,000 feet on the way back from Toronto. A group of us had been to the Canadian Exhibition, a three-mile long fairground with show jumping and marching bands. Alex won a massive teddy bear at one of the stalls and was taking it home for his daughter, Lauren. Then he asked me for money to go to the races because he was skint. I said: 'No, Alex. You never pay me back.' We did a deal. I fancied the teddy bear as a present for my twins, so Alex sold it to me for $200. I phoned home to tell them the good news. Unfortunately Alex had done the same before selling the bear to me.

He lost all his money at the races, then insisted he wanted the teddy bear back. Lauren was looking forward to it. I said: 'So are my boys.' There was a cold war until we were on our way home a few days later. Alex staggers down the plane blind drunk shouting: 'I want that fucking teddy bear!'

'Tough luck, Alex. You sold it to me.'

He calls my mother a whore and causes a major scene. The stewardess doesn't know how to handle it. John Virgo sits between us to prevent a fight. As we're coming into Heathrow, Alex says: 'All right, babes. If I can't have the teddy bear, no-one's having it.' He gets off the plane, goes to customs and tells them Willy Thorne's carrying a teddy bear with drugs inside it. The officer has no choice but to rip it apart. I could have killed Alex. He had a mind like a mousetrap.

Our card schools were something else. Alex just didn't know when to stop. We'd get to midnight and he'd urge us carry on. He didn't want to go to bed. We'd carry on till two o'clock and say: 'Okay, Alex, that's enough.' He tried to keep us going till 5.00 am until he'd either lost all his money or got hold of ours. Cliff Thorburn had fights with him over it. God bless him, he went to his deathbed owing me hundreds. I'd sometimes give him £500 to bet on a race. I hardly ever got it back.

He was addicted. I was addicted. Gambling's a disease. I should have had therapy. I had a fabulous house near to Engelbert Humperdinck when I first got married. Then the property crash happened and I was losing heavily at the bookies. I split up with my wife and was declared bankrupt. Although I only won one tournament, the Mercantile, I was earning £40–50,000 from the highest break prizes.

I was part of Barry Hearn's stable around the time he turned his attention to boxing. I suddenly found I owed £30,000 in tax and the same amount in mortgage arrears. I thought I could win it back. I lost £100,000 trying to win £60,000. The hole got deeper and deeper.

I didn't see Alex win very often. If gamblers don't win, they normally stop gambling – for a while anyway. That was me, but it didn't apply to Alex. He was losing £3,000–£4,000 a time and coming back for more. He stayed in the bookies all day. I had to drag him out, often to remind him that we were supposed to be playing that night. He was compulsive. He bet on every race – the dogs as well. In the last decade he was betting £1, even 50p. It was pathetic really.

A gambler thinks of his winnings as a bonus. It's holiday money or a chance to buy the wife something nice. The biggest win I had was £38,000. I felt fantastic. When you lose, you hit a deep depression. It makes you deceitful and ashamed of yourself.

You live a Jekyll and Hyde existence. I tried to keep it from my wife and my management team. That meant telling lies and forever making excuses like: 'Don't worry, the money will be here tomorrow.' It meant waking up in a cold sweat. It was horrible. I had two accounts – one my wife knew about and a gambling account I kept secret.

You think the only way out of it when you're losing is to gamble some more. You're well and truly trapped. That's how Alex was. The difference was that I always had enough in my pocket to buy a meal. I was never down to my last fiver like Alex. I didn't have to beg, steal or borrow.

Gambling not only ruined my marriage, it destroyed any respect my wife had for me. She hated me for years and my sons thought I'd let them down. Those are hard things to take. A few of that snooker generation had problems of one sort or another but Alex Higgins was the most tragic case of all. I saw him in 2007 at Paul Hunter's funeral. My first thought was: 'You should be dead, Alex.' He looked worse than Paul and *he* was in a casket. Even so I was shocked when I got a text to say he'd died. It choked me. It was the end of an era.

What's really sad is that Alex wanted to be part of the Legends tour. He could have earned some money and got back to doing what he liked best. But he could hardly get around the table. He couldn't hit the balls hard enough to play the shots he wanted. It was dreadful to watch. They had to let him down gently. The organisers told him: 'People are paying good money to see you play and you can't do it. We're sorry but we'll have to replace you.' They did – with Dennis Taylor.

Barry Hearn persuaded BSkyB to cover the legends. Cataracts have stopped me playing any more so I hosted the shows on television. It was fabulous to have so many of the old boys back in the same room – Joe Johnson, Jimmy White, Cliff Thorburn,

Defiance burns in his eyes. Alex's world took an irretrievable turn for the worse after the Paul Hatherell hearing.

Alex could only look on enviously as Barry Hearn (*left*) helped to create an empire for Steve Davis.

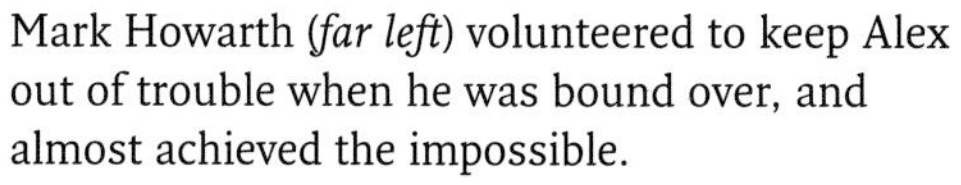

Mark Howarth (*far left*) volunteered to keep Alex out of trouble when he was bound over, and almost achieved the impossible.

Howard Kruger thought he could market snooker's black sheep but both went bust.

Alex and the 'love of his life', Siobhan Kidd. By the time he damaged himself jumping out of her apartment window, the relationship was doomed.

'I've been stabbed in the back so often, I didn't feel a thing!' Alex declined to bring charges against his on-off girlfriend Holly Haise after this assault in 1997.

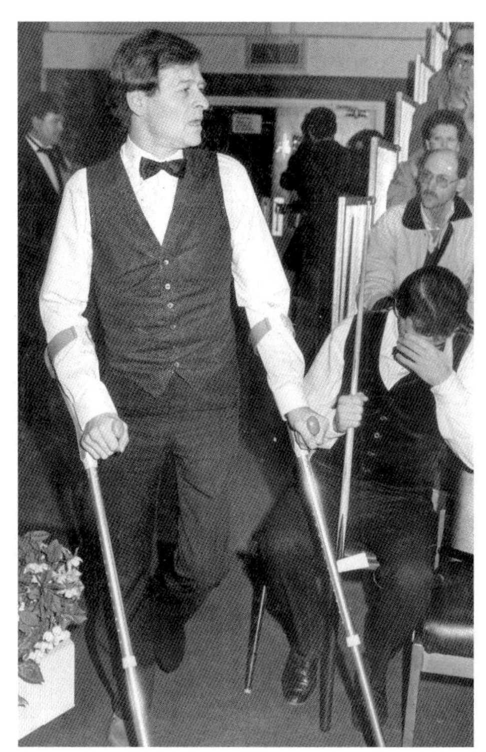

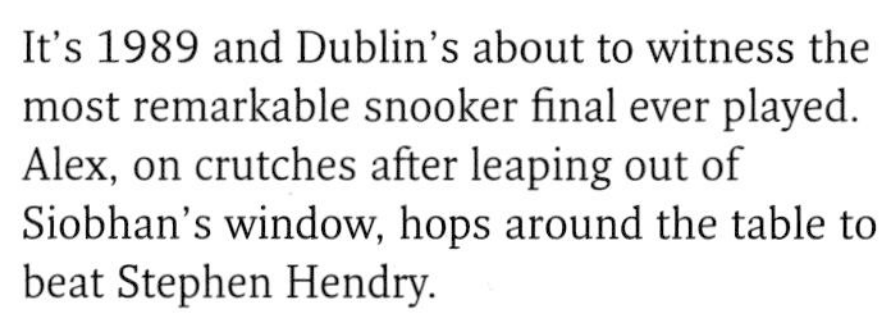

It's 1989 and Dublin's about to witness the most remarkable snooker final ever played. Alex, on crutches after leaping out of Siobhan's window, hops around the table to beat Stephen Hendry.

Siobhan shared his unlikely triumph in the Irish Masters but was unable to share his life and failed to attend his funeral.

It's been said that Alex was the best drunk player ever to grace the table.

He tried to sue cigarette manufacturers for giving him cancer but he'd been inhaling smoke since he was a kid at the Jampot.

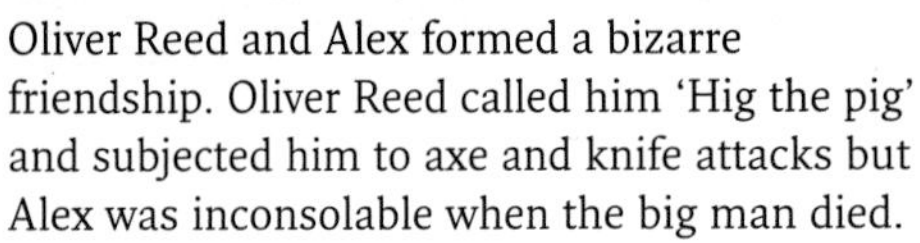

Oliver Reed and Alex formed a bizarre friendship. Oliver Reed called him 'Hig the pig' and subjected him to axe and knife attacks but Alex was inconsolable when the big man died.

In the south of France admirers queue up to give Alex freebies.

At the other end of the spectrum, Blackpool was a soul-destroying place for a former world champion to go through the qualifiers.

Still the best-dressed man at the racecourse – gambling was Alex's most destructive addiction.

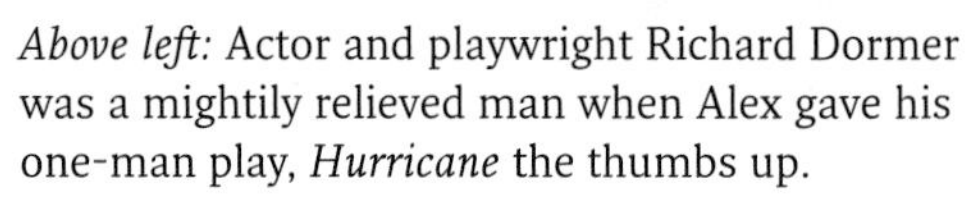

Above left: Actor and playwright Richard Dormer was a mightily relieved man when Alex gave his one-man play, *Hurricane* the thumbs up.

Above right: Alex wouldn't have missed Peter Madden's wedding for the world. He said the jockey was 'the brother he never had'. Although barely able to talk, Alex wowed guests with his best man's speech.

Left: After giving portrait painter Alan Quigley hell, Alex was eventually pleased with this impressionistic work.

Below: Tom McCarthy (*left*) and Ken Doherty (*centre*) made sure the Condolence Book was signed by players, colleagues and friends from all parts of the country. They're joined by Jim Carrick from the Republic of Ireland Billiards and Snooker Association

Above: In a rousing tribute to a neglected hero, the funeral cortege winds its way through the streets of south Belfast towards St Anne's Cathedral.

Right: Will Robinson (*far right*) came in for plenty of stick from Lynn and Lauren for organising Alex's 'state' funeral. Ken Doherty was among the pallbearers.

Below: Family feuds forgotten for a day, Lauren Higgins is supported by two of Alex's sisters, Jean (*left*) and Ann (*right*), as they enter the cathedral. Jordan Higgins is front left.

This photo was taken in a Belfast park just round the corner from where Alex died alone and half-starved in a warden-assisted flat.

Alex spent most of his last days studying form at The Royal, a pub on the corner of Belfast's Sandy Row and Donegal Road, close to where he grew up.

This home-made mural outside The Royal is the only lasting memorial to the people's champion. Belfast has said no to a statue.

Steve Davis, etc. Alex should have been a part of it. He was the one who made it all possible.

Ken Doherty

That aborted Legends event has bittersweet memories for the 1997 world champion, Ken Doherty, who was also inspired to take up the game by The Hurricane. The bitter part was seeing Cliff Thorburn reduced to tears after beating Alex 4–0 in a sorrowful encounter which signalled the end of Alex's involvement. He couldn't pot a ball. Ken was also playing in that event at St Andrews Hotel in Scotland.

Thorburn was horrified when he walked into the hotel reception to meet us all. He hadn't seen Alex for years. They were never best mates but Alex held out a hand to greet him. Cliff hesitated. The hand was so frail, he didn't know whether to shake it or not. Their game was awful to watch. When he came back to the dressing room, Cliff was sobbing. He said he couldn't believe how a person could deteriorate so much. It was as though someone had produced a cardboard cut-out of the real Alex Higgins.

What made it more difficult to comprehend was that inside that withered body and sunken face, Alex's mind was as sharp as ever. When we were interviewed before the event, the interviewer said to Tony Drago, who's quite a big lad: 'You were no slouch in your day, Tony. You played as fast as Alex.' Before Drago could answer, Alex dived in with: 'Yes. He's a gazelle in a buffalo's body!'

We all fell apart laughing. Poor old Drago tried to catch up: 'Sorry Alex, what did you say?'

Ken Doherty was part of a strong Irish contingent at Alex's funeral. They shared a table at the wake – Eugene Hughes, Patsy Fagan,

Stephen Murphy and Joe Swale among the mourners. The English players – Tony Knowles, Willy Thorne, Stephen Hendry, John Virgo, Tony Meo and David Taylor – sat at an adjoining table. As Ken recalls, the mood was refreshingly upbeat.

> Everybody had a funny story to tell. One memory sparked another. If an outsider had seen us laughing, he'd have thought it was a celebration party. Although we were devastated that the game's great pioneer had gone, it was perhaps only at the wake that we realised what a fantastic legacy he'd left us. Above anything else, Alex was a great source of amusement. Even the burial had its lighter moment. We were at the graveside for nearly two hours before the priest arrived. He got a slow hand-clap which didn't please him. Someone joked that only Alex could keep us waiting after he was dead. When the coffin was finally lowered into ground, the joking stopped and the tears flowed. I think every player was overcome. My mind went back thirty-odd years to the days of *Pot Black*, when I was glued to the screen as an eight-year-old watching Hurricane Higgins and dreaming of being a professional.
>
> My greatest sporting memory was seeing Alex hold the trophy in 1982 with his baby girl in his arms. I was thirteen, watching it at home with my mum and dad. What the public didn't know was what happened when Alex came to Dublin for a series of exhibitions shortly afterwards. He was booked into the Gresham Hotel for two nights but stayed for three weeks. He and Jimmy White bumped into Phil Linnett from Thin Lizzy. The three of them had a ball. A pal of mine was sent to collect Alex from the hotel and bring him to the National Boxing Stadium where a huge crowd gathered for one of the exhibitions.
>
> There was no answer when they knocked on the door. The porter opened up. Alex was stark naked and comatose on the

bed. He was so pissed he didn't know where he was or who he was. He was due on stage in an hour. They scraped him off the bed, gave him a cold shower and got him dressed. He couldn't stand up. The exhibition was delayed but Alex staggered to the table and Jimmy broke off. What happened next was just unbelievable. Alex potted a long red and cleared the table with 136! He probably didn't remember it.

I first met him about a year later while working as an usher at Goffs. I was an up-and-coming player and the boss thought it would do me good to savour the atmosphere at the B & H. Meeting Alex was the highlight of my life up to that point. It was my job to get his drinks. The instructions were: 'If I ask for an orange juice, it means *vodka* and orange. If I *ask* for a vodka and orange, it means bring me a double!'

Several years later I played him at Goffs. He went down the tunnel ahead of me. We were live on air on RTE. Everything was timed to the second, as it has to be on television, but Alex realised he was missing one of the three pigs he always wore on his fedora. They were his lucky charms. He wouldn't play without them. The floor manager was doing his nut, but Alex wouldn't budge. The tournament director says: 'We're ready for the introductions, Alex. We can't wait.'

'The Hurricane can't go on without his third pig.'

'Where is it?'

'Dunno. It might be in the dressing room.'

The temperature in the TV gallery was soaring. Eight hundred seated spectators and another 1,500 standing on the balconies were getting restless. The director grabbed one of the ushers and shouted: 'Run down to the dressing room and find that fucking pig!'

Lo and behold, it was in the dressing room. The lad sprinted back, Alex pinned the charm to his hat and announced: 'Okay, babes, The Hurricane's ready.'

He had a tremendous sense of theatre. Not only was he one of the all-time great players who'd still be a problem for any of the top sixteen if he were alive and well today, but he was by far the greatest entertainer. Even when the other guy was at the table, most eyes would be on Alex. There was something mesmerising about the way he took a drink or a drag of his cigarette and threw back his hair with his whole body twitching.

Alex was a very difficult guy to fool. I tried and failed on an RTE show called *Anonymous* which was a bit like *Candid Camera*. The plan was that three so-called priests would play an exhibition against a pro. Alex was in town so I gave the producer his number. Alex wanted £1,500 to appear. That was over-budget but I told the producer he wouldn't regret it. He'd be great television.

I dressed up as sixty-year-old Father Sean O'Donoghue with white collar, robes and mask. I tested the disguise on my mum, my brother and my wife. They were all fooled. Only the dog knew it was me. On the night, Alex bounced into the studio carrying a pint of Guinness. Before we started the game, he leaned over and said: 'You've got eyes like that snooker player, Ken Doherty.'

It had taken him seconds to notice what my entire family missed. Anyway, he hadn't completely rumbled me so we carried on. The deal was that he would give Father O'Donoghue a bit of coaching. The presenter asked him what advice he'd give to the holy man. Alex replied: 'I've been called the devil many times so he'll need divine inspiration to get past me today!'

I broke but bashed the balls around the table and allowed Alex in. He was on a break of 40-something. It looked like I wouldn't get to the table. I did everything to put him off. I stood in his line of shot and put on my best disguised voice:

'Give the priest a chance. All the brothers in the parish will be watching this.'

Alex missed and I began to play more seriously. The camera was on Alex in the chair. He mumbled: 'Good shot, Father.'

When I got to a 50 break, he really started twitching. He was studying my cue action. Then he got out of his seat.

'I know who you are. You're not Father O'Donoghue. You're Ken Doherty dressed up!'

I went to shake his hand and apologise for the joke. He smiled and whispered under his breath: 'Father Sean, you're a cunt.'

Thankfully it was too soft for the microphones to pick up.

Although there were twenty years between us, we became good friends. I was always a bit in awe of him. I loved to hear his tales. They were always funny because Alex had a mischievous sense of humour. There was nobody better at one-liners. He had the world eating out of his hand. He could treat people hatefully, but they'd still do anything for him. That was the magic of the man.

We once travelled together to Navan for some exhibitions and stayed in a small hotel. Alex invited me out for 'a little Guinness'. I said I didn't want to drink before a match but he persuaded me. I went for the company. There was a bookies next to the pub. Alex ordered a pint of Guinness and 'a half for the young lad'. He wrote his slips, then sent the owner of the pub to place his bets while he watched the racing on television and told me a few more of his adventures. The poor landlord ran backwards and forwards all afternoon. Higgy didn't have to get off his stool!

He did an exhibition in my village once when I wasn't there. Apparently, some kid came up with a pound note for Higgy to sign but he put the note in his pocket and signed a piece of paper instead. The lad was devastated. They still talk about it in the village.

I'll never forget how he opened his heart to me the second time we met. Louis Copeland invited me to join them at Bloom's Hotel where Alex was staying in Dublin. Louis said Alex wanted to see me. I caught the bus into town. I was as nervous as hell. He looked serious. He said he was feeling down because Siobhan had finished with him. He told me he was madly in love with her. Then he reached into a little pocket in his cord trousers and took out a lovely diamond engagement ring: 'I offered her this and she threw it back at me. I wanted to marry her but she won't have it.'

He was broken-hearted. I'd never seen him like that before. I met Siobhan at Goffs when Higgy beat Stephen Hendry in the final. They seemed very close. It was certainly a change from a couple of years earlier when he stopped everyone in their tracks by making a grand entrance into the bar by way of the kitchen! He had a real scrubber on his hands. He'd picked her up at the races. Everyone stopped what they were doing to watch them. It was another of Higgy's dramatic arrivals, even if his partner didn't come up to scratch.

In his later years, I had him down to my snooker room in the Radisson Hotel, Dublin, to get some practice in. He had all the accessories: *Racing Post*, cigarettes, pint of the black stuff. He was still in remission from his cancer and quite weak. We played a frame, then he opened the fire doors and wandered out to roll a fag. We played another frame, then took a rest. Higgy put on his glasses and inspected the pictures around the room. There was a big one of George Best and me. Alex studied it and came up with the immortal line: 'Ah, Georgie Best! What a waste. If only he'd stuck to the Guinness like I told him!'

Alex was always good to me. I took him for what he was, warts and all. He always gave me a hug and a kiss, as though I was his brother. When I pre-qualified for the world championships in 2009 after missing out the previous year, his was the first message on my voice mail: 'Congratulations. It's good to see you back, babes.'

I thought that was a lovely touch. Alex did so much to inspire me and put snooker on the map that I offered to organise a testimonial for him. I'd reached the pinnacle of my career. It was time to give the maestro something back. He'd been living in a caravan at the bottom of Holly Haise's garden. He came to Dublin after she stabbed him. Mum invited him round for tea. He told her all about Holly's attack on him and offered to show her the scars. She told him in no uncertain terms: 'Pull your trousers up Mr Higgins. I don't want to see your bare arse!'

The guy was at his lowest ebb. I didn't know that the WPBSA had offered him a rent-free house and he'd refused it. Anyway, the *Belfast Sunday Post* asked if I was serious about the testimonial and said they'd sponsor a show at the Waterfront, a beautiful concert hall where the docks used to be. It would be the People's Champion versus the World Champion. It was a fantastic night. We sold 2,600 tickets. The *Sunday Post* gave Alex a cheque for £10,000 up front. He could have made £20,000–30,000 in total that night.

A pub called the Goat Grill laid on buses to bring a big crowd of supporters from Dublin. Louis Copeland dressed Higgy up in a white suit and hat. He looked a million dollars. There was a big cheer when I walked in with the trophy but they made ten times the noise when Alex walked in!

With a bit of help from me, Alex won 5–4. The crowd just went wild. I signed autographs for about an hour and a half afterwards but Alex disappeared. Some of the fans complained that they'd paid good money to meet their hero, but he was nowhere to be seen. I knocked and opened his dressing room door. The smoke was blinding. Through the cloud I could make out Alex, his family, friends and hangers-on going through a crate of champagne like there was no tomorrow. I suppose there wasn't for him. I told him we were driving back to Dublin now. He replied through the haze: 'Cheers, babes. Thanks for tonight. We should do it again in Dublin.'

Typical Alex. He was always thinking of the next money-making scheme. The last time I saw him was at the World Six-Red Championship in Killarney. It was the Christmas before he died. I knew he wasn't up to it, but I always insisted we invite Alex because it guaranteed television and newspaper coverage as well as putting a few Euros into his pocket.

There was a good crew, including John Higgins, Mark Williams and Stephen Hendry. Alex lost in the first round but seemed to be enjoying himself. On the last night we had a Christmas dinner and party in the hotel. Alex sat in the bar on his own. He was reading the paper and holding a pint of Guinness. He couldn't eat. I think he stayed in the bar because he was embarrassed about his teeth.

I brought him into the dining hall to sit at our table. He pulled a few crackers and had a good time. I know Christmas was a painful time for him. He had no family to go home to. The next day I was waiting for my train to Dublin when Alex bounced down the platform. We spent the three-hour journey playing Kaluki. Alex kept score. He had a little flask of rum in his inside pocket, a bottle of Coca Cola and a glass he'd taken from the hotel. He was coughing and spitting the whole way.

He won £30 off me but refused to take it when we got to Dublin. I knew he needed it but couldn't persuade him. He gave me a hug and a kiss and walked off to Louis's shop. I didn't see him again. I'm glad to have had so many good times with him. It was a real privilege.

17

HE WAS MY BIGGEST MISTAKE

'This is the first time I've spoken about Alex Higgins since we parted company in 1989. I suffered a lot of abuse from him. He told many lies. He claimed I owed him money! For someone who was a quarter of a million in debt when I took him on, that was astonishing. I didn't retaliate because there was no point getting involved in a slanging match. I didn't take him to court because he didn't have a pot to piss in. Now it's time to put the record straight.'

Howard Kruger was an ambitious twenty-seven-year-old product of the Thatcher generation when he decided to branch out into the snooker business. He drove a Roller, lived in a luxury pad in Brighton and his ear was glued to a mobile phone the size of a Danish pastry. Flash or what? He admits it himself. Howard came from a family of showbiz entrepreneurs with a string of well-known bands and pop singers in their portfolio. They hadn't, until then, dipped their toe in the sporting ocean.

Encouraged by the success of Barry Hearn's Matchroom and attracted by snooker's rising profile, Howard established his own agency, Framework Management. It began with Tony Knowles and included the former world champion, Joe Johnson. The *crème de la crème* would be Hurricane Higgins. He was a huge risk – moody and unreliable but eminently marketable (you might think). How could Howard fail with the most charismatic figure in the game by a considerable distance?

The answer is easily. *Nothing* was quiet on the Western Front. In fact, Alex was embarking on a period of trouble and turbulence almost biblical in scale. For reasons he can't quite fathom, Howard became embroiled in Alex's divorce from Lynn. This messy affair ended with Framework being wound up in the High Court. It was Lynn, *not* Alex, who inadvertently brought the company down.

In the middle of the separation even bigger trouble was brewing. Howard was thrust into the role of defence witness in the case of the Crown versus Alex Higgins which followed his attack on Paul Hatherell. Before long he'd have a banned, demoralised and deeply depressed client on his hands. The best days of The Hurricane were well behind him. Alex was coming unstuck. In the meantime, Howard's notoriety, by association with the nation's Bad Boy earned him an unwanted television appearance on *Wogan* immediately after the court case. The BBC devoted the entire show to Alex but he was too sozzled to be coherent. Since the programme was live, there was no alternative for Terry but to address most of the questions to Howard and for the studio director to keep Alex out of shot. The show was an embarrassment and an abortion.

Howard invited me to the Surrey office of his Elm Street Media Productions to inspect a pile of documents which had been locked in his bottom drawer for two decades. It was the paperwork from three torrid years with The Hurricane. Blowing dust from the files, he said: 'I kept them in case Alex Higgins came back to haunt me. Now I want you to see for yourself that we did everything right by him. Stories about me costing him money or withholding it from his wife are bullshit. Typical Alex. When I sold his contract to a management company in Scotland, I thought it was the end of my association with him. It was a relief. I had no interest in chasing him through the courts. Unfortunately, those stories resurfaced after his death. I should have sued *The Guardian* and *Daily Telegraph* but what was the point of opening up old sores?'

The files are revealing. They give us an insight into Alex's modus operandum. They underline his opinion that the world owed him a living, his conviction that life beyond the green baize was someone else's responsibility and his lack of basic arithmetic. Framework paid all his bills, from solicitors' fees to fines to school fees for his children. They paid the long-suffering secretary of the Alex Higgins Fan Club, Gina Howes. Among other bills, the poor woman had to pay printers' costs of £155.49 out of her own pocket. She sent Howard a letter saying that her husband had been out of work for three years so she couldn't afford these bills. She continued: 'I'm not all certain about continuing as Fan Club leader unless I get some co-operation from the new manager. I've been out of pocket for the past twelve months.' Howard reimbursed her, though Alex had left his stable by then. He'd have paid Lynn's maintenance if there'd been enough money in Alex's coffers.

Back to Howard: 'From the moment we took him on, he was in debt – to the Inland Revenue, to Lynn, to the bank and to a whole series of people he'd borrowed money from with unfulfilled promises to pay it back. It never got any better. We became a charity for Alex Higgins. We deducted the bills from his winnings. That would have been okay if he'd been winning anything, but he wasn't!'

A letter from Alex's accountants, Gerald W. Hulme, put things into perspective. It's dated October 1988: 'Alex's situation has deteriorated considerably over the last 2–3 years to such an extent that his recent divorce, the continuing saga of the court settlement, his ban, etc., have had a disastrous effect on him with a consequent loss of income. He is at present rock bottom, finding himself with heavy Inland Revenue liabilities and personal pressures.'

The letter, addressed to Howard, reveals that a writ had been issued for £93,000 tax arrears which were accruing interest daily. On top of that were two further tax liabilities likely to be in the region of £75,000 each and a bank overdraft of £112,000. The total debt was expected to be at least £350,000. That of course excluded all his personal debts. Howard showed me a final summary of Alex's accounts during the three years he was with Framework. His total earnings came to just over £500,000. By the time the company deducted the £113,000 Alex had already received from them, Framework's commission of £106,000, and more than £260,000 of expenditure on Alex's behalf, he was left with a mere £21,000.

Framework paid him the £21,000 but Lynn took out a garnishee order claiming that Howard's company still owed Alex, and therefore her, £50,000. Although Framework had sold Alex's management contract to a promotions company in Kilmarnock for £65,000 with the understanding that the Scottish agency would take on his liabilities, their cheques weren't honoured. Howard received nothing from the promotions company. The upshot was that Lynn wound up Framework for £50,000.

Howard explained: 'We did everything right. We paid Alex all the money owing to him but Lynn wouldn't accept the evidence. We weren't in a position to challenge the winding-up. We had Higgins telling everyone we owed him money and that *he'd* wound us up. He was continually slagging us off.

I was tempted to ask: 'Apart from that, Mr. Lincoln, how did you enjoy the play?' but resisted. Listing Alex's virtues didn't detain Howard for long.

> When he wanted to be, he was charming but I didn't socialise with Alex like I did with the other players on my books. He was a constant headache. I'd get phone calls saying my client was drunk – what should they do with him? There's no answer to that. We almost had a diplomatic incident in Beijing. He was found with a woman in his room during a tournament. They wanted to deport him. Tony Knowles was concerned that Alex was giving Framework a bad reputation. I don't blame him.

> Whenever I ticked him off, he'd say: 'Okay, babes, I've been bollocked' – then carry on as before.
>
> If anyone could have harnessed his talent, Alex would have been a brilliant client. If anyone could have got order and discipline into his life, he could have earned three times as much. As it was, event organisers and advertising agencies gave him a wide berth. He was the sort of guy who thought larking about with his mates was more important than winning prize money. I'll never forget when he lost to Dennis Taylor in the Benson and Hedges. He'd been up all night playing Jimmy White for a tenner. He was banging on Jimmy's door at 4.00 am to pay him the money. Then he went and lost twelve frames on the trot to Dennis and threw the game away. I ended up putting two minders on him. We had to lock him in a hotel room and feed him. That's the only way you could get him to produce the goods. It was like dealing with a child.

I saw the agenda of an urgent meeting Howard called to try to improve his client's prospects. He's not certain whether Alex even showed up for that meeting. If he did, these were some of the plans: Alex to start acting like a professional; his clothes should be co-ordinated; his monthly overheads need trimming; he should be put on a wage; he must do as he's told with no questions; Howard Kruger must have full control or he will pull out. And there'll be pork in the treetops tomorrow!

Alex continued to earn money from exhibitions he arranged for himself. Between February and November 1987 he pocketed nearly £17,000 in cash. It was hardly what you'd call a purple period but Alex was off-colour and off-form. He was suffering on most fronts. His assignments included £1,500 for opening a shop in Scunthorpe and £750 for an exhibition at the Civil Service Club in London. Howard warned him that this money had to be paid into Framework and properly declared, otherwise he'd be in more serious trouble with the taxman - and so would Framework. Alex took no notice. His cash earnings were spent as soon as he got them.

All of this paled into insignificance when he was asked to undertake a random drugs test at the Tennants UK Championship in Preston. Howard couldn't make the trip, but received a midnight call from Alex after he'd lost to Mike Hallett:

'Hi, babes. I've struck a blow for posterity. I've nutted the tournament director!'

'You've done what?'

Paul Hatherell wasn't merely the tournament director, he was the managing director of the WPBSA. A disbelieving Kruger made his way up north next morning. How the hell would this shake down? His dreams of a snooker stable to rival Matchroom were already in tatters. Now Framework would be scorned the length and breadth of the country - and beyond. Howard retained the court transcript of Hatherell's statement which read like this.

> About ten to fifteen minutes after the match had finished, I was approached by Alex Higgins in the backstage area. He was abusive to me and challenged me over why he had to take a drug test as he'd given a sample in an earlier round . . . he continued to be abusive and said he wanted a bottle of brandy and would stay there till four o'clock in the morning. The doctor wouldn't be able to get a sample out of someone who falls over. He also said: 'I hate your gold fillings. You've cost me five grand over the last month . . . your gold fillings will be coming out of your arse! . . . I hate you more than I hate Steve Davis.'
>
> . . . Higgins confronted me and put his face very close to mine. He shouted: 'What are you doing here?' I said I'd come to collect my coat. He shouted back: 'I suppose we pay for that

> fucking thing as well!' I moved to get my coat . . . as I did this, Higgins head-butted me over my left eye . . . I was stunned and fell backwards . . . Higgins was very aggressive and I can say almost hysterical . . . my eye at this time was bleeding.

So much for posterity. Alex seemed to think he'd done the world a favour. If nothing else, the incident catapulted Howard into the headlines. Who said there was no such thing as bad publicity? Howard continues:

> Knowing that our press conference would be on national television, I contacted the mobile phone company to tell them there'd be a great opportunity to get their product on the news. They agreed to pay us £5,000 if it worked. I made sure it did. I got one of my staff to call Alex's mobile during the TV interview. I signalled to him to answer it. There were a few tense moments before he did but it worked like a dream. Both TV channels used the clip.
>
> The *Wogan* experience wasn't so successful. I left Alex in the Green Room for ten minutes while I spoke to the producer of the show. When I came back, he was wrecked. The floor manager called us onto the set. Alex said: 'I'm not going on without you, babes.' Suddenly I'm live on prime-time television. Alex is as pissed as a rat. He's leaning on my shoulder mumbling incoherently while I talk to Terry Wogan for half an hour. Terry thanked me wholeheartedly afterwards. He said it wouldn't have been possible without me.
>
> I didn't speak to Alex after 1989. There was nothing to say. I haven't opened up before about my time with him. I took all the flak but kept every single piece of paper. Once we parted, I had no interest in him. I'd have predicted that he'd end his life in turmoil. What other way was there? I don't know why he had

it in for me when we did so much to help him. I was only twenty-seven when I signed him. I guess you could say I was naive. It could have been a great exercise for him and me. He turned out to be my biggest mistake.

18

HE WAS OUR BROTHER

Alex's sisters are a powerful force when they're together. I met them en bloc after his funeral. Isobel, the eldest, was over from Queensland to spend time with Ann and Jean. It was one of those rare family rendezvous that only weddings and funerals can bring about. The sisters were three quite different characters united in grief for a brother whose joys they shared, whose agonies they couldn't bear to watch and whose extremes they defended up to and beyond the day he left them.

Ann and Jean were both in therapy six months later. Isobel too has been having a hard time of it 10,000 miles from the heartbeat of the Higgins dynasty. The wretched emptiness of Alex's last hours kept returning to haunt her: 'I wanted to be there with him. I wanted to look into his face and hold his hand. I can't sleep for thinking about it. It was such a lonely and miserable way to go. He told me a couple of times in Australia that he'd had enough and wanted to die. When we were clearing his flat, I found CDs about preparing for death. It's awful to think he went through that on his own.'

Jean said: 'It's not like an ordinary person dying. I keep seeing him crumpled in bed with his foot sticking out of the covers. We couldn't pull the sheet away from his face because they weren't sure how long he'd been there. I've told Ann to stop blaming herself for not being with him. It could easily have happened when he was out of the country.'

Ann lost a stone in weight and came close to breakdown after being her brother's principal carer for so long: 'My son took me by the shoulders one day and told me to look in the mirror. I looked a mess. He said if I didn't slow down, I'd be dead before Sandy. I miss him so much it hurts. Sometimes it feels as though he's still here though realistically I know he's gone away.'

Jean's the feistiest of the three. She and Ann sometimes see things differently. Jean was also regularly at odds with Alex. Who wasn't? That's not to belittle the affection they had for each other. Two strong wills were bound to clash. Alex often disapproved of the company she kept, and told her so: 'He watched us like a hawk. If he saw anyone chatting me up or offering to buy me a drink, it was curtains for him and a severe talking to for me. Sandy had to be in control. He hated people straying from his script. I got annoyed with him because he was unbearably bossy with his sisters and nieces. He was always telling us we shouldn't do this and we shouldn't do that. And yet he did as he pleased. It was one rule for us, another for him!'

Ann had the job of finding Alex somewhere to live when he came out of hospital, preparing his food, doing his washing and cleaning the house. That was usually on a weekly basis. She was also party to his most private thoughts during those last tortuous years. Before she leads us through Alex's darkest period, Ann first escorts us back to the 1950s and happier times in Abington Street.

We kids didn't have much, apart from food in our bellies and lots of love. I'd get a cowgirl outfit and a toy post office for Christmas. Alex would get the cowboy hat, belt and gun and a perhaps a painting set. He and I shared a room. He regularly woke me up and sneaked downstairs in the middle of the night. If he heard noises he rushed back to bed and dived under the covers. He wasn't very brave, especially when it was dark. That fear stayed with him. One night he made cigarettes from rolled up brown paper and invited me to have a smoke. Then he heard our daddy coming downstairs and threw the burning paper under the settee. It caught fire. Isobel put it out with saucepans of water. We were terrified.

In winter we broke off icicles from the inside of the bedroom window and sucked them as lollipops. There was no central heating in those days. We kept the fire going with food scraps. They were very happy days, though. On Sundays in the better weather our daddy took us on the train to Carrickfergus to stay at Aggie Rooney's. She was a friend of Mummy's who lived by the sea. Daddy took us on the beach collecting cockles and willicks [winkles]. If Sandy saw a crab he ran a mile. We came home with two bucketfuls of shellfish. We picked them out with a pin and had them for tea.

At Easter, we were taken on the bus to Holyrood. We went to the zoo, then joined hundreds of others rolling eggs down the hill. It was an annual custom. Sandy saw an opportunity. He'd tell Jean to open the eggs and take out the sweets because no-one would notice. That was Sandy – getting someone else to do his dirty work! Jean did as she was told.

Jean:

He was no better when he grew up. He loved playing pranks. You daren't take your eyes off him. He once put my daughter's pet gerbil on the record player to see it go round. The poor creature could have been flung anywhere! He also poured Pernod into the goldfish bowl for a laugh. The worst trick was when he almost drowned my chickens by slipping vodka in their drinking water and dropping the birds into the kids' swimming pool.

I got a hell of a surprise when I answered a knock at the door at three o'clock one morning. Sandy stood there saying he had 'a big bunny rabbit' for me. I looked down and a greyhound stared back at me. Sandy helped it onto the settee and told me it needed looking after! I'd never had dogs so I didn't know what to do with it. Sandy said bread and soup would be a good idea so the two of them sat on the settee in the early hours having soup for breakfast.

It was a racing dog he'd got from a rescue home. He wanted to get it well again. If I know Sandy, he was hoping to race it and win money. What it had to do with me, I'll never know but he told me to look after it and gave me £100 to get 'whatever it needs'. Then he left. My husband got up to go to work a few hours later and shouted upstairs: 'Hey, Jean, there's a greyhound in here!' He wasn't pleased. I was panicking so I decided to take it for a walk. It bared its teeth at me. I ran across the road to my friend Kate who knew about dogs.

She put a lead on and I took it out. It was still snarling at me. I was terrified. Eventually we walked past a church where a wedding was taking place. Just at that moment, the dog had diarrhoea and let everything go. I had nothing to clean up the bloody mess! Then my mobile went. It was Sandy checking to see if everything was okay. I shouted down the phone: 'No, it isn't! The bloody animal's baring its teeth at me and now it's shat all over the pavement.'

He was killing himself with laughter: 'I can't do anything, Jean. It's very funny!' I said it might be for him. Not knowing what to do next, I took the dog to the vets. He said it was past its sell-by and ought to be put to sleep. I called Sandy back. He said I had the £100 so I was to do what I thought was best. As if the dog had been my idea all along! No wonder Sandy was still laughing.

Back at Abington Street, Ann found herself running the house at the age of fourteen while Mum was out cleaning cinemas and

Isobel was busy with her new job. Ann was responsible for cooking everyone's dinner, including Sandy's. What a thankless task that was:

> He was hardly ever there to eat it. His eating habits were chaotic. We kept meals in the oven until he came home but it was usually too late. I tried to get him out of the Jampot. When you opened the door, the smoke was unbelievable. You couldn't see anyone. I'd call out:
>
> 'Is our Sandy there?'
>
> 'No.'
>
> 'His mammy says he is and he's to come home.'
>
> 'Sorry, not here.'
>
> I knew he was there and he knew I knew. He had them warned off. The Jampot was an awful place for a child to spend his time. That's where he started smoking. Breathing in all that stuff killed him in the end.
>
> Sandy was the original wheeler-dealer, good at money-making schemes. He could only have been eight or nine when he ran a Christmas raffle. Somehow he got hold of sweets, chocolates and fruit for nothing, wrote out the tickets and sold them at the Jampot. Those guys couldn't afford much but Sandy made a nice little profit. His other successful scheme was selling potato skins to a pig farmer. He and I would go round the streets with a cart collecting peelings from door to door or out of dustbins. He got 6 pence for his trouble. I got 3 pence.
>
> At one point he was a runner for Linfield Linen Company, taking samples all over Sandy Row on foot. He literally ran everywhere. He knew the back doubles and said that's where he learned to be quick around the snooker table.
>
> I'd often go up the Shankill to see Aunt Rosie. I was her favourite. She gave me money. Then Sandy came sniffing around,

> telling her he was Annie's brother so could he have some too? He played the same trick on Granny Smith, an old woman in a black hat and shawl who waited on the corner of Melrose Street to give me 6 pence because I sang at the local clubs. She'd go up Library Hill with Sandy chasing after her: 'Don't forget me, Granny. I can sing!'
>
> Actually, he was tone deaf. I was doing four to five shows a week at the Empire. At the age of twelve I was resident singer at Clarence Place Hall on Saturday nights. I sang 'Lipstick on my Collar' and other Connie Francis songs. I even went on tour to Londonderry with a hypnotist called Edward Heath. I earned £2.50 on Saturday and £3 on Sunday. All the money went to our mummy. She gave us spending money back. Mummy dressed me in the finest hand-made frocks and a pair of gold slippers. I don't know how she afforded it. The kids from school just went: 'Wow!'
>
> But Mummy didn't know how to handle Sandy. She left him to his own devices. She didn't really have any choice. Although he wasa rascal, he wasn't a troublemaker. He was quite shy to be honest. You'd never see him in a fight. He was a coward and ran the other way. I had to fight his battles for him! The boy who left home to be a jockey, then a snooker player, wasn't the man who came back.

Being ten years older, Isobel had less to do with Alex's playing days, but watched his development closely. 'When he left home at fourteen, Sandy knew nothing about the outside world. He was adventurous, though. He was ready to take a chance, which was good. I didn't like school either. I left when I was fourteen. I just wanted to get out and work. Looking back, Sandy could probably have made something of himself because he was extremely bright. He read a lot of books. I saw his gentle, more relaxed side many times. We squabbled like all families do but we were very close.'

Ann:

> Over a period of time, people let him down. He lost his trust. I think that's when the troubles began. He started to snarl back like a cornered animal. Everyone he met seemed a potential snake in the grass. He was on the defensive as if to say: 'Come on then. I'm ready for yous.' He needed help out there in the snooker jungle, but so-called agents and managers just saw him as a money machine. They didn't care about the person underneath. He never got the financial side under control. How could he when he was out playing seven nights a week?
>
> He ended up with huge tax arrears. Sandy told me that when he went into the tax inspector's office, it was plastered with newspaper cuttings about his exploits at different venues. He couldn't deny anything. If he'd had good management from the start, he'd have been a better person. He wouldn't have thought the world was against him. Rightly or wrongly, the only people he trusted in his life apart from us were Jimmy White, Cecil Mason, Tom McCarthy and Charlie Hawley. But he fell out with them too!

The subject of Lynn makes their hackles rise. It may be because they thought she had it easy, enjoying the money and the fine living that didn't come their way. On the other hand, Lynn calmed a wild man who didn't want to be calmed. She also had to bring up two children pretty much on her own. Jean spent a year at their house. She was expecting her first daughter and was grateful for the support. Nevertheless, she finds it difficult to be sympathetic with her sister-in-law.

> Marriage wasn't a good thing for Sandy. I'm not sure why he did it. I'm not sure why Lynn did it either. It's not Sandy's fault that the relationship went sour. You know when you marry a celebrity that life isn't going to be sitting by the fire watching TV. Snooker's not a nine-to-five job. Lynn didn't go into it blindfold.
>
> He was a good dad but he was on the road a lot so he didn't see so much of his kids. His work sheet was relentless. He was up and down the country every day of the week. He didn't drive so he relied on lifts and train connections. Sandy worked all night and travelled all day. Lynn knew what she was taking on.
>
> I never saw him put his arms around her. He only kissed Lauren. There wasn't much love from Lynn to Sandy either. They weren't touchy-feely. After the divorce, he wasn't allowed make amends. Lynn didn't want him near the kids.

In actual fact, Lynn was keen to encourage a relationship between Alex and his children but not when he was drunk and aggressive, which, sadly, was the usual state of affairs.

Isobel got a better view of Alex's first wife, Cara, whom he met and married in Australia. That was another mismatch. She was the daughter of a Sydney racehorse trainer, Baden Hasler. Right up Alex's street! She was also very amorous. By his own admission, he couldn't handle her physical demands. He stayed up watching late night videos to avoid the bedroom. This, in Alex's words, is how they met.

> A pal from the *Sydney Morning Sun* arranged a blind date. We met in an Italian restaurant. My head was turned as soon as I saw Cara. She was glamorous with a lively personality. We had some marvellous times around the clubs and at the races but, as with most of my relationships, we had serious ups and

downs. It became a long-distance love affair, which suited me fine. I spent several months in Sydney and the rest of the time sharing a flat with Cara in Manchester. After a couple of years of this, she talked about getting married. It's *all* she talked about!

While playing a tournament in Australia in 1974, I agreed. Cara's family arranged a big white wedding at Darling Point Church and a dozen Aussie jockeys formed an arcade when we came out. Ray Reardon was among the guests. The wedding night was hilarious. We were going to the Great Barrier Reef on honeymoon, but I suggested we drop in for a thirst quencher at the Sebel Townhouse where The Who were celebrating the launch of their musical, *Tommy*. We were still going strong with Roger Daltrey and company into the early hours. I was still in my morning suit and Cara was in her wedding gown! The honeymoon could wait.

The marriage wasn't too successful. I wasn't ready for settling down and starting a family. Cara was. We travelled backwards and forwards across the globe with the inevitable arguments and tears. It dragged on for three years but I ended it when I met Lynn. The Cara thing was a mistake but no-one got hurt.

Isobel: 'It was a strange marriage. There was some thought that Cara was pregnant. There's a girl claiming to be Alex's forgotten daughter. We don't believe it. The timing's wrong. Even Cara said it wasn't Sandy's baby. I think she wore him out. I discovered it was all over late one night when Sandy hammered on my door. He asked me to help him into the house with a pile of suitcases. I expected to see Cara but he was on his own. He told me he'd left her. I was dumbfounded. Sandy stayed with us in Sydney for a while and got up to his usual mischief. His favourite trick was waking my young daughter in the middle of the night and scoffing all the ice cream from the fridge. Julie loved it when Uncle Sandy was in town. It meant she didn't have to go to bed.'

An Aussie entrepreneur called Peter Wake was best man at Alex's Australian wedding. He was part of the Legal Eagles gambling syndicate to which Alex belonged. As the name suggests, most of the others were lawyers. Peter told me: 'Cara was like a young Maureen O'Hara. I think she got pregnant by Alex. We were never sure. Alex was so unpredictable and was out for a good time, not marriage. He brought Sydney to life with his snooker, his boozing, his gambling and his women. There was more than one woman. Some people play the field and some don't. Men who brag about it are all talk and no trousers. It's the quiet ones you have to watch. Alex kept very quiet!'

Ann and Jean didn't see an awful lot of Cara but they saw plenty of the woman Alex called the love of his life - Siobhan Kidd. They were very fond of Siobhan and still can't explain what went wrong. She's the subject of another chapter but here's a flavour of her relationship with Alex. It comes from Jean who was with Siobhan the night Alex proposed - at least, one of the nights.

'We'd been at a charity golf do in Belfast. It was a lovely day. Frank Carson was there. Siobhan met me in the bar that evening and announced that Sandy had proposed. She had a huge grin on her face. I asked if she'd accepted and she said yes, she wanted to get married. She was in love. I was over the moon. Siobhan was a great girl, of Irish descent. I think one of her parents came from Bangor just down the coast from here. Sandy loved her till he died. He never got over the break-up. They had rows and fights but we don't know why. We haven't seen or heard of her since. I hoped she might come to the funeral but there was no word from her. She knows she's always welcome at our house.'

It's no secret that the sisters are partial to the odd drink. They can hold their own with the men - not an uncommon phenomenon in Ireland where they give you a bell to ring and hang an 'unclean' label around your neck if you can't hold your liquor. It's social death. I was interested to hear Isobel's view of her brother's drinking habits. Alex never registered as an alcoholic. He wouldn't, would he? Yet he gave a good impression of one.

Isobel:

> Just because he took a few drinks to help him relax didn't mean Sandy had a drink *problem*. An alcoholic needs his first drink when he wakes up in the morning but Sandy was never like that. He preferred a cup of tea. I don't believe he had a self-destruct button either. He suffered because he didn't have a good woman or a good home to come back to. If you're happy in your home, you're happy in your life. He wanted it but he didn't achieve it. He drank instead of going back to his family.
>
> Lynn has said it was the beginning of the end when he became world champion again. I think that was jealousy on her part. She knew he'd become an even bigger personality and she couldn't take it. She sat on her backside and devoured food, especially cakes and takeaway curries. She put on a lot of weight which was bound to alienate Sandy. He hated fat people.

Alex's father is only mentioned in dispatches. Yet he outlived Alex's mother, Elizabeth, by several years. He had the misfortune of seeing Alex waste away. Father and son lived close to each other in the latter years, but hardly fraternised.

Ann again:

> In many ways, Daddy and Sandy were alike. He'd flare up just the same. He was a wee man with size six shoes but they were smart shoes. Daddy loved his clothes – especially ties and

waistcoats. That's where Sandy got it from. They both took the news about Sandy's cancer without a fuss. I don't think it was ever discussed. Our daddy was too old to visit him in hospital. They fell out a lot but Daddy wouldn't hear a word against our Sandy. He went to many of the tournaments to support him. He liked a wee bet but didn't go crazy like Sandy. He lived on his own in Matilda Avenue, not far from Sandy's flat. Sandy bought the house in Abington Street. They sold it to make some money and moved into another council house. Sandy and Daddy occasionally had a drink together. My daddy died in 2002 when he was eighty-three. He smoked like a chimney but he was fit and well until the last year of his life.

When he was earning well, Sandy always sent our mummy and daddy money. He also gave his great niece, Alexandra, money and jewellery. He saw it as looking after his family. That was the legacy from my mummy who said you should take care of your children first and stick together when any member of the family was in trouble. Unfortunately the bottle got *her* into trouble and we couldn't do much about it. Mummy started drinking heavily at the wrong time of her life. She was too old to cope with it. She did it to cover up the pain over Sandy. She daren't read the papers or watch the television when he was on. She hated the WPBSA. We all did.

They wanted to destroy my brother. The press goaded him too. It was a good story for them if he over-reacted. That head-butt was an odd one. Sandy wasn't a fighter. Did Paul Hatherell deliberately taunt him? Did he dive? It sounded like a set-up to me. The officials didn't like it because Sandy wasn't a 'yes' man. They thought he was bad for their image. What image? Anyway, they got their wish. Sandy had no hope of getting his ranking points back. My mummy was inconsolable. She reached for the bottle again.

> She was too old and shaky to carrying on doing Sandy's laundry. She'd done it all his life. Whenever he was in Belfast he dropped it on her. Now I got the treatment. He'd say: 'I'm off to Balmoral for a golf event. I need these done for tomorrow!'
>
> I'd have the washing machine and the tumble drier thumping away in my hairdressing salon. I'd be ironing at the same time. It was like a Chinese laundry!
>
> Sandy disrupted the place whenever he came home. Everybody had to jump to it. If he was playing at the Ulster Hall I usually cooked him a steak to eat after the tournament. Once he left the hall and forgot about the steak. It was in his dressing room wrapped in tin foil so nobody could see what was inside. Security thought it was bomb. They called the police and before you knew it, the bomb disposal squad was investigating 'a suspicious package' They were hyper-sensitive about that sort of thing in Belfast but they only had to ask the doorman. He knew I always brought Sandy a steak.

Those were the good old days when he could eat. That pleasure, not to say necessity, was denied him little by little by a combination of circumstances. First, the after-effects of the cancer operation which left him with scar tissue in the throat; second, prolonged radiotherapy treatment; and third, his disinclination to eat because food was rarely on his agenda.

The family have often questioned the amount of chemo and radiotherapy Alex received, Ann in particular.

> If anyone else had been given forty doses of radiotherapy, it would have killed them. I think Sandy survived because his body was used to turmoil. It was a difficult job getting him into hospital when his throat first began playing him up. His doctor

examined him and tried to refer him to the Belvoir Hospital. Sandy replied: 'I'm not going till *Coronation Street*'s over!' Doctors were only relevant when he decided they were. *He* had to be in charge of his health. Maybe this control thing cost him his life. He was terrified of hearing the word cancer. After he died I found an appointment card to a chest clinic but I don't remember him going.

The night he had the sore throat, he was in a very bad way. I was so worried I phoned Lynn to say I didn't think he'd last until the weekend. They had a shock when they saw him in the Belvoir. As always, his eyes were bright and alert but his cheeks had disappeared. Lauren told her dad he had to start eating. It was no good. The ward doctor said Sandy was also refusing treatment so they'd have to let him go because they needed the bed. My brother was his own worst enemy.

Lynn, Lauren, Jordan and Sandy stayed at my house. I cooked a Sunday roast dinner the next day. We were around the table but Sandy sat in the armchair with a bowl of soup. He had a couple of spoonfuls but that was all. A few days later, his consultant, Dr Brooker, decided to operate. Sandy liked Dr Brooker. He trusted him, which was a relief. We got the thumbs up. The operation had been a success.

Under pressure to provide accommodation for someone who insisted on his own space but wasn't capable of looking after himself, Ann found Alex a council flat close to where she lived in Lurgan. She received a £300 allowance to furnish it. The council paid his rent. With help from Alex's old pal, Cecil Mason, Ann took care of the rest. She was on call 24/7 and the stress began to tell.

My son told me to get things in perspective but there was no-one else to do it. Sandy's GP had an awful time trying to sort it out.

My brother refused to have carers visit the house. He said I was his carer, end of story. Getting him settled in the bungalow was a struggle. It had a glass-fronted fire. They were called Silent Killers because the fumes leaked out. The first day there was freezing. I lit the fire but it went out. Sandy threw himself onto the settee. He was shivering uncontrollably. There was no flesh on him. I was crying and trying to relight the fire. I was at my tallow's end.

Thankfully a neighbour got the fire re-lit and I was able to go home. I called in every morning before going to work to check the fire and make Sandy his tea. He didn't get out of bed. I used to tiptoe around the room to see if he was still breathing. He'd wiggle his fingers under the sheet to let me know he was all right. That was his sign. Then I went to work but came back at dinner time to do the same again. I put Build Up in his tea because, apart from a wee bit of Madeira bun, that's all he was taking.

I stayed till ten o'clock at night, then Cecil took over. He was there all night. Sandy started to recover a bit. I saw a wee chink of light once he was on his feet. He watched the television again. He talked a bit. He was studying the *Racing Post* and wanting to put his bets on. He'd tell me to do it for him. I said I'd never been into a bookies in my life but he pleaded with me:

'Please, please, please. I'll make you a cup of tea when you come back.'

I went into the bookies, hiding my head behind my sleeve. I felt ashamed. I told them it wasn't for me, it was for my brother.

There were signs that Sandy was getting better. He didn't want anyone coming to wash him so I gave him bed baths. Eventually he was able to go into the shower by himself. Cecil took him to the Hertford, a nice little pub in Lurgan where the landlord made sure no-one would bother Sandy. He could put his bets on and have a Guinness again.

However, when there were periods of calm, you knew a storm was coming. He had no control over his outbursts. One moment he'd be nice, the next impossible. Then he'd apologise and say: 'I can't do this without you, Ann.' I found a book on his shelf, *How to Win Friends and Influence People.* I couldn't believe it. According to Cecil, the doctor told Sandy his mood swings were an illness. I think schizophrenia was the word mentioned.

While he was losing weight, he asked us not to buy small size clothes. He wanted medium to give the illusion that he was normal. He'd put several layers on. He was very proud of his appearance. He wore smart shirts and jackets and had some lovely shoes. Then he put on his nice aftershave. It upset him when his clothes didn't fit. He looked in the mirror and said: 'Oh my God!' It must have been devastating for him. I don't know how he managed to carry on.

Things took a serious turn for the worse at Easter 2010. Alex contracted a chest infection. It coincided with his hopes of getting back on the circuit with the Snooker Legends. He told Ann he thought it might be pneumonia. Could she get him some fresh pyjamas because he was going into hospital to get it sorted out. Then he could play in the Legends. There was good money to be earned. Jimmy and co. were doing well out of it. Alex thought he could see the glimmer of a comeback. He ignored the prognosis, which was bleak. Jean could see the writing on the wall.

I could tell he was dying. When I got to the hospital, Sandy had the sheet over his head. I thought I was too late. Then he pulled it back. He was heavily drugged. I let him sleep and went home. I got a call the next morning that he wanted to sign himself out. I went back to the hospital and told him no. He agreed to stay another day, as though he was on a weekend break! The woman doctor said the infection had spread because food was going directly into his lung. They needed to put him on a drip. She said if he went home, he'd be back within an hour – that's if he could make it to a phone to call an ambulance. He was a very sick man. I went back onto the ward and Sandy was out of bed. He said: 'There's my bag. I'm going home.'

'No, you're not.'

'Yes, I fucking am!'

'I'm not taking you home to put you in a box, our Sandy.'

He threatened to call Cecil to collect him. I started to cry. I screamed at him: 'If you want to die you can do it here. I'm not taking you home to have it on my conscience.'

The ward sister held his hand and explained that there was no choice. He had to stay in hospital. Sandy closed his eyes then opened them again to say: 'I'm only staying because she's crying.'

He was pointing at me. The sister and I went outside and did high fives. A couple of days later, I get a call from Cecil to say that Sandy had been discharged after all! He'd signed himself out and gone straight to the Royal. I went to find him. His skin was cream coloured. Death was written all over his face. He sat with a Guinness in his usual seat. I said: 'Didn't they give you any medication?'

'They'll bring it down to me.'

'No they won't, Sandy. They've got better things to do than run around after you.'

He lived in a dream world. He told me he was getting a flight to Manchester the next day to join the Legends. What was I supposed to do? It was either madness or raw courage and defiance on Sandy's part. I'm not sure which. He probably thought there was nothing to lose. He'd told me a few weeks later:

> 'There's nothing worth living for. I can't eat, I can't talk and I can't play snooker.'

The cold war between both sides of Alex's family threatened to erupt into something more serious after he died. Funerals, like weddings, can bring out the worst in people. The fact that Alex's children and ex-wife were on the other side of the water aggravated matters further. They felt left out. Jean couldn't understand their grievances.

> They were annoyed because I asked Will Robinson to help with the funeral. What was wrong with that? Will was a good friend of Alex's and knew about event organisation. If Lauren thought they could do it better, they should have jumped on a plane. They treated Will with no respect instead of thanking him for a difficult job well done.
>
> I thought the funeral did our Sandy justice. There was no way he'd have wanted anything quiet. He was an actor. Sandy didn't just arrive anywhere, he swept in with a flourish of his cloak. The horse-drawn carriage was just right.

Ann's keen to encourage contact with Jordan. He's been to Belfast a couple of times and says he feels at home. Says Ann:

> I think he likes the freedom he gets over here. He's shy but so was his father when he first went away. That's why he took a drink. Jordan's lacking in confidence. We want to help him find it.
>
> A big part of my life has gone with Sandy. In some ways he was more like a son than a brother to me. Sometimes I wouldn't see him for months but that didn't matter. Sooner or later he'd be on the phone asking me to sort out his visa. I won't have counselling because I need to go through this my way.

I've thought a lot about Sandy's battle to stay alive. It was never easy to know what he was thinking but he probably gave up in the end. He must have known the COPD [chronic obstructive pulmonary disease] would kill him. He did nothing to help himself. He thought he could be his own doctor, dosing himself with antiseptics and herbal concoctions just like my mummy would have done. I found unused packets of amoxicillin in his cupboard. That was the antibiotic to treat his pneumonia. He had one packet marked June and the other July. As soon as the pain eased, he must have stopped taking them. He just didn't get it.

As we all know, Sandy could be horrible to people, but when he turned on the charm, he could twist you around his little finger. You couldn't refuse him anything. He'd whisper: 'It's the smile, Ann.'

He was right. The Higgins' smile was irresistible. It helped him throughout his life. He would have liked to get rid of that dark side of his character, but he never did. He couldn't. He didn't talk about it either. He knew it was something he couldn't control.

On New Year's Eve 2010, Jean bucked up the courage to watch the funeral CD for the first time. She thinks Alex would have been pleased. Then she started the painful business of going through his effects. She burned a lot of the stuff because she didn't want documents falling into the wrong hands. She was amazed that someone auctioned one of Alex's betting slips for £2,000.

Even stranger was a letter she found among her brother's medical records. In it, Alex pledged to donate his organs to medical science! Trust him to come up with a twist in the tail.

Incidentally, Jean kept Alex's mobile in a drawer after he died. The following Christmas she heard it ringing!

19

HE WAS OUR RESPONSIBILITY

If you mentioned snooker's governing body to Alex Higgins, steam came out of his toes, never mind his ears. Mention Alex Higgins to the WPBSA and they pretend they don't speak English. Until I contacted Martyn Blake, the former company secretary who sat in on many of the disciplinary hearings, I didn't think it was possible to *hear* someone turn pale.

Many of us believe British sport would better off without its ruling elite. We wouldn't bankroll incompetent Swedish coaches or equally lustreless Italians who really *don't* speak English, to teach us a game we invented. We wouldn't saturate cricket with a Twenty20 match in every drinks break. We might have brought tennis within reach of families outside the higher tax bracket – and produced a winner or two. The World Professional Billiards and Snooker Association are right up there with the FA, the ECB and the LTA.

Many of us sympathised with Alex Higgins when he took on the stuffed shirts. Who can pretend they didn't smile when he told them to stick their crooked game up their jaksi? WPBSA directors may not ever have relieved themselves in a plant pot, but I bet they've been glad of a tree here and there. And for Paul Hatherell, read any jobsworth who didn't understand timing or performers. That's not to condone head-butting, just to suggest there are ways of bringing it on.

Loose cannons are exciting when they're not your responsibility but a pain in the backside when you're trying to run a sport on behalf of several thousand members. Alex would never knuckle down to authority. He didn't do it at Kelvin School on the few occasions he graced them with his presence, so why would he start now?

He firmly believed the WPBSA had it in for him and that a combination of envy and spite drove certain officials to make life as difficult as they possibly could for him. Was that paranoia? Was he doing his usual trick of blaming everyone except the culprit when things went wrong? Certainly there were questions to be asked. Among them:

> *What did the association do for him when he was sick and homeless?
> *Why was there only a token presence at his funeral?

To find out more, I spoke to the current chairman, Barry Hearn, Rex Williams who was in the chair at the height of Alex's notoriety, and a former director, David Taylor, aka the Silver Fox. This was the Alex Higgins *they* knew. Barry takes us back to the days when *he* was as big a gambler as The Hurricane.

> Some people forget what snooker was like in the early seventies. The world championships lasted a year and players arranged their own matches. The image was downbeat. My mum would have given me a clip around the ear if she'd caught me going into a snooker hall. And yet, at the other level, it was upmarket and strait-laced. Aristocrats invented it and played it on snooker tables in their ancestral homes. When I bought Lucania Temperance Billiard Halls Ltd in 1973, my daytime customers consisted of the sick, the out-of-work and the out-of-prison. At six o'clock in the evening the clientele changed. Exit thieves and vagabonds, enter the white-collar brigade.

When Alex came onto the big stage, he and his background were unique. His contemporaries were Ray Reardon, an ex-policeman, Rex Williams, an aristocratic Midlander and Eddie Charlton who carried in the Australian flag at the Commonwealth Games. They were pillars of society. All of a sudden, this scrawny little kid arrives from Belfast with attitude and no respect for the system or the people in the game. His respect was reserved for the balls, the cue and the table.

I didn't meet him until 1974. It was clear this was someone who mirrored Muhammed Ali with his inner desire to be recognised, be famous and be loved – all the things he missed in his native land. He'd spent his time in Belfast billiard halls which were rough places. Billiard halls everywhere were rough places. I remember the first time I walked into one. Four blokes were playing with a shotgun under the table. That was only in Lewisham!

So into the professional game breezes this enigma called Hurricane Higgins. It transformed snooker. A real-life hurricane was whistling through our game. People everywhere were talking about him. 'Have you seen this kid?' Snooker players' heads work in definite ways. They automatically assess the reward/risk ratio of every shot. Different players have different percentages of risk-taking. Up until Alex arrived, there was minimal risk-taking. The game revolved around long periods of safety play. Opponents jockeyed for position.

Alex rewrote that. His percentages were hugely towards attacking snooker. He could play safe if he wanted to but usually he didn't want to. His opening shot got you thinking immediately. He was already several moves ahead. In the middle of break-building, a player might think: 'I won't screw back on that. I'll play it safe.' Alex took the opposite view. He kept the break going as long as possible because that's how you won the frame. This gave him a massive advantage over the Steady Eddies, as long as he didn't miss. Other players were frightened of him. They daren't leave a ball out in the open because Alex would get it.

Steve Davis learned from the Joe Davis manual. It was full of things like: 'Don't go for that, play safe; leave this one alone, play safe.' Alex would have binned it. Added to his new style of play was an off-the-wall personality. He was as mad as a hatter but he had this tremendous desire to be loved. He didn't play snooker to win. He played to be loved. He wasn't disappointed when he lost a game but he was crestfallen if he hadn't given the crowd what they wanted. He needed the appreciation and the backslapping. The downside was the hangers-on. All that: 'Come on, Alex, let's have a drink' stuff. It was part and parcel of being admired.

Because he saw himself as the Mohammed Ali of snooker, he had to be a rebel. He had to be outside the system. The People's Champion could say what he thought and do as he wished. Stuff the consequences! He wanted to be a folk hero like Ali and George Best. His game was a way of fast-tracking that, literally. With no formal education behind him, there was no other way he could make a mark in life. There was no-one else remotely like him. We had to wait ten years for Jimmy White.

Alex was already world champion and established on the circuit when Matchroom got started. From 1975 it was obvious that Davis was going to be something special. I invited lots of pros to the Matchroom because my boy needed as much practice as he could get. In those days I used to gamble a lot. I paid Steve £25 plus a bonus out of the winnings if we won. We always won – against Spencer, Reardon, Mountjoy, Thorburn, whoever. They were paid an appearance fee but that was usually all they got. Steve wiped the floor with them. Higgins too. When he breezed into Matchroom, the conversation would be:

'How much am I on tonight?'

'You're on £500, Alex.'

'And what price am I?'

'Five to four.'

'Right. I'll have my £500, plus *this* on me to win.'

He'd empty every pocket. There'd sometimes be two, three of four thousand quid in his hand. That was a lot of money in the seventies. I remember once when he came to settle his account and pulled 14s 6d out of his pocket. He put it in my hand and said: 'Call that a pound.' He bet every single penny he had on himself and lost every time. Davis on his own table in Romford was unbeatable but Alex never learned his lesson. Steve was given a 10–14 point start because he was a rookie and no-one knew him. It was a licence to print money. That's how he came to be known as 'Nugget' because all the local boys backed him knowing he was a nailed-on cert. Alex took it well but at the end of the evening he'd say: 'Can you lend me £50 for the train fare home?'

We played the best of nines or the best of elevens and, one glorious time, the best of sixty-five. Davis and Higgins played every afternoon and evening for four days. It was the finest snooker I ever saw in my life. They were level for the first four sessions, then Higgins pulled away. But you knew he'd have a bad session some time.

You couldn't get into the place for people. The actual matchroom was just a little space on the first floor. There were no windows and no fire escape – just a tiny door to squeeze through. We had 300 spectators every session paying £5 or £10 a ticket. You couldn't see for smoke. Every now and then a hand would appear out of the smoke and a voice would call: '£300!' Big money was changing hands.

The knees of the crowd were only eight feet away from the edge of the table. Players had to say: 'Excuse me!' We had four nights like that. After the sixth session, Alex was trailing by seven or eight frames and Steve needed two more to win. The crowd were giving Alex some stick because all their money was on Steve. He turned to them and shouted: 'Right, you cockney bastards. I'm not coming back tomorrow so if you've bought your ticket, you've wasted your fucking money!'

There was nearly a riot. I took Alex downstairs to cool off. He said: 'Ignorant bastards. I'm getting no respect. They don't love me. I'm not having this.'

Trouble always flared up when he didn't play well. People say he was a bad loser but that's not true. He was frustrated when he couldn't entertain to the level he'd set himself. Again, he wanted to be loved. He carried on shouting. He said he'd fight anyone. He tried to nut me. I had him up against the wall.

'You little prick!'

'I'm not coming back!'

'You've been paid. You're coming back.'

'I'm *never* coming back.'

'I'll see you here at twelve noon tomorrow.'

He wriggled free and left. People were wondering whether to get a refund. I told them he'd be back. Sure enough, he walked in at the appointed time: 'Hi, Bal. You okay? I feel good today.'

Then Steve beat him.

Alex gave us all a reality check. The dinner-suited image didn't reflect the game any more. It had gone through a class change. What Alex brought to the table was the reality of the working man's snooker. That meant fags, booze and fights. He was connected. The WPBSA were the ones out of step. That's why he was acclaimed as the working-class hero. People who played snooker all the time looked upon him as one of their own. Sticking it up the Establishment always goes down well.

Alex asked me three or four times to be his manager. He wasn't an idiot. He could see that the game was moving forward. He saw that Matchroom was going all around the world with my Famous Eight, having it off, making money, but more important from his point of view, getting the adulation. Bangkok, Tokyo, Sao Paolo, the sky seemed to be the limit. It was a sword in the guts to Alex. He wanted to be there. He wanted to be the one walking out into the Queen Elizabeth stadium with 3,000 Chinese going mad like they were with Jimmy.

Alex and I had some mutual respect but I had to tell him he'd be a disaster to manage. I couldn't spare the time to be with him 24/7. Someone had to be. Snooker was so professional that he couldn't mess around the way he did. I'd have spent half my time picking him up from railway stations. To be fair, he never let me down but I wouldn't have slept a wink at night. Most of my grey hairs are named after Jimmy White. With Alex on board as well, I've have no hair at all!

He was completely uncontrollable. Unmanageable. He had a lot of wishy-washy management. Del Simmons was a nice guy, though. He could have made a difference. In those days, Alex was picking up £3–4,000 a night and working four or five nights a week outside the tournament circuit. That's heading for £1 million a year. It gave him a distorted view of money.

I remember bumping into him at Ascot when he'd blown £20,000 in readies on the first two races. His view was: 'Never mind, I'll get it back next week.' I'm all in favour of a glass half full but he needed someone like me or Del to say: 'I'm taking your money and putting it away.' We'd have come to blows. Alex always insisted on stuffing notes into his pockets. I'd be amazed if he even had a bank account.

His relationship with Steve was interesting. Steve's a total percentage man. It's all technique and method. He had no idea what Higgins would do next. None of us did. They played each other a lot and although Steve had the whip hand, Alex won a few. Steve had the utmost respect for him. He'd watch some of his shots and say: 'I couldn't do that.'

But Alex wasn't consistent enough to get the better of Steve over a period of time. Being a genius isn't enough. If anything the Higgins way of playing made Davis *more* methodical. It was a case of: 'Okay, he goes for the flair shots – I win the game. He pots great balls – I build big breaks.' It was like watching Spain beat Germany in the World Cup. Keeping possession of the ball might be boring but you sure as hell aren't going to win if you can't get hold of it. Higgins can be the greatest genius there's ever been but when he's sitting down, it's not much use to him. The Grinder wins in the end.

We became ashamed of Alex at the WPBSA. He paid us so much in fines, we should have named a tournament after him! Actually the money he got back from the Benevolent Fund may have left us even-stevens. By the time he head-butted Hatherell he was a liability. His game had largely deserted him, though he still won the Masters and the Irish Championship on one leg. In some ways that victory over Stephen Hendry was the most amazing of the lot. From being world champion in 1982, Alex began to go downhill. His excesses got worse which is peculiar because 1982 was probably the happiest he'd ever been. Lynn was a nice girl. She gave him the foundation. Perhaps the adulation he craved went to his head. He began socialising with footballers, pop idols and film stars. Alex was easily led astray.

Despite his nasty side – and it could be *very* nasty – he and George Best are still regarded as superstars, flaws or no. I've seen Higgins go up to geezers and whack them in the face. I often tried to figure out why he did it. I'm none the wiser. He usually got his blow in first because he knew that in a crowded place, the fight would be stopped. Maybe he wasn't as stupid as we think he was. As he got older, his relationships grew more and more volatile.

Should we have done more to help him at the end? I suppose you can always do more but people should remember that Alex had tens of thousands of pounds out of the Snooker Benevolent Fund. I didn't know that until last year. Every time he wanted something they gave him money. Unfortunately, most of it ended up in a Belfast bookmakers. The WPBSA began to say: 'Hold on a minute. This isn't helping us or him.'

People often ask me what snooker did for Alex Higgins. The answer is a hell of a lot. A sum of £20,000 had been approved for his teeth. There was no need for a fund-raising operation. We'd have used that sum to pay for the funeral but I was told by someone from the Save Alex Higgins Fund that there was £10,000 left over. I was asked if we'd pay for a tombstone. Of course we would. I didn't hear any more. Loads of Higgins fans wanted a statue of him in Sheffield. Did they honestly think I could use Alex Higgins's image as an inspiration to youngsters? Do they really expect me to put up a statue to a drug addict, alcoholic, gambler and wife-beater?

Paul Hunter who died from cancer was the nicest young kid you ever met. We haven't even got a *trophy* named after him. I don't want to decry Alex's contribution. His biggest achievement was to get people talking about snooker. They're still talking about Alex Higgins now, which is truly remarkable. The fellow hasn't been competitive for ten years! The game's been getting more coverage off the back of Alex's death than anything else. Notoriety doesn't necessarily deserve a statue. You wouldn't put John Terry's statue up at Stamford Bridge would you?

It's odd that he was catastrophic in his life but a total legend now he's gone. He pressed the self-destruct button and got away with it more times than any human being I've ever heard of. There was undeniably something magical about Higgins. The way he beat Jimmy in that world semi-final still has to be seen to be believed. You wouldn't have thought there was a one-visit clearance on offer in the entire frame, yet Alex found it. I remember watching the match live and thinking: 'This can't happen!' People don't play those shots any more. Most of them don't exist!

People asked me why, as chairman of the sport's governing body, I wasn't at Alex's funeral. I don't do celebrity funerals. I don't like any kind of funeral. The whole entourage puts me off. Jeremy Beadle was a good friend and one of the nicest guys I knew but I didn't go to his funeral. Having said that, I'd have gone to Alex's funeral if I could. I had an important appointment in New York and that was the only free day before the middle of November. The *Daily Mail* were right when they said the occasion was best judged by the people who *weren't* there – me, Steve Davis, Dennis Taylor, Terry Griffiths – all people who knew him at his worst. It wasn't the greatest incentive.

People lined the streets of Belfast weeping for a total arsehole. A horrible drunk. Snooker wouldn't have been the same sport without him, which is a huge compliment to the man, but there were many times when snooker would have been a better place without Alex Higgins.

Rex Williams was WPBSA chairman during the worst of Alex Higgins. Nobody would have wished that on the genial Black Country businessman. I got to know Rex while presenting ITV snooker and often marvelled at the way he could turn up in the television studio bright eyed and bushy-tailed after emptying whisky and brandy bottles with John Pulman into the wee small hours! I'm not suggesting Alex Higgins drove him to drink, but you wouldn't blame him for using it as an excuse. The worrying thing is that John was also expected in the studio, sometimes as early as 12.30 pm. Rex claims that if it hadn't been for him giving Pully three alarm calls each morning, the old maestro wouldn't have made it.

Rex's introduction to the game wasn't too dissimilar to Alex's, although the family background was very different. Rex's father owned a printing works near West Bromwich. At the age of nine, he found his way to the local billiard hall in Blackheath and also honed his technique on the table in his dad's factory. Once established in the professional circuit, Rex enjoyed two key things denied to Alex (or should I say that he denied himself?) – family life and a home to come back to. On the face of it, they were galaxies apart, yet there was empathy between them. As you'll hear, Rex still has a tinge of regret that he didn't manage Alex. Yes, he *is* serious. Here's Rex's take on The Hurricane.

> There was genuine hatred for Alex among players and members of the Board. I used to plead his case in those disciplinary hearings. I felt sorry for him. I told colleagues: 'He's trapped inside that body. Would you like to be trapped there for one day? He's got it every day of his life.'
>
> Alex often wasn't responsible for his actions. They were the products of a head that was mixed-up the first day he came into the game and never got untangled. I remember when he joined the Association. I'd heard about him through the grapevine. He walked into the WPBSA office and said: 'We've met before, Rex. You came to Belfast with Fred Davis and played at the Queen's Ballroom. I came to watch you. Afterwards, I asked you how to become a pro.'

Then I remembered. I had lots of pimply faced kids asking me the same question but this one seemed more focused. There was no hint of what was to come when we accepted him into the ranks. He was twenty-one. A few months later he beat me in the semis on his way to winning the world championship in his first year. It was extraordinary.

We stood at 30-all in the best of 61. I missed the blue in the final frame and he won 31–30. It's a compliment to Alex that if he hadn't beaten John Pulman in the quarter-final – much to everyone's surprise – he wouldn't have been in a position to beat me. Pully was a great player with loads of experience but Alex was the quickest learner I've ever seen around a snooker table. I don't say he was the greatest player, but he had the quickest brain. He was raw as far as the tactical side of the game went. He hadn't played at that level before. Playing with the top pros was a different league from Belfast. I was 5 frames in front in our semi-final but he pegged me back. I was playing safety shots that he couldn't have known or understood unless he'd picked them up from Pulman. Towards the end he was playing the same type of safety as me. He was learning from me as the match went along – and beating me too. It was quite unnerving – like dealing with a creature from another planet!

That's meant as a compliment. He did some silly things in his career but when he played snooker, there was always method in what he did. I'd have underestimated him if he hadn't beaten Pully. That was a warning. Unfortunately, I didn't heed it well enough. Not many people thought Alex could beat John Spencer in the final. From what I'd seen, I thought he could. And of course, he did. Alex said to me many years later: 'That blue you missed changed our careers. I won the world championship and you didn't.' That was my last chance. I was forty then. My career was going down. I'd been a pro since 1951.

I used to study Alex as others did. We couldn't understand how he managed to strike the ball so accurately. He jumped up as he made contact but we reckoned that on the point of impact he must have been doing something right. Spencer and I took Alex into the practice room and tried to get him to keep his head down. He missed the shots and said: 'Look what happens when I keep my head down!'

I enjoyed playing him. The speed of his shots and his constant twitching didn't bother me. I liked players who got on with the game. It was a real battle but you'd get a few chances, unlike playing Fred Davis. Alex took risks but people should remember how good his safety play could be. I commentated on a famous frame between Higgins and Cliff Thorburn which lasted more than an hour. You'd think that would be boring. In fact it was one of the most fascinating frames of snooker I've seen. Thorburn would play a fantastic shot to put Alex in what he thought was deep trouble, only for Alex to return the favour with interest.

I don't think you can say Alex was responsible for the increased awareness of snooker around the country. The reason we had a surge of interest was *Pot Black* which started in 1969. Alex arrived when the boom was already underway. I concede that the game benefitted from having him there, but if he'd arrived ten years earlier, no-one would have noticed. I'm not sure you could say that snooker *needed* him either. There's room for one Alex Higgins in professional sport, but no more. There's no doubt he was the main reason snooker continued to grow. People watched because of him. There were only two players who could pack a place out – Joe Davis and Alex Higgins. Joe was just as quick. He was the Rolls-Royce, Alex was the clapped-out Ford. They both reached their destination.

Five years after that Higgins final in 1972, Pulman was invited to tour Australia with Imperial Billiards. They rang him from

Sydney to ask about the whizz kid. Would he bring Alex as well? John replied in that low key way of his: 'I don't think that's a terribly good idea. He's such a hellraiser, he won't live to see thirty!'

He sensed big problems and didn't fancy being on the other side of the world with someone so irresponsible. However, they talked him into it and John made all the arrangements for Alex to go. What a combination, Pully and Alex! They both liked a drink but intellectually they were chalk and cheese. Their hotel rooms were next to each other. As early as day two, the chambermaid complained to John: 'Mr Higgins is a dreadful man. He knew I was in the bedroom and came out of the bathroom wearing only black underpants!'

Pully replied: 'It's terrible, I know. They were white when he left England!'

Alex got into all sorts of trouble down under. He pulled a gun on two girls during a tournament in Melbourne. The police were called but he'd scarpered. They knocked on Ray Reardon's door in the early hours of the morning to see if he knew where Alex had gone. Eventually they found him and put him on a plane back to the UK with an order not to come back. He did of course – to Sydney anyway. He got involved with the local mafia because casinos were illegal in New South Wales. He fell foul of the mafiosi too. He was found unconscious in the street after being chucked downstairs. Most of Pully's nightmares had come true!

I once got in a fight with Alex myself. I was playing spoof and having a few drinks with Pulman, Thorburn and a couple of others. Alex charged into the room. He was buzzing around looking over our shoulders and being a real nuisance. We were all getting exasperated so I told him to fuck off. At least I tried to tell him. Before I could get the words out, he hit me on the side of the head. I got him by the throat against the wall. It was only because Thorburn held my arm that things calmed down. I'm not proud of that episode. It would take someone like Alex at his most irritating to get me that wound up. Afterwards, Thorburn said: 'I don't know why I was holding you back, Rex. I wanted you to hit him!'

Though the evidence might point the other way, Alex was wrong to say the WPBSA had it in for him. *I* certainly didn't. I thought we should have swept the pot-peeing episode under the carpet, if you'll forgive the pun. There'd been an official complaint about the incident so we were obliged to take it seriously. Word went around that the WPBSA were going to punish Alex hard. That wasn't my view. He'd just won the world championship. We'd had a great event and lots of publicity. The celebrations with Lynn and Lauren were shown worldwide. I couldn't see the point of washing our dirty linen in public – nor of humiliating the new champion. I thought we should give him a rap on the knuckle and forget it.

I couldn't believe the strength of feeling at the meeting. One of the players on the board wanted the fine to be £1,000. Another said £2,000. Then it went to £3,000. I stood up and said: 'Any advance on £3,000?'

It was ridiculous. Just then the door burst open and a waiter walked in with half a dozen bottles of champagne. We hadn't ordered any. The chap said: 'With the compliments of Mr Higgins, gentlemen.'

Alex was walking around outside almost in tears. I later found out the champagne had been organised by his agent, Howard Kruger. I can't remember whether we drank it or not. Doug Ellis was on the board at that time. I thought it was a good idea to get business people involved. The other members were Reardon, Spencer and Griffiths. Del Simmons was chief executive. I still think the £1,000 fine we agreed was too heavy. Peeing in a plant pot was a small misdemeanour, even though there were courtesy girls in the area. The press went mad with the story. I was on Alex's side. I definitely *wasn't* on his side over the Paul Hatherell head-butt. That was a serious offence. So I called an emergency meeting the next day.

The board said: 'Chuck him out of the UK championship now.'

I told them they couldn't do that. They wouldn't listen.

'He's got to go. Throw him out!'

'If that's what you intend to do, I'll resign here and now. I won't be part of it. You have to keep within the rules or Alex can come back at you and break this association.'

We had to go through the proper procedure. You can't have players meting out drastic punishments on other players. We were criticised over the plant pot issue for that very reason. I told them the head-butt had to be handled independently. They still wouldn't believe me. They'd have gone ahead and thrown him out if it hadn't been for a stern warning from the company lawyer. He said: 'Listen to the chairman. If you go outside the rules, you won't have enough money to fight the court case.'

We never saw behaviour like Alex's before or since. The explanation wasn't as simple as drink and drugs although he was heavily into both. He was just unable to control himself. He got it into his head that the authorities were against him. He hated the WPBSA, despite the things we did for him. It all blew up after I beat him in a tournament at Warrington. He went mad in the press conference, claiming the game was crooked and threatening to expose it. He charged out of the conference as I was going in. He went to shoulder charge me but I sidestepped him. Then he walked into a live TV interview with Dickie Davies and made the same accusations. Dickie asked for my reaction. I said it was a pity Alex couldn't lose more graciously.

Later, I was having a drink in the Green Room with Del and Gordon Ingham from the WPBSA when the door burst open. Alex turns on Gordon: 'You limping bastard!'

He then mistakes the company lawyer for the tournament sponsor and gives him both barrels: 'I wanna be paid! Where's my fucking cheque?'

The lawyer said he was so disturbed by Alex in that rage that he nearly gave him one. A cheque I mean! I went to Alex's room to try to reason with him. Unfortunately the telly was on and my interview with Dickie Davies came up. As soon as Alex heard me saying the bit about losing graciously, he went barmy again.

I don't think anyone could have straightened out his life. He wouldn't let them. Barry Hearn was the wrong temperament for Alex. He wouldn't have stood for the tantrums. There'd have been no sympathy. Del tried to handle him with sensitivity but it wore him down. A typical example was when he organised a car for Alex because he wanted to learn to drive. Del fixed it with Sid Faulkner, his mate in the car trade. A couple of days later, Alex rang Del: 'I don't like the car. Tell Sid to fetch it back.'

Sid did as he was told but reported back in a state of shock: 'This must be a joke, Del. There's no front end to the bloody thing!'

Apparently, a truck pulled out in front of Alex and took the bumper, headlights and radiator grill with it. Alex didn't mention the collision. He hoped no-one would notice.

I always wondered whether I should have managed him. There was one brief period of stability when he and Lynn started a family. That was the window. It's easy to say his instability was his own making but when you're away from home for such a long time and living out of a suitcase, it's perhaps not surprising that he was a rolling stone. If I'd have been his manager, I might have helped him to stay on a level plane. I thought about it many times but didn't get round to suggesting it. I know he'd have been a nightmare but there was a slim chance I could have saved him from himself. I'm sorry I didn't try.

Contrary to what some people think, the WPBSA *did* try to help him. We offered him a rent-free home for the rest of his life and we offered to split the profits from one of our tournaments. When he was suffering from cancer and in a financial mess, we agreed to dedicate the Irish Championships to Alex. We didn't have a sponsor so we could call it the Alex Higgins Irish Championships and give him 50 per cent of the gate money. The rest would go to a charity of his choice. Ray Reardon thought it was bad idea to give him cash. It would end up on the favourite in the next race.

Nevertheless, Martyn Blake, our company secretary, wrote to Alex explaining our plans. Martyn brought his reply to the next meeting and said: 'Before we go any further, gentlemen, perhaps I should read Alex's terms to you!'

That made us laugh for a start. We were offering to help and he had his *terms*? Point one was that he would present the winner's trophy. Point two was that he'd have his own stall within the arena, selling photographs and memorabilia. Point three was that if we didn't comply, he'd run naked through the Wembley Conference Centre at the next Benson and Hedges Masters! Reardon gave me a knowing look. I said: 'Not a word, Ray! I know that look. It means I told you so.' The plan would have netted Alex £5,000 but he threw it in our face. We should have known better.

I've often been taken to task on the issue of snooker players drinking. It wasn't against the rules. Players were allowed to drink what they liked. Look at Bill Werbenuik. On second thoughts, don't look at Bill Werbenuik, or Rubberneck, as Alex called him! On reflection it probably wasn't a good idea, though we were dealing with grown men who had choices. Alex was the only one I knew who could play better after a drink.

A classic case was the UK final when he came back from 0–7 to beat Steve Davis. I was commentating for the BBC. The match went crash, bang, wallop – 7–0! Del rang on his way to the venue and asked gingerly: 'How's it going, Rex?' When I told him the bad news he said: 'Oh God! He'll be impossible when I get up there.' The pair of us met in the Long Bar at Preston Guidhall just before the start of the second session. Alex wandered in as cool as you like: 'I couldn't do anything about it, fellahs. Everything he did went right – everything I did went wrong.'

It was true. I asked Alex if he'd been drinking during the interval. He said Lynn wouldn't allow it. I told him he should. I got him a half-pint glass two-thirds filled with vodka and topped it up with coke. I said: 'Get it down you!' He downed it in one. Del said: 'What have you done, Rex?' I said: 'Given him a chance to get his pride back.' Alex beat Davis 7–1 in the evening session. Before the next day's play got underway, he came up to me and asked: 'Has Dr Williams got my medicine ready?'

I got him a smaller one this time – more coke, less vodka. He didn't know. He went and beat Davis to win the tournament.

I also commentated on part of the 1982 final when he beat Reardon. Ray told me the pressure was too great for him at the end. I distinctly remember being on the microphone for Alex's match against Doug Mountjoy in an earlier round. He produced one astonishing shot. Alex had a free ball. To our surprise, he nominated the brown when he could have put Doug in all sorts of trouble. Alex rammed the brown into the top right-hand corner pocket at 200 mph and won the frame. Afterwards, I asked him why he took on the brown when there was a much easier option? He said: 'I had to prove to myself that I still had the bottle.'

That comment sums up Alex's game – daredevil and brave. That's why he could rouse a crowd like nobody else. That's why people flocked to see him. I was reminded of the tremendous support he engendered during a match I had against him in Preston one year. There were two tables in the big arena. Only a handful of spectators were at the second table, but there must have been a thousand waiting for us. I said to the referee: 'I can still pack 'em in, can't I?' Alex potted a ball about eighteen inches from the pocket and the crowd erupted. When I knocked in a long red I was really proud of, one solitary voice pierced the silence: 'Good shot, Rex.'

I turned to the fellah and said: 'Oh, I've got one supporter then?'

Another voice called out from the back: 'No, there are two of us!'

Alex deserved the adulation. Some of the shots he took on under pressure were breathtaking. He must have had nerves of steel. My first reaction when he died was: 'At least he won't suffer any more.' He had a sad, tormented life, without much of a break. I don't think he was a horrible drunk. There was a streak of kindness in him. I saw him volunteer to visit sick children in hospital. He was good at that. And yet he could be nasty to his best friend, Jimmy White, who did more than anyone to help him. Right to the end, Jimmy still thought the world of him. That says something.

Very few people, even his sisters, were aware that Alex could have spent the last quarter of his life in comfort. He didn't need to doss with friends or shiver in council houses. He didn't have to die in a soulless apartment whose warden was allegedly unaware that Alex hadn't surfaced for a few days before his body was found. Alex compared the place to a prison cell. He hated living there. If he hadn't been so stubborn, he could have been living rent-free in a Cheshire bungalow with free meals and a cleaner. Who would have provided it? None other than the WPBSA.

Let's go back to the late eighties when Alex's life was crumbling. Snooker brought him embarrassing defeats sprinkled with meaningless wins. His children were fast sliding out of his life and he'd finished with Siobhan Kidd. What's more, he was broke. David Taylor, a colleague of Alex's from the late sixties and a director of the WPBSA when he hit rock bottom, revealed this hitherto confidential information.

> We got a call from a friend of Alex to say he was in a dreadful state. He was living rough and couldn't afford to feed himself. I hated the thought of the former world champion without a roof over his head. I wanted him to finish has days with respectability. We had the cash to do it. We put together a rescue plan. The Players' Benevolent Fund, which had nearly half a million in its coffers, would buy a bungalow in Cheadle close to where Alex and his kids were living. The WPBSA would own the house but Alex could live in it rent-free for the rest of his life. He'd have no bills to pay. We'd provide two meals a day free of charge. They'd be delivered to his door. He'd also have a housekeeper to keep the place spotless, again at our expense.
>
> Rex Williams passed it as chairman. Ray Reardon was apprehensive. He warned: 'He might throw it back in your face, David.' I told him he must be kidding. What a great opportunity this was for Alex. He knew he'd have a roof till he died. The letter Alex sent back was shameful. It contained the f-word. He said he didn't want the house: 'Just give me the money.'

Ray Reardon was right.

I could tell from the first day I met him that this was no ordinary human being. I received an invitation to play the Irish wonder kid in Belfast in 1968. I hadn't heard of him but a trip to Ireland sounded like a nice break. The McMordie Hall was packed with 1,500 fans. I asked an official who this guy Higgins was. He replied: 'Good player.' Out stepped this skinny, anorexic-looking kid with a spotty face. He wore a big black studded belt. He was shaking so much he couldn't pot a ball. I won the first frame quite easily. In the second, I left him a red over the corner pocket. He had to pot it and get back on the black with the reds all over the place. He hit a terrible shot and left himself with the white over a corner pocket. The black was out of the question. I expected to him to play a safety shot because the pink was on its spot and straight.

Alex walked around the table, drew back his cue and hit the ball so hard, the pink disappeared. I asked the ref: 'Where's the pink?'

'It's in the pocket, David.'

'You're joking.'

'Really.'

It was too. Alex made a break of 80 in just over a minute. I'd never seen anything like it. He finished up beating me 4–3 and got a standing ovation. I looked round and thought: 'I'm glad I *didn't* win.'

After the game he asked if he could come to my hotel for a chat. He knew I'd just turned pro after winning the world amateur championship. He wanted to known how the system worked. I thought the lad was something special. He was bound to make it as a pro. I told him Australia was the place to go. He'd love it and they'd love his style of play. I told him I'd fix it with Eddie Charlton but Alex came over to Bolton to play in the Players Number Six instead.

It just took off for him there. Snooker suddenly looked a different game. He was giving Dennis Taylor 21 start and still beating him. I'd never seen anyone give so much of himself to one shot. Alex gave blood. And we'd never seen anyone watch his opponent so closely. Alex studied their hands, their eyes and their body language. It was intense.

It's amazing how quickly he adapted to the pro circuit. He started to upset the apple cart. The established players, Reardon, Spencer, Gary Owen and co. didn't like it much but they weren't daft. They knew he was putting bums on seats. Once that happens, the money follows. Alex broke the mould in many ways. Not just the speed. After two shots he'd have his bowtie hanging out of his shirt. When they tried to stop it, he came up with a certificate saying dress shirts gave him a rash on his neck. Snooker's popularity went through the roof. The BBC did blanket coverage when Terry Griffiths met Dennis Taylor in the world final. If you thanked Alex for helping to give us a good living, he'd say: 'Pay me then. Give me some money.'

That strikes a chord with David's wife, Janice, who travelled the circuit with him. She even played a bit of snooker – maximum break 35. The couple became good friends with Lynn and Alex. They'd visit each others homes regularly. She told me: 'You couldn't get a penny out of him. He was as tight as hell. He wouldn't buy a drink. I was a bit scared of him because you didn't know what was coming next. He shouldn't have married Lynn or anyone else. He wanted to carry on being a bachelor, then come home to find everything was as he left it. It was bound to end in trouble. I was there once when it blew up. Alex picked up one of his golf trophies and hurled it at Lynn. Lynn hurled it back and it hit the wall and smashed into smithereens. Alex sat on the floor surrounded by pieces of glass. He spent an hour gluing it back together. He wouldn't give up. When it was three-quarters done, he lifted it up, examined it and said: "It's fucked." He chucked it back at the wall.'

20

HE WAS OUR PASSPORT

Blackpool is no place to be when you're under the weather, so Alex adopted his customary position in the corner of the bar and ordered a Guinness. His good friend Damien Kelly had crossed the water from Dublin to lend moral support. They felt sure nobody would bother them here. They were wrong. Alex noticed movement out of the corner of his eye and swore under his breath: 'Bastards! I've only just found out and they're onto it already.'

Two tables away, a group of journalists had materialised out of thin air. More of them than you'd expect at the qualifying rounds. In normal circumstances, you wouldn't find the People's Champion here. Life hadn't been normal since he was banned and stripped of his ranking points. Attempting to claw his way back into contention was infra dignitatum. It was Lord Olivier playing the back end of a horse in the village panto.

Qualifying rounds are a snooker transit camp where upcoming hopefuls, all ambition and acne, square up to the downsliding hopeless, all thread veins and prostate. A place in the top sixty-four is either a foggy remembrance or a glittering aspiration, depending on which category you belong to. But Higgins on the road to oblivion was an old story. The media must have got wind of something else.

Has-beens like Alex couldn't have chosen a grimmer cemetery for their morale than Blackpool's Norbreck Castle. This mock - and mocking - fortress of a venue is guaranteed to squash your spirits at the first glimpse of its breeze-block battlements awash with seagull faeces. The faint aroma of Dunkin Donuts and the crash of Britain's most radioactive waves against the sea wall, combine to make it a five-pronged assault on the senses.

To give him his due, Alex took the tackiness in his stride. If the snooker authorities he despised were resolved to humiliate him, this was as good a place as any. It sharpened his loathing.

These thoughts however were overtaken by more serious ones. All he could hear were the words of the consultant repeating themselves over and over.

'I'm afraid the results are positive, Mr Higgins. It's cancer.'

He knew anyway. Several small growths had been removed from his mouth. He kept quiet about it. Even his sisters didn't know. Alex tended to leave unpleasant realities alone. His throat had been bothering him for some time. His voice had been growing weaker. In Blackpool, of all places, he received the phone call he'd been dreading. How did the press find out so quickly?

Damien, a former sales executive who latched onto Alex through their mutual love of snooker, golf, drink and gambling, was a member of that loose circle of friends prepared to drop everything when he called. They could be in Belfast or Dublin, London or Manchester. They were his chauffeurs, gofers, confidants and money-lenders. He was their passport to mischief.

Unaware of any hidden agenda, Damien exchanged pleasantries with the journalists while Alex tried to make himself as inconspicuous as possible. Damien said:

> They seemed a nice bunch. They made idle chit-chat and asked if Alex was in good health. I told them he was fine. He immediately put down his half-empty glass and growled at me: 'Drink up. We're out of here.' I wasn't about to argue. It's useless when he's in that mood. As we left the bar, Alex whispered: 'Those *nice* blokes you've been talking to are reporters, but they're not

snooker writers. They're newsmen and they're here for a reason. Why do you think they asked about my health?'

I had no idea until he told me: 'I've just been diagnosed with throat cancer. Those bastards knew before I did!' I told him how sorry I was. It hadn't occurred to me. I asked him how serious it looked. He said: 'I might make it through the qualifiers, but don't hard boil the eggs! Listen, babes, I'll beat this. There's no way the Big C's going to get *me*.'

And it didn't. Cancer and inordinate amounts of radiotherapy would damage his body but fail to destroy it. There was no sign of cancer when Alex died fifteen years later. Damien told me: 'He was the most fearless man I ever met. He was afraid of nothing and no-one.'

Damien and I met up in the railway diner at Dublin's Heuston Station. (Is there a Hedgeware Road and a Hislington somewhere?) The oak-panelled room with its subdued lighting and dark reproduction furniture was reminiscent of Milford Junction, the fictitious station in *Brief Encounter*. Celia Johnson could walk in at any moment!

As Damien stirred his Lapsang Suchong, I played my usual guessing game. What could this besuited, middle-class gentleman have had in common with a gunslinger like Alex Higgins? Damien was a retired executive, a devoted husband and a father of several. In other words, the last person you'd expect to find in the fug of a snooker parlour. Then the truth came out. It was delivered in a soft Irish brogue, refreshingly distinct from the harsher twang of an Ulsterman: 'I have a weakness for booze, women and the gee-gees.'

Enough said. Who had led whom astray? It emerged that Damien was a good amateur snooker player and once made a break of 131. He'd also sponsored an Irish professional, Stephen Murphy, and tried his hand at management. Somewhere down the line, it was suggested that managing Alex might benefit both. He replied: 'Not in a million years. That would be like minding sheep at a crossroads!'

However, as Damien discovered, it was infinitely preferable to minding Alex in a nightclub when he was half a dozen vodkas the worse for wear. That was like shepherding a herd of buffalo through Harrods' glassware department. There were many times during his adventures with Alex (1973–2010) when poor old Damien found himself on the horns of such a dilemma. It went with the territory. 'I avoided nightclubs like the plague. My idea of a good time is a sing-along in the pub. That was no use to Alex. After playing an exhibition match I'd organised for him in County Tyrone, he demanded a slice of the action.'

The nearest nightclub it was. Damien's discomfort was made more acute when Alex began chatting up an attractive blonde who was obviously spoken for. Naturally, this incurred the wrath of her boyfriend. He was ordering drinks when The Hurricane nipped into his parking space. It was classic Higgins with a classic outcome. Two rutting stags shouldered each other with increasing venom as tension mounted on the dance floor.

Before he could play peacemaker, Darren was hauled off his stool by Alex and shoved unceremoniously towards the enemy. Alex took cover behind Damien's back and shouted: 'If you think you're big, hit him not me!' Worryingly for Damien, the boyfriend *was* big. About six feet five inches. Damien's life flashed before him.

'I'm a confirmed coward. I'm wondering how the hell I got into this. I'd never hit anyone in my life. If someone went to hit me, I'd probably die from shock. I tried the diplomatic route but Alex pushed me closer and closer to this man-mountain. He kept telling him to hit me. It was my great good fortune that he took me for

Alex's official bodyguard and backed off. He said he didn't want his picture in the papers. That was a very narrow escape!'

It's part of the initiation process to fall out with Alex. He tested people. Most of his relationships began with negative equity. Damien's was no different. As usual, the issue was minor. Damien worked part-time selling snooker tables for BCE. In one particularly successful campaign, he sold thirty tables and agreed a deal which involved Alex putting on an exhibition for a nominal £1,000. His usual fee was double that, but this was a return favour to Damien.

The exhibition coincided with the birth of one of Damien's sons. Alex produced two bottles of champagne to wet the baby's head. He wanted Damien's son christened Alex. Damien had no intention of obeying this command but nodded politely. His wife couldn't stand Alex. The idea of naming her child after such a renegade would have been laughable. For no discernible reason, Alex had one of his turns. He hit the roof about his £1,000 fee.

'I've had to turn down £3,000 for you. Make it worth my while.'

'Stick it up your arse. I'll get someone else.'

Damien left Alex and went to the bar. Five minutes later, Alex swept into the bar wearing his signature long coat and fedora. Damien ignored him. Alex sidled up to him all smiles again. He apologised and agreed to accept £1,000. There was a pregnant silence. Alex fixed Damien between the eyes and joked: 'I suppose this means you won't be calling your son Alex?'

Damien's wife tried to persuade him to keep out of Alex's way, but to no avail. Despite being married for thirty-five years, he saw himself as a social freelance and enjoyed the spin-off potential when Alex went 'socialising'. He also liked the jeopardy.

> It was never far away. Alex was witty and great company much of the time but you had to be on your guard. He changed like

the wind. It was definitely a case of a spilt personality, though people made it worse by goading him. I warned them to stop but they couldn't help themselves. Then, sure as hell, Alex would rise to the bait because he had no fuse. That's when it was dangerous.

One night, Alex, me and the Irish snooker coach, Ritchie Dunne, went to a filthy old pub somewhere up country. A young invalid in a wheelchair started needling Alex. On and on he went. He thought he was being clever. He knew Alex couldn't hit him. There was a group of gypsies in the bar. They were big fellahs. Alex eventually lost his rag and called the lad spastic. The travellers jumped up and came for him. Two of them threatened to take Alex outside and kick him up and down the car park. There were ten of them against three of us.

Ritchie took control. He warned them that if we started a fight, someone would get badly hurt. What Alex had said was unforgiveable but would they be placated if *he* hit Alex on their behalf? A novel idea, I thought. They said yes, as long as Ritchie hit him properly. He promised he would because he was upset at Alex's remark too. He thought he should be taught a lesson.

Suddenly, he gives Alex a whack on the jaw and sends him reeling. Alex slowly gets to his feet and shouts: 'What are you doing, cunt?'

'Saving your fucking life!'

Two of the gypsies shake Ritchie by the hand.

'Fair hit. The matter's settled.'

Damien was Alex's guest at most of the big snooker events, including the world championships at Sheffield and the Coral UK in Preston.

He made sure I didn't pay for anything. I toured England and Ireland with him and hardly put my hand in my pocket. There again, Alex was getting it all for free. In the late seventies and eighties every club wanted him. They gave him a private room, free drinks – anything he wanted. In the latter years, it all changed. They wouldn't let him in!

I drove him miles. Very often it was on a whim. Once, after playing in Dublin, he decided he wanted to go to the north side of Belfast. Would I take him? We set off in the dead of night. At about 3.00 am, I noticed I was nearly out of petrol. All-night garages didn't exist in those days. Alex yells: 'Let's get into that hotel, quick!'

He bursts in on the night porter demanding a room. The porter says he's full. Alex says: 'I want a room and I want it NOW!'

The porter says he'll get us one but we'll have to share. He starts filling in a form for us to sign. Alex isn't waiting for that. He gets out a ten pound note. 'Fuck the form. Put this in your pocket and keep quiet. We'll be gone as soon as the petrol stations open at 7.00 am.'

We slept for three hours, filled up and eventually got to Belfast. Crazy days. And there was I, a father of seven, running around like a college student. I didn't see much of Alex in the last five years but I miss his energy and his sense of humour. It got harder and harder to understand what he was saying when he voice changed. He'd crack jokes and wonder why I didn't respond.

One of my fondest memories is of Alex and his Irish soda bread. He loved the way they baked it at the Arcadian Hotel in Newbridge. It's dark brown, almost black, with treacle in it. You can't get it in England. Alex would order bread and soup. That's all I ever saw him eat. He'd say: 'I'm over next week, Damien. Can't wait for some more of the black bread.'

It saddened me that he didn't have much contact with his kids. I think the adulation of people meant more to him than the love of his own family. That's why he always made the big entrance. He was larger than life and larger than death. Despite the common perception, he was rarely lucky with women. He couldn't hold a conversation with them. He sometimes made an idiot of himself. The usual trick was to get them to go back with him to the Kedean Hotel which was an hour out of town. He hoped once he got them there, the distance would persuade them to stay the night. He wasn't very subtle.

Later on when he couldn't have a sex life, all his energies went into gambling. When you get up in the morning, you need something to look forward to. Even when he only had small amounts of money, gambling was still the buzz. That's all he had. What a contrast to the freewheeling days when he'd blow ridiculous sums at the Curragh. I remember wearing one of those big Aran sweaters the Clancy Brothers used to wear. I belted it across the middle, stuffed £11,000 inside and pulled the belt extra tight. It was all Alex's cash. There wasn't even a fiver left in the sweater when we came home. Alex had done the lot.

He was unlucky with horses *and* women. He knew the trainers and studied the form. He was so knowledgeable he could have been on *Mastermind*. What good does it do you? Half the time the trainers don't know what they're doing themselves. It's a mug's game. There were plenty of dramas and plenty of tight corners but I wouldn't have missed my time with Alex for the world.

Michael Gaffrey, who, as we have seen, rescued Alex and Siobhan Kidd on a Marbella road late at night, also knew it was a dubious privilege to play chauffeur and host to a national institution. Michael was The Hurricane's guest at premium events in New York, Dubai and Los Angeles, but his first outing was nearer home. It began with a typical Higgins phone call on Easter Sunday. He was on the train from Belfast to Dublin. Would Michael pick him up at Heuston? It was more of an all-points bulletin than a request. Michael agreed. It might be fun.

The first shock was seeing Alex on crutches as he hopped off the train. He was recovering from his death-defying leap from Siobhan's first floor window. The second shock was that Alex had gone on the wagon - maybe not for life but for the foreseeable future. In preparation for the B&H Irish Masters that Easter holiday, he'd kept off the booze for a whole week. Michael and Alex ended up at a pub in Malahide with Alex drinking alcohol-free cider. Michael thought it rather strange that sobriety should be his priority when the inability to walk appeared more of a threat to his victory hopes.

Be that as it may, Michael's wife Breda took Alex's mind off the bottle with a slap-up dinner. He scoffed the turkey and asked for more. He never did that. Perhaps the teetotalism made food more appealing. Michael describes the rest of the week.

> We went to Fairyhouse for the Irish Grand National on Easter Monday. Alex had tickets to the inner sanctum. He told me Siobhan would be joining us the next day, in time for his match in the B&H Masters. He had a wild card entry because he'd been stripped of all but one of his ranking points. They thought taking the lot would have denied him his livelihood. Alex lost a fortune at the Grand National. He was in a filthy mood. I said: 'Let's have a pint and forget it.' It was the worst thing I could have said.
>
> He went doolally: 'Michael, I've told you I'm not drinking!'

'Come on, one won't hurt.'

He stormed off, swearing he wasn't coming back. I removed his things from my car and left them by the roadside for him. Then I felt guilty so I went back to see if he was all right. There was no sign of Alex, his bag, his cue or his crutches. He only had to raise his hand and passing cars would queue to pick him up. The tiff was forgotten the following day. He phoned to say he had tickets for Breda, me and our three children to watch him play. Alex was a 33–1 outsider for the Masters but I had £50 Irish on him. The bookmaker said: 'Are you joking? The guy's on crutches.'

'I know. He's living with us.'

He won of course. When he reached the semi-finals, I arranged Siobhan's air ticket from Manchester. When we took our seats, Alex was already playing. He looked up at me and said within in earshot of everyone: 'Siobhan's over there.'

We joined Siobhan and had a quiet chuckle about Alex's damaged foot. Breda dressed it for him during the match. Siobhan told us how he came to jump from the window and injure himself. Apparently, he'd been gambling at the casino and came back to the flat to get more money. She refused to let him out because she didn't want him losing again. That's when he jumped.

The final was an incredible affair. He was limping and hopping around the table but Stephen Hendry was ahead at the break. Siobhan, Breda and I went to his hotel room to chill out. He was lying on the bed watching the omnibus edition of *Coronation Street*. He ordered prawns and scampi for us all but no alcohol for him. He had his usual collection of good luck charms, post-cards and letters on the dressing table.

We set off for Goffs and the evening session. The crowds were six deep. We daren't risk the main gate or Alex would be

> suffocated. It was dangerous in there. Supporters were hanging over the rails. I'd never seen anything like it. It went 8–6 to Hendry. In the dressing room, Alex looked nervous. He said: 'I don't know what to do. What do you advise?'
>
> 'Try to enjoy it. You came here with no expectations. You've won £20,000 already and there's another £15,000 if you win. No pressure.'
>
> He was behind twice in the final frame but came back to win 9–8. The place erupted every time he went to the table. It was mayhem when he won. Everyone had forgotten about the bad foot and the crutches. Hendry said Alex's limp seemed to vanish the better he played. Damien Kelly ran on stage to give Alex a kiss. He had money on him. Siobhan was there to hug him.

It was like a repeat of the Lynn and Lauren scene at the world championship but with a different blonde. Hearing the deafening roar for Alex at the end! For a 33-1 outsider with a bandaged foot, it was almost surreal. The wily old John Pulman, who'd seen just about everything in his time, wrote: 'One of the most extraordinary scenes I've ever witnessed in snooker was Alex Higgins winning at Goffs in 1989. He beat Stephen Hendry in the final while hobbling around the table on a broken foot. That was the most amazing sight you could imagine. He was dead and buried three times but fought his way back to win.'

Michael Gaffney won £3,000, Damien slightly less. Alex came down to earth with a bump. He had to be in Blackpool the next day for yet more qualifiers. He was going from the sublime to the faintly ridiculous, from a delirious crowd to emptiness and silence. How would he motivate himself? Alex only had time for a celebratory sip of champagne then it was an early night followed by a 6.00 am alarm call next morning. Less than twenty-four hours after being hailed by the whole of Ireland, he was dumped unceremoniously out of the qualifiers.

Goffs would be his last hurrah. For Michael, however, it was only the beginning. Next stop was Dubai. Alex had qualified for the national championship. Michael broke a business trip to Hong Kong to join him in the Middle East.

> They had a beautiful snooker centre with cushioned seats. Alex introduced me to the sheikh, a fine looking fellow more than six feet tall. We went out every night to rock concerts or cabaret bars and played golf during the day on the most magnificent course. The sheikh gave us free equipment. After every three holes there was a bar, food and as many women as you could want. As Alex said: 'Yer man the sheikh has a knocking shop in the middle of the fucking course!'
>
> I'd hardly got over that when Alex's agent, Doug Perry, phoned to say there was a first-class ticket to Los Angeles waiting for me. Alex was off to Las Vegas for a week. It coincided with the Tyson-Ruddick fight, though we didn't have tickets for that. Neither Siobhan nor Doug could go, so he wanted me there. I wasn't sure I could spare the time. I'd only just come back from another trip to Hong Kong. Fortunately, my boss was an understanding chap. I checked on the computer. My name was already on the passenger list before I got the invitation.
>
> Alex had never been to the States. He was scared to go on his own. He was scared to go *anywhere* on his own. I don't think I've met such an insecure individual. Alex gave Heathrow officials his autograph and they fast-tracked us through customs. We had a marvellous champagne-fuelled flight before being collected at the airport and whisked away to the Four Seasons Hotel in Beverley Hills where only the rich and famous stay. I discovered that the trip had been organised by a wealthy English

fan of Alex's. He invited us to lunch in Rodeo Drive. Demi Moore and Bruce Willis were there. I had to pinch myself. I was in Hong Kong on Monday, Beverley Hills on Wednesday.

The next day just happened to be St Patrick's Day. I got up early and went for a long walk. I came across an Irish pub with a queue outside. Everybody in LA is Irish on St Patrick's Day! I called Alex and told him to get there sharpish. There was time for a quickie before we left for Las Vegas. Alex carried £6,000 for the trip. He kept four and gave me two in case we were mugged. He took one look at the line of people waiting for the pub to open and changed his mind.

'Fucking hell, Michael, I'm not queuing.'

He went up the man on the door.

'Do you know who I am? Alex Higgins, the world snooker champion.'

The doorman gave him a blank look. As luck would have it, the pub door was open and someone inside recognised him. He shouted: 'There's Alex Higgins!' The doorman let us through. We had two wonderful pints of Guinness, then flew to Vegas with the millionaire fan who arranged it all. We booked into the MGM Grand where the fight was being staged. As we walked around the hotel, our host kept leaving us for the loo.

I asked Alex if the guy was okay: 'Has he got a cold? Look at his nose.' How naive of me! He was doing coke. I was astonished when he invited us duck shooting at his ranch. I told Alex to count me out. There was no way I'd go shooting with a coke addict. Then the guy went missing in the hotel and we didn't see him again. His wife picked up the tab. She didn't reimburse the £2,000 Alex lost at the tables!

The treats continued. Alex invited me to New York. He had tickets for the Prince Naseem-Kevin Kelly fight at Madison Square Gardens. He sometimes overlooked the fact that I had a full-time job and wasn't as free as he was, but how could I refuse an offer like that? We got to NY a couple of days before the fight. Alex said: 'I wonder where the Prince is staying. I'd like to meet him.'

I made enquiries at reception and managed to get Naseem's number through Brendan Ingle, his Irish trainer. I told one of his entourage that Alex Higgins wanted to meet Nas. He thought it was a wind-up. I put Alex on the phone. A few minutes later, we were in a fabulous pool club in downtown New York. The Prince and Alex played about ten games into the early hours of the morning. Alex let him win a few. Nas asked what tickets we had for the fight. We said the normal package-tour tickets. He said to forget them. He'd leave ringside tickets at reception. The Prince was knocked down in the first round but won in four.

Pierce Brosnan sat near us and couldn't believe Alex was there. Pierce comes from Navan in the Republic and was a big Higgins fan: 'I've followed him since I was a boy. I'd love to meet him. Can you introduce me?'

He flung his arms around Alex. The Americans couldn't understand what was going on. They knew Brosnan but they'd never heard of Alex Higgins. Why was a superstar hugging a stranger?

I kept in touch with Alex for years. The trouble was, you never knew when he might drop in. He flew to Dublin late one night with nowhere to stay. Instead of knocking at our door, he decided to stay at Gibneys, a pub in Malahide. Old Jack Gibney had a nasty shock the next morning when Alex ordered breakfast. They'd no idea he was there. He'd climbed onto the pub roof and broken in through a skylight. Alex seemed to think it was perfectly normal behaviour. He took a fancy to Jack's oil lamp in the bar. He said he wanted it and would Jack leave it to him in his will? Jack replied: 'I'll do better than that. When you win the next world championship, I'll *give* it to you.'

Alex never got the oil lamp. Nevertheless he was a big hero in Malahide. They all wanted a piece of him. One day when Siobhan was over, Alex and I were having a drink at the golf club. They were about to pull the shutters down in the bar when the club captain asked Alex for a game of snooker.

Alex responded positively. He told the barman: 'Okay, shutters up!' Then, turning to me: 'Get Siobhan and Breda down here. Tell them to bring my cue from under the bed.'

It turned into a major exhibition. The bar stayed open all afternoon and evening. Alex played dozens of members. Amazingly, the snooker room had tiered seating. The place was full. They all wanted to play Alex Higgins. They still talk about that day in Malahide. It's the biggest thing that ever happened.

Alex invited us to his mother's funeral. It was at the height of the Troubles. I asked the advice of one of our store managers in Belfast. He warned me not to drive a southern registered car in the Sandy Row district. They'd attack it. The manager gave us a lift to the house. Alex's mother was laid out in the lounge. The only person from the snooker world was Len Ganley. We marched with the coffin through the estate. There were loyalist slogans everywhere. It was quite an eerie experience for me. I didn't know Alex's mum but I met his dad at Goffs. I remember Alex giving him one of his dress suits to wear. Alexander senior was a real gentleman.

Not long after his mother died, Alex went down with cancer. As soon as I heard they'd admitted him to Belvoir Park Hospital I knew it was bad news. I went to see him after his first treatment. He was using a false name – Mr. Jones. When I walked in he was chatting to the nurses. He saw me and jumped up to put his clothes on. He was skin and bone even then. They allowed him out for a while so I drove him to a pub with guess what next door? A bookmaker. He suddenly remembered he couldn't take me in because I was Catholic. I felt uncomfortable.

I saw him again when he came out of hospital. Ann had set him up in a little council house. I knew it wouldn't suit him. It was too far out of town. There was no pub or betting shop and he didn't stay there long. Somehow he got down to Dublin for my daughter's wedding but he was very sick. I put him on the celebrity table with Louis Copeland and a sports writer from the *Irish Times*, Peter Byrne. He was there most of the evening looking like death. Instead of leaving him, I stayed in the same hotel room to keep an eye on him. I didn't think he'd survive until the morning.

21

HE WAS MY WARD OF COURT

Keeping Alex out of police stations and law courts was such a recurring challenge they could almost have marketed it as a computer game. He came within a whisker of being detained at Her Majesty's pleasure after decking the tournament director, Paul Hatherell, in 1985. Alex called it 'the most expensive head-butt in history'. It did him more harm than Paul.

His punishment from the WPBSA made a large dent in his wallet and hurried his demise as a serious sportsman. But it could have been worse. At the Hatherell hearing, Alex had the benefit of a good lawyer, Anthony Burton, and an Olympic smooth-talker, Howard Kruger. Between them they conjured Alex's escape from Alcatraz. He was bound over to keep the peace and ordered to undergo psychiatric tests.

The man appointed to guarantee his stainless behaviour from that moment on seldom gets a mention. Maybe he should have got a knighthood! His name is Mark Howarth. He stepped in where angels feared to tread. And yes, he kept his sanity!

Mark entered Alex's orbit by accident in 1982. Six years later, he staggered out of it with a sore head. In between, there was danger and excitement in equal portions as Mark became Alex's minder, chauffeur and event planner. I should throw in butler, gardener and bottom-wiper for good measure. To begin with, he did the job on a voluntary basis while running his own DPC business. It stands for Damp Proof Coursing. Alex could have done with some of that too.

Mark's friends thought it was the blind leading the blind. You could see their point. He was expelled from Rugby School as a teenager and led his parents a merry dance before getting his life together. Alex too was expelled - from normal society. Two black sheep were in the same pen. Could it possible work? Mark tells his story for the first time.

We got off to a good start. The WPBSA asked me to put on a trial snooker event at Trentham Gardens to see if it could be a suitable tournament venue. I wanted the two biggest names in the game – Alex Higgins, the current world champion and Steve Davis, the world number one. Barry Hearn agreed to a £2,000 fee for Davis but Del Simmons warned me that Alex would rather swallow his cue than have any dealings with the Ginger Magician.

I knew Alex drank at the Europa Hotel near Manchester airport so I spent three days waiting for him to show. On the third he did. With some trepidation, I approached him at the bar. I needn't have worried. Alex was agreeable. It turned out to be one of the easiest deals I ever did. Del couldn't believe it. The event was a big success and Trentham became a popular venue for ranking tournaments. After that, Alex and I bumped into each other in Manchester clubs. We were nodding acquaintances. One day he asked for a lift. Some lift! I spent the next five hours running him around Cheshire. I didn't mind. It was an honour to chauffeur the world champion. It didn't do my credibility any harm.

He was a lonely individual. Lynn had left him and taken the kids, then Del Simmons stopped managing him and Alex stopped practising. He was rudderless. It was obvious he loved his kids and the stability of a family, even if he treated it casually. I liked the guy. He was quick-witted and had a good sense of fun. He was also knowledgeable. His reading ranged from Robert Ludlum and Freddie Forsyth to biographies of jockeys and magazine articles about the Troubles in Northern Ireland. He devoured the newspapers. For someone who hardly went to school, he seemed very well educated.

I soon realised that all the good things invariably went out of the window when he drank. One sip too many and his eyes glazed over. Then the shutters came down. Trouble was inevitable. The most common trigger was fans outstaying their welcome once he'd given them an autograph or posed for a photograph. I used to say enough is enough and shepherd them away. I got a lot of stick for it. They didn't know the explosion that was waiting to happen. I did.

There was a knack of dealing with Alex. It needed forward planning. If you wanted him to do something, you planted the seed two days beforehand. The following day he'd adopt it as his own and on the day in question, he'd do it, claiming it was his idea all along. Alex had to be in control. QED.

He liked to test you. His favourite trick was waiting until you'd taken the first mouthful of your meal then inventing some spurious errand that had to be done urgently. It might be checking for a message at reception or running up to his room to bring his cigarettes when you knew he already had two packs in his pocket. I soon got wise to it. It was a ploy to unsettle you, especially if we had two attractive girls at the table with us. He didn't want *me* chatting them up. He wanted both of them for himself. He enjoyed your discomfort. There was a big grin on his face when you came back to find your food had gone cold. It showed he was Mr Big. Sometimes I joined in his game by exaggerating my annoyance to see his face light up. It was a game of double-bluff.

I often thought he was more relaxed in the company of men than women. He wasn't competing with them. When he was with men *and* women and everyone was trying to impress, there was an element of 'mine's more beautiful than yours' which could make him aggressive.

Psychological jousting was a big part of his life. If you watched Alex coming out of the dressing to play a match, he'd jump ahead of his opponent to maximise his entry into the arena and make the opponent feel inferior. Then he'd hang back to make sure his opponent was introduced first so *he'd* get the full applause afterwards. He didn't want to be sitting in his seat waiting for the other chap to be cheered. Very calculating.

Before long, Alex asked me to be his manager. I refused because I didn't have the expertise or the funds to set up a management agency. In any case my DPC business was doing well. To my relief, Howard Kruger appeared on the scene. He wanted to create an agency to rival Barry Hearn's Matchroom. It would be called Framework and be built around Alex. Tony Knowles, Joe Johnson and Mike Hallett were lined up but it all depended on Alex. Without him, Kruger said he couldn't do it. It was pandering to his ego. We all knew how much Alex envied Jimmy White's experience with Matchroom.

He was in two minds because he didn't know Kruger. He insisted he wanted me as his manager: 'Come on, babes, you can do it.' Kruger had a showbiz background and lots of money. Or so it seemed from his lifestyle. I advised Alex to go for it, then went on Kruger's payroll as Alex's official minder. The going soon got rough. A story broke in the red tops that Alex was in Malta doing a grand of coke a week. While he was away, I was looking after the shop at Delveron House. I woke up on Sunday morning to find twenty-six reporters and six camera crews on the doorstep. I told them the story was ridiculous. The guy from *The Star* got aggressive. The footage was shown on BBC and Granada that night. My mother got a shock. She hadn't seen me for weeks. She told friends she'd found her missing son – on the telly.

Alex had the odd dabble with coke but not to the tune of £1,000 a week. He couldn't afford it. He needed work but winning prize money was a rare luxury. When Framework set up an exhibition somewhere, he'd order them to set up three more in the same part of the country. If *they* couldn't, he would. That was the hustler talking. No one understood the system like he did. He was his own agent.

My most dangerous assignment was a month's tour of Northern Ireland when the shootings and street riots were going on. I went with Alex to Enniskillen, Belfast and Derry. Being an Englishman in Ulster wasn't clever. In typical fashion, Alex organised an exhibition on an industrial estate at the north end of Belfast. The deal was £1,200 in cash but the atmosphere was threatening. Two guys demanded the money from me. I said: 'No way!' It was naive of me. I knew there was a police presence down the road, but I didn't realise these thugs were armed. The last thing you did if you valued your life was stand up to them. It could have been very nasty. Alex got me out of the mess. They only tolerated me because of him.

Despite the obvious dangers, Alex had no qualms about going into Catholic areas. He knew how to wind them up and make them laugh. In the middle of war, that's an astonishing gift. I can't imagine anyone else pulling it off – or having the nerve to try. He was in demand. We couldn't get enough tickets. He must have earned £20,000 that month.

On the domestic front, Alex was living with Siobhan but agonising about Lauren and Jordan. Lynn didn't like me because I was in Alex's corner. I suppose that's fair enough. The first time I met her was when Alex got to the quarter-final of the Dulux in Derby. We'd had a great day. He forced himself to practise and was cueing well. The mood changed when he announced, in the middle of the tournament, that he wanted to see his kids. I drove him from Derby to Cheadle in a hurry. He went into Lynn's house saying he wouldn't be long. I sat in the car for ages.

Eventually I knocked on the door because we had to get back for the match. I could hear shouting and banging from inside. They were having a massive row. Alex told me she ran upstairs when she heard us arrive and kept the children in a bedroom. She wouldn't let him see them. He was so screwed-up he was in no fit state to play snooker.

Lynn could tie him around her little finger. Towards the end of my time with him, he couldn't get to see his children at all. Once, we were halfway to Preston for another tournament when he thumped the dashboard and said: 'Turn the car round!'

'What for?'

'Don't ask questions, just turn the fucking car round. I'm going to sort that bitch out!'

'Alex, you're on the table in half an hour.' Thankfully, that brought him to his senses.

He was desperate not to miss the kids. It gnawed away at him. The worst moment was when Alex picked up a rumour that Lynn was taking the children out of the country. There's some half-baked message from Lynn through Siobhan to Alex that she's not coming back. Alex is in a flat spin. We hare off to Ringway and he's dashing around the airport desks trying to find out which flight they're on. In the meantime, I go to see Lynn's parents. They're a very nice couple and scotch the rumour. What's Alex talking about? Lynn's due at their house in a few minutes. I call Alex to put his mind at rest.

'It's okay. Lynn's not emigrating. She'll be at her mum's soon.'

'No, babes, I tell you, she's leaving the fucking country!'

I get a few rounds of abuse, then he hangs up. I hear later that he's been arrested at the airport. He'd been trying to break through security. They took him to the nearby police station and kept him in overnight. As you can imagine, he was in turmoil. I immediately drove over to collect him. The police refused to let him go because Alex had been charged. I said: 'I'm sorry but you have no right to detain him.' They came up with some silly excuses, so I got hold of a solicitor who used the right phrases and persuaded them to let Alex go. He was released into my custody. The emigration rumour was just another wind-up.

I was used to having Alex in my custody. After the Hatherell hearing a couple of years earlier, Alex was bound over to me for three years. I volunteered to do it. The alternative would have been prison. It meant being with him at all times to make sure he stayed on the straight and narrow. I remember the judge looking at me as if to say poor sod, you must be mad!

I wasn't mad, I enjoyed the responsibility. The first engagement was an appearance on *Wogan*. Alex was pissed. He dragged Kruger on stage with him. Wogan and Kruger were worried – with good reason. Alex was slurring badly, but he loved being the centre of attention again. Howard hadn't had so much publicity in his life. I'm not sure he wanted that kind of fame!

Part of the condition for Alex's lenient sentence was that he received medical attention. He had fortnightly visits to a psychiatrist in Withenshawe. I'm not sure what good it did. Alex said he told them what he thought they wanted to hear. He hated medics. They prescribed betablockers. When the psychiatrist's reports were read to a court official, I was asked to leave the room. It made no sense.

To me, Alex always seemed more of a man's man. He worshipped Oliver Reed and was in awe of him at the same time.

He admired Oliver's hellraising and the way he got away with it. More often than not, Alex didn't get away with it. Whereas *he'd* upset people, Oliver made them laugh. He and Alex phoned each other in the middle of the night. I'd hear these enormous belly laughs which went on for an hour or more. They laughed until they couldn't speak. They tried to outwit each other. Oliver was streets ahead.

Alex could never have a lasting relationship with a woman. Lynn offered him all the security he wanted and it still went belly-up, and love affair with Siobhan was bound to end in tears. His strange on-off relationship with Holly ended in blood. It just wasn't going to happen for him. He lived on a knife edge. *He* was the most important person in his life. Being the star of the show was his biggest drug. In his own mind he was the People's Champion, at home or at play. It didn't matter who else was in the room or how famous they were, everyone had come to see *him*. His trophy cabinet's pretty bare, but if they'd awarded trophies for public adulation, it would be full. Being accepted was important to him. It went back to the Jampot when the cheeky kid was trying to get a game against the men.

Preferring adulation to trophies didn't mean Alex was a good loser. He *hated* losing. I remember we were playing doubles with friends and I mistakenly potted the blue. I'd miscalculated the scores by one point and left us needing a snooker to win. You'd have thought it was a ranking final. Alex went bonkers.

I had a terrific time with him, though. I saw places I'd never have seen. I met famous people I wouldn't have been near. I was extremely proud to have kept him out of serious trouble and mostly out of the headlines for the three years I promised the judge. The WPBSA thanked me for calming him down. And yet it ended on the sourest of notes. I got the same treatment as Paul Hatherell. (*He* deserved what he got – I didn't. There are ways of asking someone for a urine test, and there's a time to do it. Hatherell went in with the subtlety of an air raid. If Alex hadn't twatted him, I would have!)

I received several abusive phone calls after tearing up my professional relationship with Alex in 1988. I didn't see him again. That was twenty-two years without contact. I saw Lauren when she was about twenty and was working at a beauty counter. I hadn't seen her since bouncing her on my knee when she was five.

Del Simmons died in 1997. He was a highly regarded contracts negotiator for the WPBSA and brought home several of their sponsorship deals with tobacco companies. Trying to balance his responsibilities to the board with his responsibilities to its most flagrant 'sinner' eventually persuaded him it was time to let Alex go. Ten years with The Hurricane was beyond the call of duty. Alex was fidgeting for a move anyway. This is what Del told me at the time.

I was sorry to say goodbye to Alex. It was like losing a son. People thought I was mad to take him on in the first place but in some ways he was the easiest person in the world to deal with. It was all a question of timing. If you caught him at the right time, he'd do anything for you. I learned very quickly that if he'd just lost a game he should have won, there was no point going within a hundred yards of him. When he gets wound up, he has to cool down in his own time.

Alex was often misunderstood. He opened lots of events and refused payment for them and encouraged children in hospital without seeking publicity. His lateness for appointments is legendary but he usually made it up to exhibition organisers by playing extra frames.

I don't know how he's managed to run around the country like he has since 1972 without keeling over. The lifestyle would have destroyed a lesser person. Alex has quite incredible reserves of energy. When I started with him, I remember looking at a map and thinking it wasn't that far between Manchester and Grimsby where he had back-to-back exhibitions. Then it was a manageable trip down the east coast to Dover before popping across to London on his way back to Manchester via Leicester. When you actually *do* those journeys either by road or rail, they're exhausting.

The worst thing that happened to Alex was splitting up with Lynn. She's a strong woman – stronger than him. I was delighted when he married and apparently settled down. There'd be no more empty hotel rooms to go back to! He could be very lonely. Without a solid base, I feared he'd be lost. I just hope and pray I'm not right. I'm godfather to his children and know how fond he is of them. Lynn will cope with divorce and bringing the children up on her own. The kids will adapt too. How will Alex get on, though?

I can't see him ever retiring from snooker. His charisma is such that fans will always pay to see him. As long as they want him, he'll be there. The day he puts down his cue will be the day he dies.

22

HE WAS MY MODEL

Along with most of the population of Belfast, I was lucky enough to see *Hurricane*, Richard Dormer's one-man show which enjoyed a second run at the Grand Opera House in January 2011.

Alex saw the premiere in 2004 and, on condition that he was given a cut of the box office proceeds, gave it his approval. *Hurricane* had a salutary effect on him. He loved being the centre of attention again. He'd slipped out of the sport's and the city's consciousness for years. The play rejuvenated him. He even began to put on weight.

Alex had two works of art dedicated to him during his lifetime - a stage play and an artist's portrait. We'll hear from the creators of both masterpieces about their relationships with the model. First, Richard Dormer, a young actor making steady progress in his stage career until *Hurricane* brought him to Britain's - and America's - attention. Richard wrote the play and acted the part of Alex Higgins. It was directed by his wife, Rachel O'Riordan. The experience enriched all of their lives. The couple thought seriously about inviting Alex to live with them. Here is Richard's story.

The idea of a play came to me when I saw a newspaper picture of Alex at Oliver Reed's funeral. He was standing over the grave looking lost and broken. I remembered him strutting about in his prime – a sexy, dangerous, fast-moving guy. The picture wouldn't leave my head. It dawned on me that no-one had written a play about Alex. It was time someone did. Why not me? It had to be a one-man play because his was a one-man life in every sense. It was Alex Higgins versus the world.

I had two disadvantages. First, I was an actor not a playwright and, second, I'd never met Alex Higgins. I hadn't even seen him play. He was an image, a symbol of something both tragic and heroic. I began researching his life. I wanted to capture the essence of the man behind the headlines, not just regurgitate material already in the public domain. I realised that I could have lawsuits flying everywhere. The editor of a local paper warned me that Alex was a difficult subject. He said: 'Don't get him personally involved. He'll burst the bubble.' Rachel and I decided to give it a go.

The first task was to talk to my man. Not easy. I waited in the recommended pubs and betting shops around Belfast but always missed him. As often happens in these cases, I found him when I wasn't looking. It was in Connelly Street, Dublin, where I'd been auditioning for a part in another production. I was telling one of the pub regulars that I'd been combing Northern hangouts for Alex without success. He whispered: 'You won't believe this, but look over your left shoulder.' To my amazement, there was Alex ordering a pint of Guinness. It must have been fate. Feeling nervous, I wandered over to him.

'Let me buy that pint. I'd like to talk to you.'

'Okay, babes. Where did you get the jacket?'

Talk about non-sequiturs! I happened to be wearing a pigskin jacket that Rachel (my girlfriend at the time) had bought me. Alex was very keen on it. I told him I wanted to write a play about him. He listened in a noncommittal way then said: 'You can carry my golf clubs.'

In a slightly confused state, I obeyed his command and carried his clubs to Heuston Station. As luck would have it, we were both catching a train back to Belfast. All he seemed bothered about was swapping jackets. He tried mine on. I said he couldn't have it. He went off in a strop, still wearing it.

'We have nothing more to say to each other.'

We were the only passengers in our carriage. He waltzed up and down boasting: 'I've still got it on, babes. Look at me!'

I wasn't sure what to make of him. Getting him to co-operate in a play would be bloody hard. I couldn't even get my jacket back! Perhaps I should forget the idea. The train trundled on. This promised to be a long trip. Half an hour or so before we reached Belfast, Alex reappeared. He sat down beside me and handed me a can of lager.

'No hard feelings, kid.'

That redeemed him in my eyes. There was something about the fact that he came back. He realised he'd hurt my feelings. That image of him crying at the Crucible flashed through my mind. My enthusiasm returned. Yes, I *did* want to write this play. We chatted. I liked him. It was difficult not to. In order to write a play about someone you have to like them or there's no humanity in it. His emotions constantly fluttered and twitched across his face. It's strange being with someone like that because you're watching their inner turmoil being acted out before your very eyes. My brother-in-law who's a psychiatrist spent two hours with Alex when the show was up and running. He was transfixed by the guy. He told me: 'Alex has got everything with an "ism" in it. He's almost unreadable. The most complex person I've ever met. Even when he's being nice, there's something behind it. When he's being horrible, there's conflict.'

Alex endorsed the idea of the play with one proviso: 'As my old friend, Oliver Reed would say, I just want some crispies!'

'Of course. We're not here to take advantage of you.'

'I want £1 million cash.'

'That's half the total budget, Alex.'

'Makes sense then – you get half, I get half.'

'It doesn't quite work like that. The production costs are huge.'

'Give me £20,000 in an hour then.'

'That's impossible.'

By copyright law, we only had to give him one per cent, but we settled on Alex receiving 33 per cent of the takings. The guy was down at heel. We wanted to do our best for him. He probably only made £3-4,000 from the play but a good deal more from his signed photographs. He must have been selling 200 a time at £20 each in the theatre foyer. He brought his mates from the Royal to help him. They were scary guys, ex-paramilitaries with names like Stabber, Cruncher and Basher!

Richard and I met in the Opera House a few hours before the evening performance. The play was showing for five nights with an additional matinee on Saturday. Then it was moving to Derry. Being on stage alone for one and a half hours was a mighty challenge. Pretending to be a character as high-profile and controversial as Alex Higgins was equally tough. After its first run, *Hurricane* won the BBC Steward Parker Award for New Writing and the *Stage* Edinburgh Fringe Best Actor award. It was well received in the West End and on Broadway. Taking it to New York was a bold move. America doesn't play snooker and Alex Higgins wasn't a household name. Nevertheless, The Hurricane *had* registered on the US Richter scale. *The New York Times* devoted several column inches to his obituary: 'The rogues of sport are legion. Gifted, charismatic and reckless, they burn with hubris, flout convention, seize championships and rouse fans. Bobby Fischer at the chessboard; Mike Tyson in the ring. Alex Higgins, smoker, drinker, brawler, gambler, womanizer and two-times world champion was an exemplar. As angry as John McEnroe but more physically threatening

. . . he came to snooker when methodical play was the rule and a 100-point break took ten minutes or more. His brilliance at the snooker table was undermined by his self-destructive instincts . . .'

Richard's performance was dynamic and extremely moving. Some of the audience were in tears by the end of it. Others were splashed with sweat. The play begins with a latter-life Alex tearing up his betting slip as another horse lets him down. His opening words are: 'That's fucked that then!'

The play takes us through his hopes, agonies, aggressions and infidelities and finishes with him facing his own tragedy with supreme defiance: 'Don't pity me. I stood on top of the world.'

Minor criticisms I heard were that Richard's accent drifted towards Ian Paisley and that the ubiquitous cigarette in Higgins' fingers was conspicuously absent. I prefer the *Belfast Telegraph*'s line: 'Richard Dormer IS Alex Higgins.'

When they'd finished writing the play, and were ready to start rehearsals, our husband and wife team took a deep breath and announced it to the local press, television and radio, apprehensive about what Alex would think.

> 'We knew a press release was the hook which would bring him in. Sure enough, Alex turned up to watch our first twenty-minute run, though, at the Old Museum Art Centre. He deliberately sat in a position where I *had* to look at him. He stared back at me. They were the most terrifying twenty minutes of my life! All he said afterwards was: 'You're very fit, son.'
>
> It was an endorsement. I could breathe easily. He turned up unexpectedly to the first preview and was visibly moved by the reaction of the crowd. He congratulated me on my impersonation of him but told me to give the actions 'less swagger, more grace'. It was fair comment. He *did* have grace. I always thought he styled himself on Marc Bolan of T. Rex. It was that

Glam Rock thing of the late 1970s. Although he was basically a street fighter as hard as nails, he had the walk. There was a campness about him. Yet when he fixed you with that stare, it was intimidating. Probably the only person who could do it back to him was an actor much more famous than me – Oliver Reed. He had dead eyes. Alex was in awe of him. He told me about the episode with the axe. Alex had locked himself in the downstairs bathroom at Oliver's house in Guernsey. Oliver's wife ran out of the place screaming because he'd really lost it. Behind his eyes was a sign saying 'no-one here.' Alex described it like a scene from *The Shining*. Oliver was trying to break the door down with an axe, shouting: 'Come out you fucking little leprechaun!'

Then it goes quiet and Alex thinks Oliver must have passed out. He climbs out of the bathroom window only to hear a deafening roar as Oliver smashes the axe into the window frame, missing his fingers by inches. For some reason, Alex loved the guy. You could see from that newspaper photograph at the funeral that he was looking down at his mate's coffin thinking he'd be next.

He looked dreadful when I first met him in Dublin, but the play raised his spirits. He loved all the attention. I suppose it made him realise that he *was* important – that he'd left an indelible mark. He was so proud that he phoned Lauren to tell her he was back in the limelight. He wanted her to come and see the show – and see him. I don't think she ever did. He came with us when the play moved to Soho and didn't miss a performance. We'd become close friends by then. I can see him now on the steps of the Arts Theatre, milking the public adulation, smoking a joint and waiting for guests to arrive. He got away with everything because he was Alex Higgins. Then he'd wait for them in the foyer as they came out – people like Val Kilmer, John Hurt and David Suchet. He'd ask them if they liked what they saw then turn to me with that knowing look: 'Right, Richard, let's go for a drinky.'

He stood on the steps with his vodka and orange in his hand, hailing a rickshaw. He loved rickshaws. Then off we'd go into the night. I had to be careful with alcohol because I was performing again the next day, but they were great times. I told him it was exhausting playing him.

He replied: 'How do you think I feel? I've been playing me since before you were born!'

That's my favourite Alex Higgins quote. It was double-edged. It made me wonder whether he actually *meant* that he was playing himself. That the whole thing was a big act? I think he probably got it into his head that the public *wanted* him to misbehave. They wanted the jeopardy. They wanted him to break the rules. He almost *became* Alex Higgins to fit the part – like me! The thing about ripping off his bowtie, wearing coloured clothes against the regulations and peeing in plant pots was Alex saying: 'This is what's expected of me. The public want me to shake everything up so I will. I'll be the kid who takes all the shit. I don't care.'

The split personality thing was very noticeable but I couldn't explore that side of him in the play. It wouldn't have been fair because he was alive and hopefully recovering. Neither did I want to make it public. The play was conceived as a tribute – a celebration of his life. He was mercurial, explosive but self-pitying too. He hated anyone pitying *him*, but he pitied himself.

An important thing I discovered about him is that he *wasn't* alcoholic. His only addiction was gambling. I think a gambler's only happy when he's thrown everything away. When you watch Alex playing snooker, as I have through videos and on YouTube, you see that he sometimes played to lose. He'd choose a shot that was fraught with hazard when he didn't need to. That's the gambler. He gambled his career, he gambled his marriage, he gambled his life. He gave it all away. All there was in his flat was the bunch of flowers we'd given him. The rest was empty. I believe in a perverse way that's the way he like it. He needed to lose everything to be complete.

At one point Rachel and I were going to take him in. He wasn't looking after himself and had no home of his own. We thought we could feed him, help him to put weight on and give him a place to come back to where there'd be someone to welcome him. But where do you stop? It would have taken away *his* privacy and ours. We had our marriage to think about!

I sat behind Jimmy White at the funeral, feeling terrible. It was a miserable, miserable end. I came to the conclusion that nobody could have helped him. I tried once and helped him earn a lot of money. Once the play ended and the money dried up, I was an enemy. I wasn't providing him with an income so he wanted nothing more to do with me. We met him at the Elbow in Dublin Road to discuss the idea of turning the play into a film. He came with a bouncer – a really dangerous-looking guy. I told him I'd written the screenplay and would like him to be involved in the project. He had a one-word answer: 'No.'

I asked him why.

'Because *you* want me to.'

That was his twisted logic. He liked shooting himself in the foot. I think he'd started to get jealous of the attention I was getting. For a while he'd enjoyed living through me while I lived through him. Then he wanted me to stop because the roles were getting confused. Fiction and reality were entangled.

He said: 'I'm the one who did it. You're just an actor.'

We had a very strange relationship by the finish. The last time I saw him was coming out of the bookies two years ago [2009].

> I didn't think he'd seen me. I thought I'd be really nice to him but before I could speak he said: 'Hello, Richard' without even raising his eyes. It was said with a cold finality. I was out of his life. It hurt. We'd been through so much together. Playing Alex Higgins was all-consuming. Perhaps it consumed him in a different way. Most nights I'd feel possessed with him. I was demented. I kept doing the facial twitches in my normal life. Alex admitted he saw himself in me. It was the greatest compliment he could have paid me. Then he must have felt I was taking over.
>
> I prefer to remember one beautiful evening in Soho. We'd just heard that the show was going off Broadway. The rain was thunderous but we bumped along in a rickshaw heading for the Phoenix Club to celebrate the news. We were singing 'New York, New York'. I looked at Alex. The words of Van Morrison came to mind – wouldn't it be great if it was always like this?

Alex didn't get on with his portrait painter for twenty years. He had a deep suspicion of artists. They had power in their palate knives and the capacity to see things from a different perspective. He had no control over that. He may also have been spooked by the film of Oscar Wilde's Gothic horror, *The Picture of Dorian Gray*, in which a handsome young hedonist sells his soul to ensure that his portrait will age but he won't. Alex made reference to the film when he saw his own half-finished portrait covered with a tarpaulin in the artist's studio.

All of the above made life difficult for the artist, Alan Quigley. It's no exaggeration to say that Alan was driven to the edge of a breakdown by his manic-depressive model. And yet Alan and Alex had plenty in common. The painter was a child of the sixties like Alex, and still sports the greying remnants of a Leo Sayer perm. He was similarly afflicted by the Irish gambling contagion and could stand toe-to-toe with anyone at the bar. They should have clicked.

They did eventually, becoming such a fixture at the Beaten Docket that the landlord was planning to put up a small plaque in their designated corner of the pub. It would be called the Higgins-Quigley Table. You'd think they were joined at the hip flask!

But that was years after their first, testy encounter. Alex was famously short of patience with anyone who had a stronger opinion than his. Alan came into that category. He was a nervy ferret with a butterfly mind and a verbal attack as overwhelming as the incoming tide. They got off on the wrong footing when Bob Kearney, tournament director of an upcoming snooker event in the Ulster Hall, commissioned Alan to paint portraits of the star attractions. They included Kirk Stephens, Cliff Thorburn, Steve Davis and Alex Higgins. Bob provided him with relevant photographs so the players wouldn't have to pose. It sounds good so far. Part of the assignment was to escort a shy, fresh-faced Davis around Belfast. It was his first visit to the city. Alan and Steve got on well, though the sightseeing was somewhat limited.

Says Alan: 'All Steve wanted after a day's practice was to go to the penthouse of the Europa Hotel where they had music, bunny girls and a large television screen showing sporting highlights. He only ate chips. I asked him why we stayed here when there were lots of interesting nightspots to explore. He said: 'You haven't noticed have you, Alan? Look at the screen.' They were showing highlights of the recent UK final between Davis and Higgins. He studied it every night.'

While Steve was engrossed in his homework, Alex was out on the town. He'd taken a fancy to one of the tournament courtesy girls, a stunning, short-skirted redhead with a tan – fake or otherwise. Snooker didn't seem to be a priority. The redhead brought drinks to the dressing room where Alan and Steve were discussing the portrait he'd just finished. They were both delighted with the end product. In breezed Alex, all cloak and looking daggers. He thought Steve's portrait flattered him.

They went to Alex's dressing room to see the picture Alan had painted of *him*. Alex had been smoking a lot of dope. He'd also been drinking. The combination didn't augur well. The conversation went like this:

'What do you think, Alex?'

'Fuck – it's terrible! You made the nose too big.'

'Oh, I'm sorry. I just went from the photograph.'

'Why the fuck did you make Davis look so good and me like so fucking bad? Call yourself a painter? My daughter could do better with a packet of crayons!'

It's worth pointing out at this stage that Davis had just hammered Alex to take revenge for his defeat in the UK final. Alex was smouldering. Alan was distraught. Having tried with the help of the courtesy girl to calm Higgins down, he asked meekly if Alex would sign the picture anyway. Signed portraits were to go on display to the public. Alex refused and unleashed another wounding tirade.

Alan picks up the story: 'He was so nasty he had me in tears. The girl put her arms around me and told me not to listen to him. Then Steve Davis knocked on the door and asked to see my work. He took one look and said: "Great painting of Alex!" Alex told him to piss off. Steve, being Steve, politely sidled out of the door with a look of horror on his face. Alex stormed off with the redhead.'

Alan slumped into his seat. Kearney, the tournament director tried to sympathise: 'What a bastard he is after all the work you've put in.'

The artist poured himself a drink and tried to retrieve his self-worth. Had he made the nostrils too flared? Maybe – but his painting was true to the photograph. Alan was deeply hurt. He couldn't stop crying. Alex came back into the room.

'Alan, I'm sorry. I still don't like the painting but I've taken it out on you because Davis beat me. That was wrong. If you do a painting of me in future, do it from the heart.'

'You got that expression from Oliver Reed.'

'How do you know?'

'I've painted Oliver Reed.'

Alex had a habit of picking up other people's expressions – sometimes, as Lynn testifies, their ideas – and running with them.

Alan was as mesmerised by Oliver Reed as Alex was. He loved actors and films. Before making his reputation as a painter, Alan tried to become a make-up artist with Hammer Films. Oliver Reed was on their books. Unfortunately Alan wasn't. Not for long anyway. His twelve-month apprenticeship didn't work out.

After such an unsatisfactory beginning to their relationship, a cautious friendship developed between artist and recalcitrant model. It was, as usual, one-sided. Alan and Alex didn't see each other for years while the former got on with building his career and the latter got on with dismantling his. Divorce, Siobhan, booze, bets, fines, fights, another suicide attempt, the WPBSA ban and cancer.

Perhaps he couldn't help the cancer. He must have passive-smoked several fields of tobacco at the Jampot before attacking the weed with such vigour himself. Nevertheless, after hearing about a successful litigation in the States, Alex tried to sue Imperial Tobacco, the makers of Embassy cigarettes, for giving him throat cancer. He engaged a Dublin solicitor, Peter McDonnell to fight the case on the basis that, as sponsors of snooker tournaments, Embassy not only encouraged players to smoke but garlanded them with free samples. It was the biggest test case of its kind in Britain. Alex challenged Imperial on behalf of 200 other Irishmen who suffered different forms of cancer from smoking.

He lost his case but wanted his battle with the tobacco industry symbolised in the seven-foot portrait Alan would paint of him towards the end of his life. (That's the one *without* flared nostrils.) Tobacco aside, Alex maintained that his voice was wrecked, not by cancer but by a mugger who struck him in the throat as he was leaving a Belfast pub. Alan lends support to that view because he too had been attacked in the same part of town - by the same man.

> We'd been cheering like mad in the pub because I won £1,000 on the horses. With hindsight, cheering was a mistake. When I went to the toilet, I noticed a couple of unsavoury characters out of the corner of my eye. Suddenly the door burst open and this huge fellah hit me. I banged my head against the wall. He put his hands straight into the pocket where the money was, which means he must have been watching me closely. I spat in his face, then he held a gun under my nose and said: 'Is this what you want?' He took the money and ran off.
>
> Alex came to see me, very upset about the incident. Six months later he suffered the same fate. The guy hit him hard in the larynx. He was in a lot of pain. His voice disappeared completely for a while. He could only communicate by passing messages to my wife, Audrey and me – usually with doodles on. He was good at drawing.
>
> Perhaps because of what I do for a living, I have a photographic memory. When Alex described the mugger to the police, it sounded familiar – tall, dark-haired, stocky with a black moustache. Both attacks happened in the same area. It had to be the same person. Then we saw the story about a former professional boxer in his seventies who was battered to death after putting up a fight. In the end, they caught the guy. He's serving a life sentence. Pictures in the *Belfast Telegraph* confirmed it was definitely the same man who attacked us.

Whether their shared experience helped them to bond, Alan's not sure, but some of the edginess disappeared. As Alex slipped out of the snooker circuit and settled back in his home city, Alan became a useful ally, both as a gambling enthusiast and a moneylender. When he wasn't in the Royal, Alex spent hours and days at the Beaten Docket - now called Brennan's - where Alan was to be found when he wasn't putting acrylic on canvas. Brennan's is one of three old Belfast saloons which stand in line along Great Victoria Street, opposite the Europa. All three are character pubs with cubicles, oak panelling and gilded mirrors and, de rigueur, television sets for horseracing and football. All three establishments are heaving. It could only happen in Belfast.

Saturday afternoons heralded the Alan and Alex show. Watched by his trusty runner and his patient wife, Audrey, Alan would set out his stall at the first table inside the door - dockets, racing papers, pens and pencils. The telly was blaring; the craic was deafening; the Guinness and the Harp were flowing.

Alan: 'Alex would bound in, all smiles and hugs to take his usual seat under the mirror. He felt secure there. When he studied the form, Alex was like a university academic. Completely focused. There could be a hundred people clamouring for his autograph and he wouldn't even notice them. We both knew a lot of people who owned racehorses but Alex always had to tap me for money. I must have "lent" him £6,000 over the years.'

Yes, Alan and a few others besides. It's one of the intriguing things about Alex that so many people gave him money or treated him to drinks, lifts, etc. as though he was a national charity. Perhaps he was. Few if any seemed to resent it, but they all made a point of telling me. I asked Alan why he kept putting his hand in his pocket.

> I was infatuated with him. He had a way of winning you over. You couldn't refuse him. He had a few successes on the horses but not

many. His biggest win was £17,000 but he told me to keep quiet about it because he had a lot of debts. He repaid me £20 out of that. I ask you – £20!

He attacked me once over money. He was catching a boat to the Isle of Man and asked if I could lend him the fare. I agreed. Next thing I know, he rings me in a panic. The ferry leaves in a few minutes, where's the money I promised him? I told him Audrey had my bank cards so he'd have to wait till she came to the pub. He came storming in from the bookies and hit me in the face! He was so frail I could lift him off the ground even though I'm only five foot six.

'Alex, we don't need to do this to each other.'

'You let me down. Why haven't you got the money?'

We had a love/hate relationship. I liked him as a person who shared my passion for horseracing. He was great company. He had a great sense of humour as well as a vicious tongue. He was as frightened of me as I was of him. He told my wife he didn't trust artists. He trusted her, though. Whenever I went to the bar I'd see him whispering in her ear. He wrote his mobile number on a piece of paper and pressed it into her hand. She was expected to ring him. He loved walking around with Audrey on his arm. Women were a trophy to him. I don't think he ever loved them. It's like the courtesy girl at Ulster Hall. He told me he slipped away to a friend's house and got her into bed while the tournament was on.

By and by the issue of another portrait came up for discussion. The Irish TV channel RTE wanted to film a documentary of Alan painting Alex. Alex had recently undergone chemotherapy so Alan was apprehensive. He didn't want his subject looking gaunt. He didn't want to expose himself to more criticism after the flare-up over the nostrils.

Finally Alex gave them the green light: 'Let's do it. I'm feeling okay and looking better. This time, I want something different.'

'How do you mean?'

'Make a few sketches and I'll tell you.'

He was keen that his hands, the tools of his trade, be displayed in a prominent and theatrical way. He wanted a grey background and was adamant that he didn't want to pose holding his snooker cue. He liked Alan's idea of hands crossed in front of him. Surprisingly, he posed in several different positions: high hands; hands low; hands in pockets.

Alan came up with a title: 'We should call it "The Birth and Death of Snooker".'

'I'm not dead yet.'

'You've missed the point. When you stopped playing, snooker died.'

'That's good. I like it.'

Progress stuttered to a halt when Alex threatened to sue RTE. He claimed he hadn't been paid for the project – or hadn't been paid *enough*. He was permanently dogged by the suspicion that people were making money at his expense. He moaned that Alan was profiteering from signed sketches, which wasn't the case. They'd agreed on a fifty-fifty split for Alan's chef d'ouevre. Unfortunately work stopped because of the arguments. The portrait was mothballed for four years. Says Alan:

> Alex saw the canvas covered up in my studio. He said it reminded him of *The Picture of Dorian Gray*. He knew the story well, especially the part where Dorian's face in the picture becomes old and hideously disfigured because of his depraved life.
>
> Alex took one look and said: 'So you're keeping my picture there to keep me alive? What if you sell it and I die?'
>
> 'You've got some imagination, Alex.'

'I just want you to finish it. I want it to be provocative. I want it displayed where people can see it and touch it.'

It was certainly a challenge. He wanted his nails painted the colour of snooker balls and suggested that his face should also appear inside the moon. He wanted it slightly mocking. And he wanted a burning cigarette on top of his cue to reflect his attempt to sue Imperial Tobacco. By this stage, Alex was getting extremely weak and his spirits were low. But he had another suggestion.

'What about painting the ace of spades in my waistcoat pocket?'

'You're a gambler, Alex. The ace of spades is no use to you. The ace of hearts is better. You know what you said about painting from the heart.'

'Yeah, good idea. Put JW on the top corner. That's my best friend.'

I didn't know what JW meant for ages. I changed 'Birth and Death of Snooker' to 'Snooker Deity'. When I told him deity meant God, he was happy. He saw the finished painting a few weeks before he died. He said it was my finest work and gave me a big hug.

It's an unusual portrait of an unusual bloke. Alan has captured the loneliness and vulnerability in Alex's face while accentuating the light in his eyes. At the time of writing, the giant picture stands in Brian Eakin's Belfast gallery waiting for a good home. I guess it's a combination of collector's item and acquired taste. Alex polarised opinion. He was either a hero or a horrible drunk. To those who knew him well he was both of those things but a lot more besides. To Audrey Quigley, the artist's wife, he was charm personified.

> In some ways he had a softer, more caring side than my husband. He liked me because I'd sit in the pub for hours with them. I didn't mind the gambling. He was always trying to chat me up – not because he wanted to take me to bed, just because he liked being affectionate and playful. Taking any woman to bed would have been beyond him at the end. He used to say he hadn't had sex for ten years. In his earlier days he'd have no time for someone like me. Not with all those women chasing him.
>
> He asked me to dance when he was barely fit to walk. I had no idea he was a dancer. He said: 'Wait till I show you.' We danced to one of his favourite tunes, 'Teenage Wedding' by Chuck Berry. He was very good. The reason he didn't find a lasting relationship with a woman is that Alex did what Alex wanted to do. Any partnership was bound to fail.

How bizarre is it that while the portrait was attracting admirers to the gallery and the one-man show was packing them in at the Opera House, the subject of both could be simultaneously begging in the street or rolling in the gutter? Several Ulstermen, my bus driver friend and Alan Quigley in particular, witnessed that side of the People's Champion. One particular moment is still vivid in Alan's recollection.

> He'd just had a heavy dose of chemo but turned up at the pub as breezy as ever. He ordered a Guinness (for which I paid) and said: 'Let's do the horses, Alan. Give me fifty quid.' Then he started to feel unwell. We got him a bowl of soup and a roll of bread. He sat crumbling the bread into the soup. Everyone was watching him. He wheezed at them: 'Stop staring at me and lift that table outside.'
>
> Alan asked why.

'Just do it. Take the chair too.'

'Alex, you're not fit enough for this.'

'I've got no money so I'm setting up a stall to catch people coming back from the bookies. I can sell them autographed pictures for £2 a time, you see.'

He wouldn't be talked out of it. As my taxi came to collect me, it started to rain. The driver pulled away and I watched Alex through the windscreen wipers. Water was dripping off the rim of his hat. His fag had gone out. He was shouting: 'Give us a fiver, boss! Give us a fiver! Fuck off then!' I don't think I've seen anything more pitiful. That image is imprinted.

So is the image of Alex in his warden-assisted flat. People don't realise how much he *hated* that place! I ask you – white walls and an old brass bed. What a way to finish your days. There've been stories about the woman who lives there now complaining that it's haunted. How stupid. It was like a mental hospital to Alex. He stayed away as much as he could. He sure as hell wasn't gonna come back and haunt it!

It took him twenty years to care for me. He was smoking dope in the Europa penthouse one night. The manager told him to put it out but he ignored the request. He turned to me and said: 'I've known you for a long time, Alan. I never liked you. I don't trust artists.'

'You like Oliver Reed. He's an artist.'

'He's an actor, that's different. He's just a drinking mate.'

'His wife chucked you out for peeing on the curtains.'

'He shouldn't have told you things like that.'

'And you reckon you don't trust me?'

'Anyway, Alan, I love you.'

'You're telling me that after hating me all your life? You've insulted me, rubbished me, hurt my feelings and made me cry. Now you love me?'

'You've stuck with me through the bad times. You brought me coal and blankets when I was freezing. You've painted a wonderful portrait. I'm glad the moon is smiling. I want people to see me laughing at myself because, in all truth, I've had a ball.'

HIGH and LOWS

1949 Born Alexander Gordon Higgins, Belfast, March 18th.

1960 Picked up his first cue at the Jampot.

1963 Leaves Belfast to begin his career as a jockey in Berkshire but is released without riding in public and returns to Belfast two years later.

1968 Wins All-Ireland amateur championship at 19.

1972 Turns professional and wins the world championship at his first attempt, beating John Spencer 37-32 in the final. At 23, Alex becomes the youngest player to win the title.

1974 Marries Australian, Cara Hasler, in Sydney.

1976 Alex's first son, Christopher, is born to his live-in lover, Joyce.

1976 Beaten in world championship final by Ray Reardon.

1980 Loses his third world championship final to Cliff Thorburn 18-16. Alex marries for the second time. This time to Lynn Avison.

1981 Alex's daughter Lauren Elisabeth is born.

1982 Wins world championship, by beating Ray Reardon, for the second time - the summit of his career.

1983 Amazing fightback to beat Steve Davis in the final of the UK championship at Preston. His second son, Jordan, is born.

1984 Loses UK final to Steve Davis.

1985 Alex and Lynn divorce.

1986 Head-butts Paul Hatherell at the UK championships in Preston.

1987 Loses Irish Masters final to Dennis Taylor.

1989 Alex breaks his ankle jumping out of girlfriend Siobhan Kidd's window but wins the Irish Masters on crutches, beating Stephen Hendry in the final.

1990 Threatens to have Dennis Taylor shot and punches a tournament director at the world championships. He's banned for the rest of the season.

1994 First signs of cancer. Alex has growths removed from his mouth.

1997 *Sunday World* newspaper, supported by Ken Doherty, puts on a benefit night for Alex at Belfast's Waterfront Hall. It raises £10,000.

1998 Alex undergoes surgery to remove a tumour from his throat.

2005/6 Appears in Irish Professional Championship but fails to get past the first round.

2010 Admitted to Belfast City Hospital suffering from pneumonia but leaves to attend his own fund-raising event in Manchester.

2010 Saturday, July 24th. Alex found dead at his warden-assisted bedsit in Belfast.

INDEX